Additive Schooling
in Subtractive Times

Additive Schooling in Subtractive Times

Bilingual Education and Dominican Immigrant Youth in the Heights

Lesley Bartlett and Ofelia García

Foreword by Angela Valenzuela

VANDERBILT UNIVERSITY PRESS ❧ Nashville

© 2011 by Vanderbilt University Press
Nashville, Tennessee 37235
First printing 2011
Second printing 2013

This book is printed on acid-free paper.
Manufactured in the United States of America

Library of Congress Cataloging-in-Publication Data

Bartlett, Lesley.
Additive schooling in subtractive times : bilingual education
and Dominican immigrant youth in the Heights / Lesley
Bartlett and Ofelia García ; foreword by Angela Valenzuela.
p. cm.
Includes bibliographical references and index.
ISBN 978-0-8265-1762-3 (cloth edition : alk. paper)
ISBN 978-0-8265-1763-0 (pbk. edition : alk. paper)
1. Education, Bilingual—New York (State)—New York
2. Dominican Americans—Education (Secondary)—New
York (State)—New York. I. García, Ofelia. II. Title.
LC3733.N5B37 2011
370.117'50974711—dc22
2010046395

To the faculty, staff, administrators, parents, and students of Gregorio Luperón High School, past and present, and to the Washington Heights community, for teaching us so much.

Contents

Foreword

LESLEY BARTLETT AND OFELIA GARCÍA's text, *Additive Schooling in Subtractive Times: Bilingual Education and Dominican Immigrant Youth in the Heights*, is long overdue. It tells the tale of the heroic struggles of Gregorio Luperón High School and a community committed not only to its survival but also to its advancement. Starting as a newcomer school for immigrant, mostly Dominican youth in New York, it later becomes a four-year high school in a context of both changing demographics and accountability demands related, in particular, to an intensification of testing.

While immigrant parents, their children, and their teachers are fully invested in the idea of students learning the English language well and quickly, their desire to see these children progress at a reasonable rate and graduate is too often frustrated by high-stakes tests with elusive and challenging vocabulary, no visual support, and historical and cultural references that these youth cannot access because of the embedded assumptions of these tests. That is, the tests implicitly assume an entire schooling experience in the English language and are thus systematically inappropriate for immigrant, newcomer youth whose exposure to academic English and academic discourse is generally not comparable to that of their U.S.-born counterparts. The authors cite this disconnect between policy and demographics as a key culprit in the insurmountable barrier that high-stakes exams present for school completion despite Luperón's higher success rate in this regard relative to its peer institutions in New York.

Notwithstanding these significant, policy-driven hurdles, Luperón's sociocultural, social justice approach to learning provides an effective counterbalance to the institutional impulse to sacrifice some curriculum in the service of test preparation. Four years is not enough time for all, or even most, children at Luperón to learn at a level comparable to the advantages enjoyed by their native-born, English-speaking peers, but Luperón's context- and language-sensitive approach is demonstrably additive, building on its students' linguistic and cultural resources.

The reader may be drawn, as I have been, to the powerful narrative of a school with a deep and abiding commitment to a newcomer, immigrant community in a challenging urban context. Every major decision is a community-based endeavor oriented by values such as social justice and an ethic of care articulated in the co-construction of "school" as a sanctuary, a home, and a family away from the homes and families the students physically left behind but to which they remain deeply connected.

How often does one hear from parents that their child's fiscally challenged, urban school creates a sense of well-being? How often is such a school characterized as a blessing and a gift? Yet these are the very terms that Luperón parents use to describe their children's schooling experiences. The road for Luperón has not been a smooth one, but effective, accessible, and caring bilingual leadership has systematically rescued it in times of trouble, alongside culturally and linguistically relevant pedagogy and a parent- and community-centered approach to schooling. Lesley Bartlett and Ofelia García weave a compelling narrative that inspires us even as it informs the direction that change can and should take if we as a nation are to address responsibly the demographic imperatives that lie ahead.

Angela Valenzuela
Professor, University of Texas at Austin
Director of the Texas Center for Education Policy

Acknowledgments

THIS PROJECT WOULD HAVE BEEN impossible without the significant assistance we received from the faculty, staff, administration, parents, and students of Gregorio Luperón High School. The principal, Juan Villar, provided us with unparalleled access to the school, encouraged us to investigate the school's strengths and weaknesses, and munificently shared his time, experience, and insights over a period of seven years. The faculty and staff patiently abided our presence and our persistent questions. This book would not have existed without their generosity of time, their probing questions, and their keen analyses not only of ongoing educational reforms but also of Luperón students' assets and the obstacles faced. We appreciate deeply the feedback several administrators and teachers provided on a draft of this book, which has improved it immensely. In addition, we thank two other significant groups: Luperón parents, who shared their heartfelt insights, and the students of Luperón, who taught us humbling lessons about the daunting challenges of immigrating to the United States as teens and trying to learn enough English and academic content so that they could pass standardized exams and launch themselves into the next phase of their lives.

This book has been a joint effort, with input from diverse people and sources. As detailed in Chapter 1, during the research and writing period, we were very lucky to work with an incredibly talented group of students at the Teachers College of Columbia University and the Graduate Center of the City University of New York, including Jill Koyama, Ali Michael, César Fernández, Elizabeth "Betsy" Cromwell Kim, Dina López, Norma Andrade, Carmina Makar, Ivana Espinet, and Natalie Catasús. The questions and ideas of these individuals contributed immeasurably to the research design and analysis. The written product benefited immensely from the editorial support of Heidi Batchelder and Briana Ronan, who demonstrated unusual dedication and powers of observation. It was a great privilege to work with and learn from these gems during the process. In addition, we wish to thank our colleagues Ricardo Otheguy, Jill Koyama, and Fran Vavrus for their careful listening and the critical feedback they provided at various stages of the project. Finally, we are thankful to the anonymous reviewers for their judicious advice.

We gratefully acknowledge support from Teachers College and the Graduate Center. Specifically, we thank Provost Thomas James of Teachers College for helping us make the arrangements necessary to write this book. Lesley Bartlett wishes to thank the Fulbright Scholars Program and the Fulbright-Hayes Faculty Fellowship program for financial support during her sabbatical; she also gives her immense thanks to the faculty and staff of Universidad Iberoamericana, and specifically to Vice Rector Odile Camilo, for providing a space to write, helpful bibliographic and demographic references, and good company.

We are fortunate to have found a conscientious editor with a keen ethnographic imagination whose enthusiasm and intellectual support enhanced the book; our thanks go to Michael Ames and the staff of Vanderbilt University Press for their incredible assistance through the production process.

Lastly we wish to thank our families—Owen and Lila Bartlett Chanas (who roamed the halls of Luperón in utero) and Brian Chanas on Lesley's side, and Ricardo, Eric, Raquel, and Emma on Ofelia's—for nearly a decade of the precise mix of patience and impatience necessary for us to complete this project.

Additive Schooling
in Subtractive Times

1

Introduction:
Schooling Immigrant Youth

In recent decades, the population of immigrants in the United States has steadily increased. The numbers of foreign-born living in the United States grew from 9.6 million in 1970 to 28.4 million in 2000 and 38 million in 2006 (U.S. Census 2006–2008). Over the course of these years, the demographics of immigrant populations have changed as well. While in earlier decades the majority of immigrants came from Europe, by 2000 the majority hailed from Latin America. From 1990 to 2000, the Latino population in the United States grew from 22.4 million to 35.3 million (Logan 2001). Many of these immigrants were so-called New Latinos—Latinos from places like the Dominican Republic and El Salvador who joined groups with longer histories of immigration, including Mexicans, Puerto Ricans, and Cubans. The number of New Latinos more than doubled from 1990 to 2000, from 3.0 million to 6.1 million, and their numbers continue to grow (Logan 2001).

The rise in immigration and changes among immigrants has resulted in a diversification of the U.S. student population as well. Immigrant children constitute a growing but often "overlooked and underserved" percentage of the American student body (Ruiz-de-Velasco and Fix 2000). The school-age, foreign-born population increased from 2 to 6 percent between 1970 and 2000 (Capps et al. 2005, 5; Fry 2007). Thirty-five percent of Latino youth are foreign-born (López 2009). Providing appropriate schooling for this growing but vulnerable population is a mounting concern across the United States as immigrants become more geographically dispersed. While in 2000, 67 percent of the total U.S. foreign-born population resided in the six large immigrant-receiving states—California,

Florida, Illinois, New Jersey, New York, and Texas—between 1990 and 2000 the foreign-born population more than doubled in nineteen other states (Capps et al. 2005; Capps, Fix, and Passel 2002; Fry 2007, 580).

One obvious issue facing immigrant children is the need to learn English. The population of English learners has increased at a rate seven times that of the total student enrollment in public schools (NCELA 2006). While this population includes diverse language groups, it is striking that nearly 13 percent of all schoolchildren in the United States speak Spanish as their home language.[1] First-generation immigrant children form an increasing percentage of the school-age population, and their specific needs (including linguistic needs) merit serious attention.

The widely varying means through which schools accommodate their changing student bodies, and the consequences of these decisions, are significant. How can schools best meet the needs of these newcomer students? How do these newcomers fare during high school and beyond? This book explores the ways in which one school has interpreted and responded to these questions.

The research presented in this monograph draws from a qualitative case study of a bilingual high school for Latino newcomer immigrant youth—mostly Dominicans—in New York City. The school, Gregorio Luperón High School, represents a unique effort to serve the educational needs of immigrant newcomer youth. For a period of four years, we conducted school-based observations; interviewed administrators, faculty, students, and parents; and traced the impact of public policies on the school in order to address the following research questions: How does Luperón support the social, linguistic, and academic development of recently arrived Latino adolescents? What challenges do the school and its students face, and how do they respond? How do students progress through the school? To what extent is the school able to facilitate social mobility for these students?

In answering these questions, by employing a sociocultural approach to the study of educational policy as enacted across various contexts, we consider the ways in which contemporary federal, state, and city educational mandates make possible certain practices within the school, even as they constrain instruction in other ways. We argue that the imposition of standardized testing and the mania for testing outcomes has required the school to narrow its curricular focus while potentially undermining political support for Luperón at a critical period in its development. Nevertheless, the school has managed to adapt to the constraints of testing, primarily by using a provision that allows their students to take most of the standardized tests in Spanish and therefore meet graduation requirements. By examining how Luperón has survived various policy reforms, we generate insights regarding the importance of flexible institutional structures and practices for the continued existence of such a school.

Furthermore, we draw on literature in bilingual education, sociolinguistics, and sociocultural studies of language and literacy to make several arguments. First, we intentionally avoid labels such as the federal *limited English proficient* and even the term *English language learners* (commonly used by academics) in favor of the term *emergent bilinguals,* in order to highlight the fact that for these students and for Luperón, the acquisition of English is about *becoming bilingual* in tandem with the culturally and geographically transnational lives the youth lead (see García 2009c; García and Kleifgen 2010; García, Kleifgen, and Falchi 2008). Second, we argue that as emergent bilinguals, immigrant students are best served by a *dynamic bilingual* approach to teaching (García 2009a) that rejects the usual linear subtractive or additive models of language education. Instead, dynamic bilingualism emphasizes the ways in which students adapt their linguistic resources to make meaning in context-specific communicative situations. From this perspective, bilingualism is not something students possess, but rather something they use with increasing levels of communicative competence. Furthermore, drawing on this case study, we emphasize the value of a *social* approach to teaching emergent bilinguals—one that situates language learning as a community (rather than individual) phenomenon that evolves within a sociocultural and sociopolitical context. Drawing on Brutt-Griffler's (2004) concept of *macroacquisition*, we discuss how Luperón affords opportunities for the acquisition of a second language by a broader speech community. Finally, engaging anthropological studies of schooling and sociological studies of immigration and schooling, we demonstrate the (limited) impact that Luperón's culturally relevant pedagogy and curricula has on the social capital and economic trajectories of many immigrant students.

Why Study the Schooling of Latino Immigrant Youth?

As noted earlier, immigration is reshaping the face of the United States. While its newer residents hail from all over the world, immigrants from Mexico, Central America, the Caribbean, and South America predominate. The waves of immigration have resulted in increasing numbers of immigrant children in U.S. schools. By 2050, according to projections from the U.S. Census Bureau, the Hispanic school-age population will increase by 166 percent, while the non-Hispanic population will grow by just 4 percent. As a result, it is expected that by 2050, Latino children will outnumber non-Latino children in U.S. schools (Fry and González 2008). Many of those Latino children will be English language learners, and a significant proportion will be recently arrived immigrants. Schools need to know how to meet their needs.

The insufficiently studied first-generation immigrant children who constitute an increasing percentage of the school-age population are the focus of this book. In the United States, first-generation immigrant children are predominantly Mexican. In 2000, 38 percent of all foreign-born children from pre-kindergarten to grade 5 were born in Mexico, 2.6 percent in the Dominican Republic, and 1.9 percent in Colombia. In grades 6–12, 37 percent of foreign-born children originated in Mexico, 3.4 percent in the Dominican Republic, 3.3 percent in El Salvador, 2 percent in Haiti, and 2 percent in Guatemala (Capps et al. 2005, 9).

Immigrant students also vary in terms of destination, meaning that schools throughout the United States are now grappling with how best to meet their needs. While the majority live in Texas, California, and New York, 21 percent live in the "new" Hispanic states such as Florida, Georgia, Massachusetts, Nevada, North Carolina, Oregon, Virginia, and Washington (Fry and González 2008, ii–iv). To give a sense of the magnitude of change, it is worth noting that in North Carolina, the K–12 English language learner (ELL) population grew by 372 percent from 1996 to 2006 (Batalova, Fix, and Murray 2007). Eight percent of immigrant students live in states with "emerging" Latino populations, including Arkansas, Indiana, Kansas, Maryland, Minnesota, Nebraska, New Hampshire, Oklahoma, Rhode Island, Tennessee, Utah, and Wisconsin (Fry and González 2008, ii–iv, 10–12). The geographic dispersal of immigrant students makes their education a concern across an increasingly wider swath of the United States.

Latino immigrant students are vulnerable in many ways. First, poverty exposes many Latino students to risk. More than 31 percent of Latino children under the age of six live in poverty (Gándara and Contreras 2009, 60). Immigrant Latinos are even more likely than U.S.-born Latinos to live in poverty: while 35 percent of the former live in poverty, 27 percent of the latter do; indeed, "compared with non-Hispanic students, native-born Hispanic students in public schools are one-and-a-half times as likely to live in poverty, and foreign-born Hispanic students are twice as likely" (Fry and González 2008, 13; see also ii–iv). Further, Latino immigrant students tend to live in highly segregated areas where the schools lack resources and well-trained teachers (Orfield and Lee 2005; Orfield and Eaton 1996). Many schools with large English learner populations also have large low-income populations. In vast urban centers such as New York, Los Angeles, and Chicago, where Latino youth make up the majority of the school-age population, they are disproportionately consigned to overcrowded, underfunded schools of low quality (Conger et al. 2007; Conger et al. 2009; Noguera 2003 and 2004; Oakes 2002).

Immigrant students also have specific linguistic needs. Forty-four percent of first-generation students speak English with difficulty (Fry and González 2008, ii–iv). Because of residential and school segregation, these students also tend to be linguistically segregated. Fifty-three percent of emergent bilinguals attend elementary and secondary schools where over 30 percent of their classmates are also language minorities; conversely, 57 percent of English proficient students attend schools where less than 1 percent of all students are English language learners (Van Hook and Fix 2000, 10). Nevertheless, schools serving these populations, with specific educational needs, are required to meet performance standards set by federal policies such as No Child Left Behind (NCLB); immigrant youth are expected to master academic English in a short time, and many are required to pass standardized tests in English in order to graduate from high school.

Furthermore, immigrant students' previous educational experiences may impede their retention and attainment. Many first-generation students did not experience continuous education prior to their arrival in the United States. In 2000, an estimated 6 percent of first-generation immigrant students reported interrupted formal education in their home country; notably, the school dropout rate for that group in the United States was 70 percent (Fry 2005, 3). Fry (2005, 8) explains that recent arrivals who had interrupted education abroad were 6 percent of all foreign-born teens, but because of their inordinately high dropout rate, they constituted 38 percent of all foreign-born school dropouts.[2] In contrast, only 8 percent of foreign-born youth who had not had difficulties before arriving dropped out.[3] Additionally, some of those without interrupted education had experienced low-quality education that frustrated their efforts to graduate from high school in the United States. Latino students who have immigrated to the United States after receiving some schooling abroad are significantly more likely to drop out of school than Latino youth who have received all their education in U.S. schools (Vernez and Abrahamse 1996; Van Hook and Fix 2000). According to the National Center for Education Statistics, "The status dropout rate of 44.2 percent for Hispanic sixteen- through twenty-four-year-olds born outside the fifty states and/or the District of Columbia was more than double the rate of 16.1 percent for Hispanic youths born in the United States with at least one parent born outside the United States, and the rate of 16.0 percent for Hispanic youths with both parents born in the United States" (NCES 2000, 14; see also Fry and Lowell 2002). This is startling, given that even Latinos schooled in the United States have a comparably high dropout rate: 15 percent, as compared to 12 percent for black youth (Fry 2003).

Foreign-born students who arrive as teens are particularly vulnerable to dropping out. According to Fry (2007), "In 2000, more than 80 percent of foreign-born school dropouts were recently arrived youth" (597). According to a Pew Hispanic Center report,

> Regardless of country of origin, youths who migrate early in childhood to the United States are more likely than their later-arriving peers to be enrolled in high school. Early childhood arrivals, who receive all or nearly all their schooling in the United States and thus have the longest exposure to U.S. schools and society, are the most likely to be in school. . . . These early childhood arrivals have a dropout rate of 5 percent, not much higher than the native-born dropout rate of 3.3 percent. (Fry 2005, 16)

Perhaps surprisingly, foreign-born children constitute a higher proportion of the high school student population than the primary school population. According to Capps et al. (2005), in 2000, foreign-born students constituted 3 percent of kindergarten enrollments but 7 percent of high school enrollments (7). The "share of children of immigrants who are foreign-born is lowest in pre-kindergarten (one in eight) and highest in grades 6–12 (one in three)" (36). Further, many of these first-generation students have been in the country fewer than five years. By the late 1990s, recently arrived foreign-born immigrants (in the country for fewer than five years) constituted 2.7 percent of the high school population and 2 percent of the elementary population (Ruiz-de-Velasco and Fix 2000, 2). Yet receiving school systems rarely have the resources or personnel they need to serve these students' needs adequately. Van Hook and Fix (2000) point out that there is a "mismatch between the number and needs of immigrant middle and high school students and the limited resources targeted to them" (17). Immigrants who enter United States schools at the secondary level are, as Ruiz-de-Velasco and Fix (2000) suggest, "overlooked and underserved."

These secondary school newcomers therefore face immense challenges.[4] While trying to navigate their schools, they must learn—and quickly—a new culture of schooling, as well as American race, class, and gender structures. In addition, they may face significant academic barriers. For example, previous experiences with low-quality education or interrupted formal education may have decreased the students' literacy abilities in their home language. Yet their educational backgrounds are often ignored. Newcomers at the secondary school level often do not have sufficient time to learn the academic English and master academic content necessary to pass standardized tests and graduate. Research suggests that it takes five to seven years to master academic language proficiency (e.g., Cummins 1981b, 1991); youth who arrive must generally begin taking standardized tests in their sophomore or junior year.

Schools with large immigrant populations too often fail to meet the unique needs of these students. Their culture and language is not reflected in the school curriculum and so they cannot identify with what they are learning. Teachers who lack an awareness of their realities have difficulty relating to them and may develop negative perceptions of them. The students often feel stigmatized by other students when they are removed from the regular classroom for language classes such as English as a Second Language (ESL). Further, many of the language education models for English learners were developed for students born in the United States, not for recently arrived immigrants.

These school-level lacunae parallel the absence of adequate policy attention for the educational needs of newcomer students. The federal government's influence on their education is restricted to preserving (halfheartedly) the legal rights of students with "limited English proficiency." The actual responsibility for educating these youth redounds to individual states, which generally lack specific policies for immigrants. As McDonnell and Hill (1993) write, "The needs and problems of immigrant students are rarely considered independent of their status as non-English speakers" (xi–xii). Based on their analysis of immigrant education in fifty-seven schools in nine school districts, McDonnell and Hill concluded that the "quality of schooling that immigrant students receive largely depends on the capacity of the local communities in which they reside. Yet most of these districts and schools lack the human and fiscal resources to educate students well" (xii). Districts lack sufficient numbers of well-trained bilingual teachers, appropriate instructional materials, plans for students with interrupted formal education, and access to the "health and social support services desperately needed by students who must cope with the effects of poverty and the traumas associated with leaving one culture and adjusting to another" (xii). As the authors conclude, "Immigrant students have unmet educational needs that are unique to their newcomer status," and yet the big-city school systems that primarily serve them rarely provide the necessary services (xiii). In an effort to remedy such situations, "newcomer schools" have emerged.

Newcomer Schools

A survey of 115 newcomer programs in twenty-nine states plus Washington, DC, provides the best available overall description of these efforts (Boyson and Short 2003; Short and Boyson 2000a). The programs generally defined "newcomers" as students who had limited or no proficiency in English (93 percent of the schools), had been in the United States from under a year to two to three years (64 percent), had low literacy skills in the home language (50 percent), or had experienced limited or interrupted schooling in their home countries (33 percent). The programs also considered students' test scores, educational background, and age (Boyson and Short 2003; Short and Boyson 2000a, 2000b). Notably, more than 95 percent of the programs had Spanish speakers, and almost two-thirds of all the programs served fewer than a hundred students (Short and Boyson 2000a).

Most of these newcomer programs (76 percent) were found in urban settings, and over 50 percent of the programs were located in four states with urgent needs: California, New York, Texas, and New Jersey. Over 54 percent of newcomer programs served high schools and students of high school age, as these students required rapid intervention to prepare to graduate (Boyson and Short 2003). In 85 percent of the programs surveyed, an astonishing 80 to 100 percent of students were eligible for free or discounted lunch (Boyson and Short 2003).[5] The economic, linguistic, and educational needs of these youth made them particularly vulnerable.

Because they respond to specific, local needs rather than operating according to policy mandates, newcomer programs do not fit a single model. Nevertheless, Short and Boyson (2000b) identify the programs' common features as language courses, instruction in literacy development, instruction that integrates language and content, courses and activities that orient students to U.S. schools and communities, qualified teachers, paraprofessional support, and connections to family. Additionally, newcomer programs tend to offer a wide range of comprehensive services that support students' academic needs and overall well-being, including counseling services, career information and skills development, parent and family support services, tutoring, mentoring, computer and technology training, information and referral services, and even immunization and health services (Boyson and Short 2003; Friedlander 1991). Programs may strive to help students acclimate psychosocially to their community.

Newcomer programs generally share similar goals of helping students acquire English skills while providing some instruction in core content areas. Ninety-seven percent of the programs surveyed by Boyson and Short (2003) provide instruction in one or more core content areas, and some provide instruction in elective areas as well. Some form of simultaneous content instruction is critical because academic achievement suffers if content instruction is delayed until the student has reached a certain level of proficiency in English (see Collier 1992; Cummins 1981b; García 1999; García and Kleifgen 2010; Mace-Matluck, Alexander-Kasparik, and Queen 1999). Among the programs surveyed by Boyson and Short (2003), sheltered instruction was found to be the most common means of teaching content (89 percent of the programs). This technique uses English as the main language of instruction, but it employs specialized strategies to assist with understanding. Only 11 percent of the programs gave content instruction primarily in the home language; that was possible only when schools had concentrations of students from the same linguistic background, as well as trained teachers and appropriate materials. As we show in Chapter 4, Luperón's faculty adopted a dynamic bilingual model in which they taught content courses primarily in the native language for the first two years but employed strategies to support English acquisition across the curriculum. Such an approach is underrepresented in the literature on newcomer schools and thus merits careful scrutiny.

Of the schools surveyed by Short and Boyson, 40 percent also instructed students in native language literacy. Native language literacy instruction is possible only in schools with large numbers of students from the same linguistic background. However, the scarcity of such instruction is surprising in a model meant to valorize students' linguistic and cultural assets. The lack of attention to native language literacy hinders not only emergent bilingualism but also the potential for developing second language literacy (see Bernhardt and Kamil 1995; Bialystok and Cummins 1991; Carson et al. 1990; Cummins 1991; Gabriele et al. 2009; Walsh 1991).

Luperón varies from the typical newcomer school in three very important ways. First, Luperón offers not only content-area instruction in the home language, but also native language literacy. As we discuss in Chapter 4, one of the reasons for Luperón's success has been its explicit attention to aligning literacy practices in the two languages in order to develop students' native academic language and to support the emergence of a dynamic bilingualism. Second, Luperón is itself a separate school: only 6 percent of the schools surveyed by Boyson and Short had such a structure (2003). Third, though it began as a two-year program to prepare immigrant students for mainstreaming into other schools, Luperón has functioned since 2001 as a four-year school. In contrast, more than 60 percent of the schools surveyed by Short and Boyson were designed to serve students for no more than a year, while only 7 percent were intended for eight semesters or more, the majority of which were four-year high schools (2000a; Boyson and Short 2003). The maintenance of a separate site with a focus on a homogeneous linguistic group for a long period has made possible Luperón's elaborate educational language policy. However, such a model also provokes controversies about the potential segregating effects of such an approach. We explore these issues in Chapter 7.

It is clear that empirical studies of the experiences of immigrant newcomer students are needed. In particular, we know little about the efficacy of particular institutional models or language policies for this population. Further, much remains to be discovered about the impact of schooling on the trajectories of these youth. The research reported here addresses these topics and more, in an effort to contribute to a public conversation about quality education for newcomer immigrant youth. Before outlining the research methods and general content of the book, however, we first present the key concepts that serve as a foundation for our study.

Framing the Study: Key Concepts

Broadly conceived, this book draws on key concepts from sociocultural studies of policy, sociolinguistics, language policy and planning, applied linguistics and bilingualism, and the anthropology of education. In what follows, we outline the ideas that ground this monograph.

Sociocultural Studies of Educational Policy

Though often analyzed as an "intrinsically technical, rational, action-oriented instrument that decision makers use to solve problems and affect change" (Shore and Wright 1997, 5), policy is in fact "a complex social practice, an ongoing process of normative cultural production constituted by diverse actors across diverse social and institutional contexts" (Levinson and Sutton 2001, 1). As Koyama (2010) demonstrates, federal educational policy is made, negotiated, resisted, and remade by the actions of multiple agents across multiple local and delocalized situations. Koyama's study of No Child Left Behind (NCLB), and specifically its Supplemental Educational Services provision, reveals how policies are "appropriated" at the local level—that is, how the actions of agents across multiple institutions are guided by the "situated logic in their contexts of everyday practice" (Levinson and Sutton 2001, 17). While influenced (but not determined) by federal, state, and local mandates, school-based responses to broad educational policies can vary dramatically.

Even as the federal government aims to direct the actions of state and local educational agencies through NCLB, those who ultimately apply policy significantly mediate implementation through their participation in collective sense-making (Honig 2006). Local actors, like those associated with Luperón, essentially make policy through the enactment of their interpretations. As demonstrated in this study, the behaviors of policy actors in various levels of New York City's system (including at the school level) were guided but not determined by policy, as they made sense of what actions they were to take and how they were to take them according to their local circumstances.

Employing a sociocultural approach to the study of educational policy as enacted across contexts, in this book we consider the ways that social actors at Luperón appropriated contemporary federal, state, and city educational policies. In Chapter 3, we show how the emergence in New York

City of Dominican political power—especially in relation to educational politics—and the desperate situation of schools in northern Manhattan made Luperón possible. We trace how, together with its seclusion within the Alternative Schools district, Luperón's function in the early years as a transitional school protected it from pressures that might have precluded its survival. We then examine how the advent of NCLB, the declaration of mayoral control, and the subsequent restructurings of the New York City system have afforded certain practices within Luperón, even as they constrained development in other ways. Specifically, we demonstrate how the imposition and subsequent intensification of standardized testing has significantly restricted educational efforts at Luperón, forcing the school to alter its curricular focus. Chapter 4 also describes the ways in which educators at this school negotiate language education policies that are externally imposed. As we will see, language use in the classrooms is continuously adapted to take into account contextual factors, while these adaptations, in turn, affect the context of use. While educators are operating purposefully, language education policies are being transformed in unexpected ways. Despite the existence of official documents, language education policies are socially constructed and dynamically negotiated on a moment-by-moment basis as a means of sense-making (Menken and García 2010).

Dynamic Bilingualism, Macroacquisition, and Translanguaging

One of the major differences between Luperón and most schools serving adolescent newcomers has to do with its approach to language development. Whereas most schools focus on individual language acquisition and development, Luperón attempts to work with the entire community of learners. While most schools rely on a linear model of second language learning, Luperón works with a more complex model of bilingualism. By rejecting individual, linear second language acquisition, Luperón experiments with a model rarely used in schools—a model of dynamic macroacquisition that works differently from what we find in most other schools. Before developing what we mean by dynamic bilingual macroacquisition, we review traditional second language acquisition and bilingualism concepts so that we can contrast them with the very different position on second language development and bilingualism taken by Luperón.

As a field, second language acquisition (SLA) studies the individual performance of second language learners in light of what may be considered "native-like proficiency," as if a static and complete set of grammar rules were available for acquisition. SLA researchers look at the degree to which a language learner's *interlanguage*—that is, the learner's emerging linguistic system (Selinker 1972)—conforms to the target language. They often catalog what is called *fossilization* behavior—that is, "errors" associated with the interlanguage. Selinker and Han (2000) name some of these fossilizations: low proficiency, non-target-like performance, backsliding or the reemergence of "deviant" forms, and errors that are impervious to negative evidence. The emphases on fossilization and "ultimate attainment" in SLA studies have influenced how second language educators view their learners—as incomplete. Too often, teachers oriented by SLA theory employ a deficit perspective: they focus on what students cannot do. Most applied linguists have adopted the SLA framework in developing educational programs for language minorities. The idea is to move second language learners to adopt language and literacy practices that are "native-like," as required by the high-stakes tests that students face.

Most ESL and transitional bilingual education models conceive of English language acquisition as individual phenomena that "mainstream" children into "regular" classes once they have achieved target language native-speaker characteristics. Because this conceptualization is so prevalent in U.S. society, schools tend to favor integrated language education programs, such as two-way bilingual education programs or programs that integrate children who are proficient in English with those who are still learning it. In these anti-bilingual times, these programs are usually called *dual language* programs. The thinking is that native speakers provide an important model for SLA and that a second language is acquired by negotiating communication with them (Wong Fillmore 1991).

But at least since the end of the twentieth century, the idea of native speech has been questioned by many (Canagarajah 1999; Valdés 2005; García 2009a). Kramsch (1997) has argued that the concept of native speech, which had been considered a privilege of birth, is closely linked to social class and education, since the language features of many non-middle-class native-born citizens are considered suspect. Proposing the concept of *multicompetence*—that is, the knowledge of two or more languages in the same mind—Cook (1991, 2002) argues that second language users are different from monolingual speakers because their lives and minds are also different.

In short, bilinguals are not two monolinguals in one (Grosjean 1985; García 2009a). Their ways of using language are distinct. Speaking of these bilinguals as *L1/L2 users*, Guadalupe Valdés (2005) adds, "L1/L2 users have acquired two knowledge systems that they use in order to carry out their particular communicative needs, needs that may be quite unlike those of monolingual native speakers who use a single language in all communicative interactions" (415).

This sort of bilingual multicompetence is not promoted by the traditional models of second language education, which are known broadly as subtractive and additive models. These models were developed in the twentieth century, specifically to describe the situation of bilingualism in Quebec, Canada (Lambert 1975). With subtractive models, as the second language is added, the first language begins to shrink, leading to language shift. Subtractive models can be rendered thus: L1 + L2 − L1 = L2. Subtractive approaches are prevalent in transitional bilingual education programs around the world. On the other hand, additive bilingualism is understood as a second language being added to the students' repertoire with the expectation that the student will have two complete language systems, as in L1 + L2 = L1 + L2. While this approach works to maintain the students' first language, and therefore can more realistically be called a bilingual approach, it does not adequately model what actually happens for many as they become bilingual.

The bilingualism that Luperón promotes is an example of what García (2009a) has called *dynamic bilingualism*, a more heteroglossic conception of bilingualism that rejects the linear conceptions of the previous models and takes into consideration the different and varying language practices for distinct purposes that are the result of the different contexts in which languaging (defined here as discursive practices) develops and functions. These practices go beyond the sociopolitical constructions of a "language" as proposed by states (Makoni and Pennycook 2007) and used in schools. Dynamic bilingualism has to do with complexity theory, which not only regards "systems as interconnected, but also as dynamic, often unstable" (Larsen-Freeman and Cameron 2008, 134). Complexity theory provides a more emic, or learner-centered, account of students' language development. Larsen-Freeman and Cameron explain that "learning is not the taking in of linguistic forms by learners, but the constant adaptation of their linguistic resources in the service of meaning-making in response to the affordances that emerge in the communicative situation, which is, in turn, affected by learners' adaptability" (135). In this regard, complexity theory follows an ecological view of adaptation. As van Lier (2000) explains, "The ecologist will say that knowledge of language for a human is like knowledge of the jungle for an animal. The animal does not have the jungle; it knows how to use the jungle and how to live in it. Perhaps we can say by analogy that we do not have or possess language, but that we learn to use it and to live in it" (253).

The insights provided by complexity theory provide a radical reconceptualization of emergent bilingualism. In this view, students do not "have" languages, do not maintain the languages as distinct systems, do not develop their communicative competence in some linear fashion, and do not approach "native-like proficiency." Instead, from a dynamic bilingualism perspective, language is learned through its use in specific social contexts; the learning is cyclical, continuous, and never ending; and the languages are thoroughly intermeshed.

Further, traditional models of language education and even complex theories of language focus on individuals. Instead, at Luperón, educators focus on language acquisition as a social process that involves an *entire speech community* within its sociocultural and sociopolitical context. In the last few years, sociolinguistic, anthropological, and anthropolitical linguistics (e.g., Zentella 1997) have revealed the utterly social nature of second language acquisition. Scholars have emphasized how second-language learners "are situated in specific social, historical and cultural contexts and how learners resist or accept the positions those contexts offer them" (Norton and Toohey 2001, 310). Canagarajah (1999), Mazrui (2004), Pennycook (1994), Phillipson (1992), and others have made us well aware that the teaching and learning of English have to take into account the sociolinguistic and sociohistorical context of the language community involved, and to resist, in Canagarajah's (1999) words, the "linguistic imperialism in English teaching" (i).

Educators at Gregorio Luperón High School recognize the way in which power relations influence linguistic interaction between Latinos and non-Latinos (Bourdieu 1991), taking into account the communities of practice in which these adolescents live and communicate, their social identities as Spanish-speaking immigrant newcomers who are learning English, and the power relations between the poorer Dominican community in which they reside and the larger English-speaking New York City. As we demonstrate in later chapters, the teachers at Luperón have developed a pedagogy concerned not with individuals, but rather with the speech community and the ways in which practices, identity, and power interact to provide a context for learning, especially the learning of English.

This model, which focuses on a speech community, promotes macro-acquisition. Speaking of the emergence of new Englishes in Asia and Africa, Brutt-Griffler (2004) defines macroacquisition as "the acquisition of a second language by a speech community. It is a process of social second language acquisition, the embodiment of the process of language spread and change, or language change through its spread" (138). Entire speech communities acquire a second language through a process of dynamic bilingualism. Such is the case of the spread of English, for example, in Singapore and the Philippines. But it is also the case in the acquisition of languages that are being revitalized, such as Māori in Aotearoa (New Zealand). As such, the language people acquire varies distinctly from the ways in which it might be used in a different geographical or historical context, but these differences cannot be considered errors, for "any language is the linguistic expression of the speech community that speaks it" (Brutt-Griffler 2004, 129).

Language change always accompanies this bilingual macroacquisition. Luperón supports a model of Latino acquisition of English in which both English and the adolescents' Spanish are changed in interaction. Through this process, English is adopted as the Latino students' own, no longer solely belonging to the Anglo monolingual community, while their U.S. Spanish emerges. Bilingual macroacquisition is a process rooted in and supported by the group's own bilingualism. By engaging with the students' social identities and equalizing power relations, the speech community model of Luperón supports the idea that one learns English best in the company of others from the same speech community who are struggling to acquire it, without competition from "native" speakers. Fishman's (2004) sociolinguistic model posits this principle (429). Fishman says, "Any nominal Xish [minority speaker] presence in upper status and power functions will more often than not be completely overshadowed (if not totally eclipsed) by the vastly more frequent and often far superior Yish [majority speaker] presence in those very same functions." Fishman suggests that the use of a language by speakers with power in a particular domain will always obscure minority speakers in the same domain. Thus, language-minority students in classrooms with language-majority students will always be neglected. Luperón's macroacquisition model of English language acquisition ensures that immigrant Spanish-speaking students are not overshadowed by English native speakers. The school pays attention to developing the English of all students, not just a few individuals, without having to compete with language majority students.

In this dynamic process, both languages are transformed. In explaining this complexity, Fischer and Bidell's (1998) metaphor of the web is illuminating: "The strands in a web are not fixed in a determined order but are the joint product of the web builder's constructive activity and the supportive context in which it is built (like branches, eaves, or the corners of a wall, for a spider web)" (473). Though the support structure and the individual strands are distinct, together they constitute an innovative joint product. In this same way, students draw on their Spanish while learning English and, in the process, transform both languages to result in distinct varieties of Dominican English and U.S. Spanish.

In part, these changes are wrought through practices that García (2009a) has called *translanguaging*—that is, fluid language practices. The term derives from work by Welsh scholar and educator Cen Williams (as described by Baker 2001; Lewis 2008), who coined the term *trawsieithu* to refer to a pedagogy that involves the hearing or reading of lessons in one language, and the development of the work (the oral discussion, the writing of passages, the building of projects and experiments) in another language or vice versa. In translanguaging, the input and output are deliberately in different languages. Like García (2009a), we extend the term here to refer to any pedagogy that intentionally uses two languages flexibly in a bilingual arrangement that promotes bilingualism and biliteracy. Most schools for emergent bilinguals mix students of different language groups: in this context, students develop translanguaging practices to communicate with each other (see, for example, García 2009a and 2009b). However, in this book we will discuss how at Luperón, translanguaging emerges as teachers slowly introduce students to English. As we will see in Chapter 5, translanguaging becomes an important pedagogical approach to developing the English language practices of students.

The Anthropological Study of Schooling for Transnational Youth

In addition to documenting the unusual language education model employed by Gregorio Luperón High School, this study also considers the extent to which the school is able to facilitate social mobility for newcomer Latino youth. In this pursuit, we are guided principally by social studies of schooling, and specifically anthropological and sociological studies of schooling immigrant youth.

Social studies of schooling have long documented how schooling too often perpetuates the status quo or, to borrow Willis's (1981) apt subtitle, "how working-class kids get working-class jobs." Drawing on Bourdieu's practice theory of the mutual and interminable co-production of overarching social structures and individuals' constrained agency, many of these studies offer an unsentimental portrait of the ways in which class (e.g., MacLeod 1995; Willis 1981), race (e.g., Fine 1991; Foley 1990), and gender (Holland and Eisenhart 1990; see also Levinson, Foley, and Holland 1996) shape students' educational trajectories. In many ways, this study is guided by the historically situated, political economic perspective employed in those ethnographies. Adopting Bartlett's (2007, 151) concept of *educational projects*, or "aggregations of institutions, financial resources, social actors, ideologies, discourses, pedagogies and theories of knowledge and learning that shape the way people think about education and its purpose," we consider the ways in which international relations, migration policy, the racialized economic incorporation of Latinos, educational politics and policies, and other social trends influence the educational trajectories of the youth who attend Luperón. Like Bartlett (2010), we consider the complex interrelationships between school, community, history, and economy, including the ways in which social class and previous educational experiences set students up to pursue particular pathways through school. Echoing Nespor (1997), we question "conventionally defined boundaries, looking for flows rather than states, focusing on networks and the layered connections that knot them together rather than on simpler linear histories of circumscribed events or settings" (xiv). We attend specifically to the ways in which social, political, and economic contexts shape educational processes. This political economic approach constitutes what, in our title, we call "subtractive times"—that is, a political moment of waning support for bilingualism and bilingual education, and an economic context in which immigrants continue to be relegated to low-paying work.

We bring this political economic, ethnographic approach to the study of education for immigrant youth. Two theoretical approaches have predominated in investigations concerning immigration and education: Ogbu's *cultural ecological theory* and *segmented assimilation theory*, developed by Portes, Rumbaut, and others. Though our study is informed by these approaches, it departs from them in significant ways to develop a transnational, anthropological analysis more consistent with the findings of our study.

Developed from the 1970s through the 1990s, anthropologist John Ogbu's cultural ecological theory tried to explain the differences he saw between the assimilation of voluntary minorities, such as immigrants drawn by the promise of the American Dream, and nonvoluntary minorities, such as African American youth. According to Ogbu, since nonvoluntary minorities were incorporated through coercion (i.e., conquest, colonization, or slavery), they were more likely to develop oppositional attitudes toward assimilation and, by extension, toward schooling. As Foster (2008) has indicated, Ogbu's work made four primary contributions to our understanding of immigrant youth:

> (a) the general idea that students' academic success is impacted by community and system forces; (b) distinctions among voluntary, involuntary, and autonomous minorities; (c) the recognition that cultural discontinuities between home and school were politically charged for involuntary minorities in a way they were not for voluntary minorities; and (d) the idea that involuntary minorities have developed survival strategies—some that facilitate academic success and others that hinder it . . . while voluntary minorities have developed instrumental approaches to schooling and have proven more adept at successfully negotiating schools in order to realize academic success. (578)

Ogbu's work influenced this study, in that we consider the importance of attending to community and system forces, the political valence of cultural continuities, and students' attitudes. Nevertheless, Ogbu failed to capture the diversity among different generations and within ethnic groups. His work did not sufficiently investigate how variations in the social context of reception influence patterns of social adaptation, which our analysis emphasizes. And, as Gibson (1988) cogently demonstrated, he did not adequately consider the pragmatic strategies that some groups use to "accommodate" school demands without assimilating.

Segmented assimilation theory, as developed by Portes and his associates, built on Ogbu's foundation. Focusing on second-generation youth, segmented assimilation theory posited three possibilities for the incorporation of immigrants (Portes and Zhou 1993, 82): second-generation youth might become acculturated into the white middle class; they might assimilate to the underclass, adopting an adversarial stance toward schooling (dissonant acculturation); or they might engage in selective acculturation, in which they would maintain their parents' culture and language and use their strong ethnic networks to maintain a positive attitude toward education and access opportunities. Recently, a group of scholars have engaged segmented assimilation theory to examine how distinctions in national origin, ethnic affiliation, and context of reception differentially influence incorporation; immigrant youth whose families experience opportunities in the labor market, and strong, active, co-ethnic communities with political influence and social support are more likely to succeed in school (Portes and Rumbaut 2001). In this study, we consider the impact of a culture of additive schooling that is posited, to some degree, on the idea of ethnic solidarity.

Further, drawing on Ogbu, scholars of immigration and education have suggested "the optimism hypothesis" (Kao and Tienda 1995), which conjectures that immigrant children and the children of immigrants, in contrast to third- and higher-generation students, perceive education as a springboard for upward mobility; this optimism buffers them, to some extent, from other risk factors (Gibson 1988). However, studies have made clear that the benefits of immigrant optimism are tempered by economic and social obstacles such as high rates of poverty, residential segregation, and limited stocks of social and other forms of capital (Rosenbaum and Rochford 2008; Alba and Nee 2005; Perreira et al. 2006; Conger et al. 2007).

While our work is informed by theories of segmented assimilation and immigrant optimism, we are wary of the ways in which the "generational" approach employed by sociologists overly homogenizes what is an enormously heterogeneous group of people and sometimes entails universalist, linear assumptions about youth development. Ethnographic attention to the lives of immigrant youth demonstrates the dynamic, dialogical nature of their identity formation and their developing educational trajectories (see Abu El-Haj 2007; Hall 2002; Sarroub 2005; Stritikus and Nguyen 2007). In this ethnographically informed study, much as we discuss the dynamic bilingualism of the youth, we also emphasize the performative elements of culture—the constant cultural bricolage in which the youth engage as they grow into their transnational lives. To reigning sociological approaches to the study of immigrants, our study adds an examination of how transnational processes influence ideas about and practices regarding schooling. Anthropological approaches to education and migration situate Latinos as a diaspora whose movement requires a critical analysis of the historical, economic, and political factors involved (Villenas 2007; see also Wortham, Murillo, and Hamann 2002; Zúñiga, Hamann, and Sánchez García 2008). Such an approach requires attention to the "constructed landscape of collective aspirations" (Appadurai 1996, 31) as well as the cultural imaginaries produced and sustained by transmigrants (Lukose 2005; Shukla 2003).

Further, as Ogbu himself noted, research on immigrant youth must pay sufficient attention to local community forces, including schools as a context of reception. In general, studies have inadequately considered the "local institutional opportunity structure" (Kasinitz et al. 2008, 143). And yet scholars have demonstrated the importance of school programs (Ancess 2003), positive relationships with teachers and other school personnel (Suárez-Orozco, Suárez-Orozco, and Todorova 2008), and peer relations (Gibson, Gándara, and Koyama 2004). In this case study, we pay careful attention to the additive culture of achievement established at the school for immigrant youth, including familial relationships between students and teachers and strong, positive peer pressure toward achievement.

It is also important to consider the ways in which schools embrace or reject the resources and identity politics that students bring to the classroom, and how these ways influence students' academic outcomes. In her striking ethnography, Valenzuela (1999b) describes *subtractive schooling,* or the way a high school with a predominantly Mexican student body systematically took away important cultural and linguistic resources from the youth through a variety of pedagogical and curricular practices. By ignoring the cultural importance of an *educación* that would include authentic caring in addition to academic training, the school failed to provide a culturally appropriate pedagogy of high expectations and strong support for the students. Further, rather than celebrating Mexican culture and language, these were disrespected: so, for example, students were considered "limited English proficient" rather than "Spanish dominant." The low status of Spanish and Mexican culture reinforced and exacerbated the negative interactions between Mexican immigrant and Mexican American students. These features were aptly described by Valenzuela as subtractive schooling, an approach that turned cultural and linguistic difference into deficit rather than asset.

In contrast, in this book, we describe an extensive case study in which educators provided to immigrant newcomer youth what might be called *additive schooling,* an approach that builds on and extends the social, cultural, and linguistic assets brought by multilingual, diverse student populations, and aims to prepare bicultural and bilingual students to negotiate their complex worlds.

Thus, on the whole, this book considers practices of *additive schooling*—including dynamic bilingual education with a focus on macro-acquisition, as well as culturally relevant pedagogy and a remarkable school culture of opportunity and success—in *subtractive times*, constituted by opposition to bilingual education, the intensification of educational policies that undermine bilingual approaches and exclude newcomers from attaining diplomas, and track immigrant, working-class students largely into working-poor jobs. The remainder of this book considers the complex interplay between these elements as they shape the lives and educational trajectories of immigrant Latino youth. Before outlining that story, however, we first explain the research strategies used to generate this study.

Doing the Study: Research Methods

This book results from a four-year, longitudinal, multi-methodological study. The early stages of research design were shaped by the input of research assistant Dr. Jill Koyama; access to the school site was facilitated by Ofelia García's long history of work in bilingual education and her deep connections to Latino educators across New York City. When we initiated the study in September 2003, we conducted a survey of fifty newly arrived students in order to get a sense of their heterogeneity, their migration histories, their early perceptions of the school and its curriculum, their use of various media, and their social relationships. During that first year, both Lesley Bartlett and Ofelia García did intensive classroom observations over a period of nine months in lower-level ESL and Spanish classes and content-area courses in order to document the school's curriculum, compare pedagogical approaches and media of instruction, and consider the overall culture of the school. To expand the perspectives included in this early phase of the study, we conducted seven focus groups with newly arrived students enrolled in ESL 1 and 2, a focus group with the ESL teachers, and another focus group with the Spanish teachers. Finally, during that first year of the study, we conducted monthly staff development sessions in which faculty explored the struggles they faced in providing bilingual education during subtractive times.

On the basis of our analysis of this early data, we decided to organize a longitudinal study of twenty newcomer immigrant youth. We stratified the sample to include equal numbers of girls and boys and to include equal numbers of students from three categories: low, middle, and high performance on a variety of English literacy tasks, as determined by their ESL teacher. This element of the study involved annual interviews with a cohort of students from September 2004 to May 2008. We also collected annual samples of students' writing. From these twenty students, we selected six focal students to follow in greater depth, interviewing them more frequently and conducting participant observations over a period of two years. Interviews and observations for the cohort study were conducted primarily by four graduate assistants affiliated with the project: Ali Michael, Norma Andrade, Elizabeth "Betsy" Cromwell Kim, and César Fernández.

In addition, we planned some enrichment activities for students from Luperón in order to contribute to their development while securing for ourselves the opportunity to get to know them and their concerns in a less formal setting. In the second year of the project, Lesley Bartlett and Ali Michael conducted an ethnography workshop over the course of three months for rising seniors at the school who were interested in practicing their English while learning qualitative research methods. The workshop offered a chance for us to interact with students outside of the classroom and many opportunities for informal interviews with them. At the same time, Lesley and Ali planned several field trips specifically for the youth involved in the project. These included a trip to the Statue of Liberty, a visit to Columbia University, and a discussion with the director of Columbia's Double Discovery program, a college preparatory program for minorities underrepresented in universities. (Two members of the cohort applied to Double Discovery, and one was admitted to the program and completed it.)

In the third year of the project, Lesley Bartlett, her colleague Lalitha Vasudevan (from Teachers College), Ali Michael, and César Fernández offered a semester-long workshop in digital storytelling, in which members of the cohort were invited to learn how to use digital cameras and recorders, as well as the software to turn their images into digital stories. Eight of the youth decided to participate. Once again, this workshop provided critical opportunities for us to see how the youth documented their lives and concerns, as well as chances for informal conversation. The third year of the project culminated with a field trip to Yankee Stadium to watch

Alex Rodríguez and other Dominican baseball players engage in the Dominican national passion. These activities, graciously funded by Teachers College, constituted our efforts to build into the research process reciprocity and relevance for the student participants; they reflect our political commitment to ensuring that the research outcome would not only assist immigrant youth in a general way but that the research process would, at least in small ways, benefit the immediate participants.

Our interests in the transition from high school to college were greatly informed by the master's thesis completed by Elizabeth Cromwell Kim. She interviewed seven graduates of Luperón about the challenges they faced as they secured spots at college and adapted to the distinctly different environment. Her findings regarding barriers to college enrollment and attendance inform Chapter 6.

In the final year of the study, while César Fernández skillfully completed the annual interviews with the original cohort, Lesley Bartlett conducted formal and informal interviews with ten teachers at Luperón. In addition, Ofelia García and Carmina Makar conducted interviews with twenty-six mothers, and they attended several PTA meetings, where they spoke with many parents about their concerns. Ofelia also interviewed the founders of Luperón. Lesley Bartlett and Ofelia García conducted a series of interviews with the principal of the school. Finally, Jill Koyama conducted interviews with several other administrators as we analyzed the data on educational policies.

The data for this book were analyzed using an analytic inductive approach (LeCompte and Preissle 1993). The members of the research team wrote field notes within one day of conducting observations or interviews. As data collection proceeded, we began to incorporate initial hypotheses and interpretations into the field notes as hunches subject to rejection or confirmation. At regular intervals of data collection, the researchers reviewed the field notes and wrote analytical memos (Emerson, Fretz, and Shaw 1995; see also Richardson 2000). These memos indicated which analyses needed further evidence, which was then collected. At this time, we consciously sought negative instances as well. The graduate students were deeply involved in this process; their interpretations have been very important to the ongoing analysis of the data. As the authors of this text, we reread the full corpus of data and developed separate analyses based on key themes. We then exchanged correspondence to discuss discrepant interpretations and instances of negative evidence.

In such a study, the linguistic capabilities of the researchers are naturally of interest to readers. Three members of the research team—Ofelia García, César Fernández, and Carmina Makar—speak Spanish as their home language. The other team members who conducted interviews in Spanish communicate easily in that language. This second group found instances when their unfamiliarity with certain expressions was productive, because it provided an excuse to elicit elaborations of key terms such as *tranca'o*, which we discuss in later chapters.

In writing this text, we made a strategic decision to refer to ourselves as "we" and to the data as gathered by "us." There are several reasons for this decision. First, we found it quite cumbersome to identify the individual researcher with each piece of data. Second, the principal investigators held regular meetings with the research assistants who collected much of the data, eliciting their written and dialogically produced analyses of the data over the course of its collection. Third, while data were collected by multiple researchers, the analyses were primarily elaborated by Ofelia García and Lesley Bartlett (in dialogue, of course, with key interlocutors such as Luperón principal Juan Villar), and this fact is reflected by the authorial "we." Finally, we have long felt that, though important, analyses of the ways in which researchers' perceived identities influence data collection end up being (necessarily) speculative as to the perceptions of participants. Thus, we felt that the gains of using the plural voice outweighed the potential losses of identifying the fieldworker in each instance. While this approach is common in many larger-scale studies, it is rather unusual in ethnographic studies that cleave to the lone researcher model. It therefore may provoke some useful debates among readers and researchers as we grapple with the changes in methodological paradigms occasioned by the move toward not only multi-sited ethnographic techniques but also research apprenticeship opportunities for students.

Presenting the Study: Chapter Outline

In the chapters that follow, we develop the themes and overall argument presented in this introduction. Chapter 2, titled "In the Heights: Dominican Youth Immigrate to New York," examines sociohistorical processes that have influenced the school and the immigrant youth who are the focus of this study. The chapter considers the economic, political, and educational contexts from which the Dominican youth hail. It then examines the integration of Dominicans into the U.S. context and the complex factors that have consigned them to the highest levels of poverty amongst Latino immigrants. The chapter discusses how incorporation into other Spanish-speaking communities as well as English-speaking communities influences students' languaging and learning and considers the school conditions to which Latino newcomer immigrants are often relegated in New York City. In these ways, Chapter 2 establishes key elements of the historical, social, political, economic, and cultural contexts for our study.

Chapter 3, "Education Policy as Social Context," explores how education policies—specifically bilingual education policy and federal, state, and local accountability measures—set the context for educating immigrant youth. We consider the political opposition to bilingual education in the United States, the changes wrought in schooling by the NCLB, the momentous educational reforms in the 2000s under Mayor Michael Bloomberg in New York City, and the experimentation in New York City with small schools and international schools. This chapter explains how national discourses on bilingualism, government policies, and localized policy responses establish a context for everyday actions in schools such as Luperón.

In Chapter 4, "From Subtractive to Additive Schooling," we recount the history of Gregorio Luperón High School from its formation in 1993, when most schools were structured around a subtractive, deficit perspective of immigrant youth, through the contemporary period. We analyze the significant social changes that have influenced the school's development, including the growth of the school's student body and teaching corps, the diversification of the student body beyond the core group of Dominican newcomers, and the expansion of gangs and drug activity among peer networks in northern Manhattan and the south Bronx. We also examine carefully how city, state, and federal policies afford certain developments for the school and constrain others—specifically the school's language education policies—in ways that influence students' learning and languaging.

The subsequent chapter, "Languaging at Luperón," considers the dynamic bilingual educational approach employed at Luperón. Here we present the strategies and techniques that have been adopted and adapted by the faculty. Luperón's approach frames students as emergent bilinguals in the process of acquiring multilingual academic literacies in ways critically different from mainstream approaches. We argue that Luperón's dynamic bilingualism offers important lessons about educating immigrant youth more broadly.

Chapter 6, "Challenges Facing Immigrant Youth at Luperón," examines key social and cultural challenges identified by students as obstacles to their adaptation. We rely on formal and informal interviews with Luperón students to describe richly how these factors have influenced their sense of self, belonging, adaptation, and academic engagement.

In Chapter 7, "Social Capital and Additive Schooling at Luperón," we draw on the longitudinal component of the study to consider how the school has helped students adapt to the challenges and stresses of immigration, family separation, and linguistic adaptation. We argue that Luperón's additive approach to schooling fosters students' social and cultural capital by encouraging their relationships with institutional agents such as teachers and community-based organizations, as well as bolstering their peer social capital as they encounter these major transitions. The bilingual high school itself has served as an incredibly valuable institutional resource, and the school culture continually produced there has fostered student achievement. However, as we note in this chapter and the next, the gains that students take away from the school are severely constrained by the social and economic conditions they face.

In the final data chapter, "The Political Economy of Education," we examine the experiences of these youth as they transition out of Luperón into further schooling, work and family obligations, or both. The chapter considers the extent to which the school is able to facilitate social and economic mobility for these students in a highly constrained political economic context. We demonstrate that although Luperón manages to shepherd a significantly higher proportion of its students through graduation than its peer institutions, and though it provides intensive college counseling support, many of the students end up taking low-wage jobs in the service and retail sectors with little opportunity for economic advancement. Thus, while the "additive schooling" experienced at Luperón is promising, the "subtractive times" severely constrain the social and economic trajectories of these youth. These sobering findings underscore the ways in which broader economic and social structures limit the efforts of schools to promote social change.

In Chapter 9, "Educating Immigrant Youth: Lessons Learned," we reflect on the case of Gregorio Luperón High School in order to draw lessons for the education of immigrant newcomer youth. We demonstrate the importance of bilingual education for immigrant youth, who often find educational and work opportunities precisely because of their bilingualism. We consider the implications of this case study regarding the value of small, committed schools; a well-trained, cohesive faculty with deep content-area expertise; and institutional agents who extend social capital to students. *Additive Schooling in Subtractive Times* offers a critique of the current socioeducational conditions of immigrant adolescents in the United States by describing an alternate possibility. Yet, this book also makes evident that the successes of schools are mediated by sociopolitical conditions that continue to limit the opportunities of immigrant youth even after they have graduated from high school.

2

In the Heights: Dominican Youth Immigrate to New York

IN 2008, AT THE CONCLUSION of our period of data collection, *In the Heights* won several Tony Awards, including Best Musical. In and through its merengue, salsa, hip-hop, and reggaeton-drenched musical numbers, the characters reflect with nostalgia on a largely imagined life in the Caribbean while they explore the economic, political, and cultural constraints of their lives in Washington Heights, New York City. Written by Lin-Manuel Miranda, an actor and composer of Puerto Rican descent who grew up in Inwood (just north of Washington Heights), *In the Heights* explores the constant process of symbolic bricolage—of using the images, language, and experiences at hand (such as those related to hip-hop, *café con leche*, street slang, graffiti, depictions of saints, and *carnaval*, to mention just a few) to produce, temporarily and on an ongoing basis, a sense of self and community. The plot revolves around two young couples. Usnavi, born in the Dominican Republic and named after a "U.S. Navy" ship his parents saw from the beach, has grown up in Washington Heights but dreams of returning to a largely imagined home; he falls in love with Vanessa, a young woman born in Washington Heights with aspirations of moving downtown. Usnavi is implicitly compared to Mina, a girl born in Washington Heights who goes to Stanford University, where she feels conflict between the values taught to her by her Cuban-born grandmother, the social environment of other American youth, and the intellectual requirements of the academy. When Mina falls for Benny, a young African American from the Heights who works for the taxi dispatch company owned by Mina's father, her father's racist reaction reveals not only the color discrimination prevalent in the community but also its struggles over social and economic aspirations. "Abuela" [grandmother], the neighborhood matriarch, reflects on her own upbringing in "the Washington Heights of Cuba," where she experienced hunger and social unrest, until she arrived in Washington Heights, where she and her mother shared a cramped space, struggled to learn some English, and worked as maids to get by. As the weeks turned into years, Abuela confronted it all with *paciencia y fé* [patience and faith].

The musical underscores the emerging pan-ethnicity of New York, such as when one character states, "My mom is Dominican-Cuban, my dad is from Chile and PR which means I'm Chile-Domini-curican! But I always say I'm from Queens!" Further, and perhaps more important, the musical's mélange of images, rhythms, and languages underscores the opportunistic, dynamic bilingualism and multiculturalism of the Heights (and, increasingly, of Latino communities throughout the States), such as when Usnavi renounces his dream of returning to the Dominican Republic and exuberantly states that "this corner"—the Heights—"is my destiny. . . . I found my island! I've been on it this whole time and I'm home!" This poignant musical, whose lyrics became very popular with Latino youth at Luperón and throughout the city, details the complex emotions—including hope, nostalgia, loss, belonging, patience, and faith—required to live a transnational life.

As we show in this chapter, themes from this musical echo in the migration and cultural experiences of students at Luperón. As a school, Luperón is infused with Dominican and, more broadly, Latino cultural elements. As we discuss in Chapter 4, it was founded by Latino educators in the 1990s. Though it includes Spanish speakers from many countries in Latin America and the Caribbean, approximately 85 percent of the student body hails from the Dominican Republic. For this reason, in this chapter we consider the specific economic, political, social, and cultural elements of transmigration between the Dominican Republic and the United States. This sociopolitical context serves as more than a mere backdrop: understanding the school and its students—their struggles and successes—requires historical contextualization and sociological scrutiny of the economic, political, cultural, and educational circumstances they came *from* and the structures and situations they face upon arrival, for the difficulties faced by the students of Luperón result from very specific social histories. These contexts have important implications for the education of immigrant youth, and especially for their linguistic development.

In what follows, we consider the conditions that fundamentally shape education at Luperón as well as the educational and linguistic experiences of its students. First, we discuss how the context from which they have emigrated—the Dominican Republic—as well as the context to which they have immigrated—*Nueva York*—have shaped the lives of students at Luperón. We consider the economic, political, and educational contexts of life in the Dominican Republic and how those have influenced the lives of the youth in our study. We then consider the overall incorporation of Dominicans into the U.S. context, in which a variety of factors have consigned them to the highest levels of poverty amongst Latino immigrants. Third, we discuss how incorporation into Spanish-speaking communities influences the language and learning processes for these youth and sets specific demands on their education. Finally, we consider the schools in New York City that these youths generally attend.

Immigrating from the Dominican Republic

Dominicans form a significant portion of the Latino population in the United States generally and New York City specifically. Dominicans are a substantial and fast-growing part of the immigrant population in the United States, where they constitute the fifth-largest Latino group, numbering 1,356,361 in the 2009 American Community Survey estimate (U.S. Census Bureau 2009). More than half a million Dominicans (549,051) lived in New York City in 2007, constituting the city's second-largest Latino group (ibid.). Dominicans are the largest immigrant group in New York City schools: they constituted almost 19 percent of the immigrant student population in 1999–2000, while Latin Americans made up 17 percent and other Caribbean students accounted for another 15 percent (Conger, Schwartz, and Stiefel 2003, 3).

Immigration from the Dominican Republic has varied widely over the past decades. Heavily restricted under Rafael Trujillo's dictatorship, it surged after the 1963 ouster by military forces and conservative political groups of the democratically elected Juan Bosch, and also after the 1965 U.S. invasion to reinforce conservative efforts to block Bosch and his supporters (Itzigsohn and Cabral 2000). When U.S.-backed Joaquín Balaguer assumed power in 1966 and began his reign of fierce repression, those on the left who wished to restore democracy were forced to flee for fear of retaliation (Linares 1989). Having made it almost impossible for them to stay at home in the Dominican Republic, the United States rather selfishly opened its doors to dissidents to prevent what the U.S. considered "another Cuba" (Smith 2007, 247). As a result, many of the people who arrived in New York City and elsewhere during this time, including some of Luperón's founders, were essentially political refugees. The passage of the U.S. Immigration Act of 1965, which relaxed immigration quotas, and the demand for cheap labor in garment factories further contributed to an influx of immigrants from the Dominican Republic (Duany 2003; Linares 1989).

Immigration in the 1970s and 1980s was also stimulated by the Dominican Republic's domestic economic troubles during those decades, provoking a diversification of immigrants in terms of class and labor background (Hernández 2002). The shift from agriculture to tourism and manufacturing ultimately exacerbated socioeconomic inequality in the Dominican Republic. When, in 1973, then-president Balaguer issued a decree that relocated residents living along coastal areas in order to develop that land for tourists, the massive displacement left many homeless. Tourism failed to promote job growth in an equitable manner, and instead deepened social and economic divisions (Pomeroy and Jacob 2004). Hiring decisions in the tourism sector were made along racial lines, privileging those with lighter skin and non-African features (Gregory 2007).

Throughout the eighties and continuing into the nineties, the Dominican Republic received an influx of loans in response to its economic troubles. These loans were commonly accompanied by structural adjustment policies that mandated funding cuts in critical social sectors. For example, in 1990, Balaguer initiated the New Economic Program, which eliminated food subsidies (Spanakos and Wiarda 2003). Similar reforms precipitated severe reductions in the state's provision of social service and employment-related benefits, particularly in education and health care. By 1990, government expenditures in education decreased to 45 percent of what they had been in the eighties (Gregory 2007). Rather than assist those living under the worst conditions of poverty in the Dominican Republic, structural adjustments "led to increases in underemployment and poverty and to a sharpening of social inequalities" (Gregory 2007, 28).

Steady immigration persisted in the 1990s, stimulated by frustration with markedly high levels of income inequality and the solid belief that familial socioeconomic mobility was easier to achieve in the United States (and elsewhere) than in the Dominican Republic.[1] According to U.S. census data from 2000, 65.9 percent of Dominican residents in the country at that time had arrived prior to 1989, while 37.5 percent entered between

1990 and 2000. Significant numbers of Dominican professionals migrated to the United States: Guarnizo (1994) estimates that fifteen thousand professionals entered the United States during the short span of time between 1986 and 1991 (73). At the same time, "the initially middle-class and elite migrants [gave] way to peasant migrants and then urban dwellers with lower income and education levels. In the United States, Dominicans have concentrated in the light manufacturing and low-income service economies" (Smith 2007, 41). Thus, while they are diverse, Dominican immigrants have generally been incorporated into low-paying sectors of the American workforce. Further, they have been incredibly generous with the remittances they have sent back home (Vasconcelos 2004). These factors have reduced the funds Dominicans have had to live on.

Economic insecurities and low levels of social investment continue to trigger a steady stream of immigrants from the Dominican Republic to the United States. As Sagás and Molina (2003) explain:

> The Dominican Republic's macroeconomic picture certainly looks better now than during the chaotic 1980s, but an underlying state of permanent economic crisis persists. Unemployment and underemployment are still high in an economy that has divested from agriculture and into tourism, free trade zones (dominated by assembly industries), and other service sector activities, but where major challenges, contradictions, and inconsistencies still persist. Fiscal frailty, high interest rates, a high external deficit, low monetary reserves, fluctuating oil prices, low tax collection rates, an inefficient and unfair tax system, burdensome and restrictive banking laws, confusing investment laws, lack of well-established rules for the protection of foreign investments, an expensive and inefficient bureaucracy, and low levels of investment in education and health are among some of the many complex factors behind the persistence of low levels of socioeconomic development in the Dominican Republic.

While many of the Dominican migrants who left the island over the past few decades headed to Europe (primarily Spain, Switzerland, and Italy), hundreds of thousands made their way to the United States, principally to New York and its environs (though increasingly also settling in Florida, Massachusetts, Rhode Island, and other locations).

Notably, as the presence of Dominicans has grown in New York City, which is sometimes jokingly referred to as "the Dominican Republic's second-largest city," so has their political clout. Dominicans represent an unusual form of what Smith (2007) calls "political transnationalism" (1097). The Dominican Republic received more than $2.9 billion in remittances in 2006, representing 9.0 percent of its gross domestic product (GDP) (IADB 2009; IFAD 2007). In the late 1990s, coveting the immensely valuable remissions from those who immigrated to the United States, who provided 60 percent of the total remittances (IADB 2009), the Dominican Republic rewrote the constitution to grant Dominicans living outside the country voting rights (though, until the early 2000s, they had to fly home to cast their ballots) (Smith 1997). These developments were presupposed by a very high transnationalization of political party life between the Dominican Republic and New York (Smith 2007, 42; see also Levitt 2001).

These political and economic forces were important "push" factors that prompted immigration. It is equally important to consider the educational conditions from which the most recent immigrants have emerged.

Public Education in the Dominican Republic

The Dominican Republic has a considerable network of private schools; many of them, especially the more expensive ones in urban centers, offer a high-quality education to middle- and upper-class residents. However, because the majority of Dominican youth who immigrate to the United States attended public schools before coming, it is important to consider the state of public education in the Dominican Republic.

The Dominican Republic has suffered from low levels of investment in public education for decades. In the 1980s and early 1990s, on average, the country invested less than 2 percent of its GDP in public schools. Indeed, in 1991, the investment rate dipped to a mere 0.97 percent of the GDP. Between 1996 and 2002, public expenditure on education as a percentage of GDP increased from 1.9 percent to 2.9 percent.[2] However, the economic crisis of 2003 severely affected funding for public schooling: by 2004–2005, the spending continued decreasing to 1.5 percent and 1.9 percent of GDP, respectively, erasing the gains made between 1996 and 2002 (Ziffer 2005; OECD 2008). Though General Education Law 66-1997 was passed more than a decade ago, no government has yet complied with the mandate to spend at least 4 percent of its GDP or 16 percent of its national budget on investments in education. A significant underfunding of the Dominican education system underlies many of the challenges its policy-makers, administrators, teachers, and students currently face (PREAL 2006; OECD 2008). Though public financing of education has somewhat increased over the past decade, the Dominican Republic has one of the region's lowest government expenditures on education in relation to GDP (see PREAL 2006).

Further, the Dominican Republic has spent most of its educational resources on basic schooling—for instance, the government spent 62.7 percent on basic education in 2002–2003, compared to 11.84 percent for secondary education and just 2.7 percent for tertiary education. The percentage allocated to basic education is the highest in the Latin American region, and the percentages going to secondary and tertiary education are the lowest (OECD 2008). This has serious implications for the quality of education enjoyed by youth who attended public schools before immigrating as adolescents.

After UNESCO's "Education for All" conference in Jomtien in 1990, the Dominican Republic embarked on an educational reform plan. The first Plan Decenal de Educación (Decennial Education Plan; 1992–2002) influenced schooling by expanding access and coverage of basic education, introducing curricular innovations, distributing textbooks, implementing school feeding programs in poor areas, increasing teachers' salaries, and investing in the professional development of teachers (Ziffer 2005; OECD 2008). The Plan Estratégico de Desarollo de Educación (Strategic Plan for Educational Development; 2003–2012) aims to expand pre-primary and secondary education and improve the quality of primary education. Its main achievements to date have been an extension of educational coverage at all levels (4.3 percent yearly on average); expansion of coverage to grade 8 in rural areas; and an increase in promotion and survival rates, along with shrinking rates of repetition, fewer dropouts, and fewer over-age students (OECD 2008).

However, according to a 2008 United Nations Development Programme (UNDP) report, the Dominican Republic continues to perform poorly in the provision and regulation of education, "which in turn has contributed to the perpetuation of an educational system that is deeply inequitable and reproduces an exclusionary social order" (UNDP 2008, 36–37). The report found that in the provinces where poverty is more pronounced, secondary school enrollment is lower. More generally, the 2002 census reported that 15.7 percent of boys and girls between ages six and thirteen do not attend school (UNDP 2008, 37). There are fifteen provinces in which that percentage is higher, with the highest gaps in enrollment recorded in Elías Piña, Pedernales, Peravia, La Altagracia, and La Romana.

Gender parity in primary school is greater than in secondary school, where there is lower coverage of male students. With respect to secondary education, a 2006 survey found that only 36.8 percent of boys and 51.9 percent of girls aged between fourteen and seventeen attended school (as cited in UNDP 2008, 177).[3]

According to the 2008 UNDP report, all forms of measurement indicate that the Dominican educational system is lacking in quality. Classrooms are overcrowded: the country needs between seventeen thousand and twenty-four thousand additional classrooms in order to incorporate the school-age population that is currently not enrolled in formal education (UNDP 2008, 62; OECD 2008). According to the 2008 Organisation for Economic Co-operation and Development (OECD) Report, the infrastructure of public education centers, which serve more than 80 percent of the nation's basic education population, is substandard. Many of the schools lack basic instructional resources (such as access to textbooks; basic audiovisual equipment; and spaces for teachers, administrators, and parents to meet). Inadequate mechanisms for the distribution of textbooks and instructional materials often result in schools receiving their materials late, and a lack of teacher training means that many educators are not able to use these tools in pedagogically effective and productive ways. For the most part, Dominican teachers work by themselves and cannot count on the support and supervision needed to address classroom issues and improve their instructional methodologies. Perhaps even more critical is the fact that although the official curriculum calls for 1,080 hours of class time for primary education, 1,250 for secondary education, and 1,400 hours for the technical professional level, it is estimated that the average number of hours that a student spends in class does not reach 500 (SEE 2008). Furthermore, though the national curriculum calls for 5 hours of class time per day, the actual average of class time hours is a mere 2.5 (PREAL 2006). A rather casual approach to school closure also continues to be a problem, and teacher absenteeism may be as high as 10 percent on any day (OECD 2008). The absenteeism is exacerbated by low salaries and double shifts. A primary school teacher earns on average about 5,200 DOP (160 USD) per month, working one shift per day.[4] Teachers are allowed to work two shifts, which about half the teachers do, while others seek to supplement their income by other forms of employment (OECD 2008).

The shift system, or *tanda,* is itself a reason for the minimal hours of time on task and the low quality of schooling. The Dominican Republic has long operated a shift system to accommodate increased demand for schooling amid a supply of too few—and significantly underfunded—facilities (OECD 2008). Forty-five percent of basic schools in urban areas operate with three shifts and the remaining 55 percent function at education centers in two shifts, offering a mix of basic and secondary levels. The shift system has both advantages and disadvantages. It allows for flexibility with school schedules, making it possible for students who work or have child care responsibilities to attend school in the evening. However, the system also poses many problems. Teachers often teach two or three shifts in different locations, wasting valuable work time in transit. They have difficulty adhering to the schedule; all too often, they simply fail to show up to teach. As a result of tardy and absent teachers, students receive fewer than half of the instructional hours they deserve. Further, with this overload, teachers are not always planning sufficiently for each course. There is no unified administrative structure for the shifts (each shift has a different principal), which gives rise to problems with school cleanliness, use of school materials, and congestion during transition times (OECD 2008; SEE 2008).

As a result of these and other factors, the quality of education in the Dominican Republic is low, as measured by standardized test scores. In 2005, a research consortium of three universities (two Dominican and one American) conducted an assessment of third-, fourth-, and fifth-grade students in a national sample of two hundred public urban, public rural, and fully accredited private schools throughout the Dominican Republic.[5] A goal of the study was to determine the level of mastery of the objectives of the Dominican curriculum, with a focus on reading comprehension and mathematics. In reading comprehension, students answered on average fewer than nine questions correctly out of a total of twenty-one questions. In mathematics, students answered on average fewer than twelve questions correctly out of a total of twenty-one questions (OECD 2008). International comparative studies also illuminate the low quality of education in the Dominican Republic. A comparative study by UNESCO found that third- and fourth-grade students in the Dominican Republic demonstrated among the lowest levels of language and mathematical competencies when compared to students from other countries in Latin America. Data from international assessments as well as the results from national tests in relationship to expected levels of performance showed a serious gap between the expectations of a new curriculum and the realities of graduates' knowledge, skills, and competencies (PREAL 2006). PREAL's *Informe de Progreso Educativo República Dominicana* (2006) took into account measures of quality such as standardized test scores, class time, distribution of school materials, and monitoring of teacher performance, and ultimately gave the Dominican education system a grade of "D" based on the quality of student learning and overall education experience.

The low levels of educational quality are linked to high levels of repetition and low levels of completion. During the late 2000s, more than 6.5 percent of the total number of students enrolled in the public Dominican educational system were repeaters (UNDP 2008). School completion rates have been increasing. However, over-age students are a problem: on average, 20 percent of all first-grade students, where the typical age is six, were nine years old or older. Estimates cite that nearly 240,000 students are enrolled in primary school when their ages correspond with higher grades (Gajardo 2007).

The percentage of Dominican students who complete basic and secondary levels of education is low when compared to other Latin American countries (PREAL 2006). The Dominican Republic is among the Latin American countries that have secondary completion levels of below 50 percent for the population aged 20–24; the country's completion rates compare favorably only to those of Nicaragua and Guatemala (PREAL 2006). Poverty affects students' access to and ability to stay in school. The main reasons that children and adults drop out of the primary and secondary levels of schooling are economic; close to 70 percent of the males and 36 percent of the females who drop out do so because they must work or lack the financial resources to continue schooling (see UNDP 2008).

The state of Dominican education influences the credentials and human capital that youth and their families carry with them to the United States. Dominican immigrants have low levels of education compared to many immigrant populations, and certainly compared to U.S.-born Latinos: in 2000, 55.6 percent of Dominican immigrants to New York twenty-five years old or older had less than a high school diploma (Hernández and Rivera-Batiz 2003). Among Dominicans across the United States, only

10.6 percent had completed college, compared to 24.4 percent of the general U.S. population (5). This low level of educational attainment has important implications for the schooling of immigrant youth.

Immigrating to New York

The economic conditions experienced by Dominican families in the United States also fundamentally shape the needs of Luperón students. Dominican families generally follow a pattern referred to as *step* or *stepwise migration*, in which one family member initiates the migration, leaving behind children, spouse, and siblings who gradually join him or her as the lengthy process of obtaining permanent visas is resolved (Grasmuck and Pessar 1991; Itzigsohn 2009). (In addition, it is not uncommon for parents to have more children during their early years in the United States, resulting in blended families with some members possessing U.S. citizenship.) Through this stepwise migration, Dominican workers and their families are gradually absorbed into low-paying jobs and shockingly high levels of poverty.

New York, the city built by immigration, continues to be a primary site for Latino—and, more specifically, Dominican—relocation. The city's foreign-born population increased by an astounding 38 percent between 1990 and 2000, rising from 2.1 million to 2.9 million (NYC DCP 2000). Latinos are the largest minority population living in New York City; at 2,315,041 people, they represented over a quarter (27.5 percent) of the city's population in 2009 (U.S. Census Bureau 2009).[6] Dominicans have constituted the majority of the Latino immigrant population since 1990; in 2000, they made up 13 percent of the entire foreign-born population in New York (Hernández and Rivera-Batiz 2003; NYC DCP 2000). They also accounted for almost a quarter of all Latinos in New York (24 percent in 2007; ibid).

As a group, Latinos in New York face distinct challenges. Latinos have disproportionately low levels of socioeconomic attainment in New York City as compared to other ethnic and racial groups, as well as the overall population (NYC DCP 2000). The average unemployment rate for Latinos in New York City in 2007 was estimated to be 5.6 percent, as compared to the 4.4 percent unemployment rate for the total population (U.S. Census Bureau 2007).

The economic situation of Dominicans in New York is particularly dire. According to Hernández and Rivera-Batiz (2003), unemployment rates of Dominicans in New York were at a high 8.9 percent for males and 13.1 percent for females in 2000. While this represents a significant decline from the 1990 rates of 15.7 percent for males and 18.4 percent for females, Rivera-Batiz concludes that it does not represent a substantial gain, given that it is still high compared to the country's 4.1 percent average unemployment rate at the time, and particularly in comparison to the 3.1 percent average unemployment rate of non-Latino whites (Hernández and Rivera-Batiz 2003; Rivera-Batiz 2000).

Securing employment does not guarantee economic security for Latino populations. According to the 2009 American Community Survey, the per capita mean annual income for Latinos in the United States in 2009 was lower than for all other ethnic and racial groups, at $14,977.[7] This was significantly below the U.S. average of $26,409, and contrasts sharply with the non-Latino white population's per capita mean annual household income at $28,960. Latinos are behind non-Hispanic black households as well, whose per capita mean annual income is at $17,700 (U.S. Census Bureau 2009). Dominicans face considerable economic constraints: The mean annual per capita household income of the Dominican population in the United States was $11,065 in the year 1999, or "about half the average per capita income in the country," a figure "significantly lower than the per capita income of the Black/African American population and even slightly lower than the income of the average Latino household" (Hernández and Rivera-Batiz 2003, 2).

In New York City, Latinos on average have incomes that are lower than the average for the city's total population, and significantly lower than the average of their white counterparts. The three-year estimates for 2005–2007 from the American Community Survey show the percentage of Latinos employed in management, professional, or related occupations in New York City to be approximately 21 percent, as compared to 54 percent for non-Latino whites (NYC DCP 2005). The average per capita income for Latinos in New York City in 1999 was approximately $12,000, as compared to New York City's total population's average of approximately $22,900 (Rivera-Batiz 2002; U.S. Census Bureau 2000).[8] The average per capita income of Dominican New Yorkers was significantly lower, at approximately $9,070 (Rivera-Batiz 2002).

As a result of high levels of unemployment and low levels of income, in 1999 approximately 29.7 percent of Latinos in New York lived in poverty, compared to 19.1 percent of the city's total population (Hernández and Rivera-Batiz 2003). In 2007, estimates show this rate dropping to 24.5 percent for Latinos and 15.6 percent for the total population of New York City (U.S. Census Bureau 2007). The highest rates of poverty for Latinos occur in families with children under eighteen years old; nearly 32.4 percent of this population were estimated to be living in poverty in 2007 (U.S. Census Bureau 2007).[9] The poverty rate for Dominicans in New York City in 2000 was 32 percent—the highest rate for all major ethnic and racial groups in the city in 2000, and more than three times the 9.3 percent poverty rate for non-Latino whites (Hernández and Rivera-Batiz 2003).

Such high levels of poverty can be partially explained by labor force participation, skill level, and the prevalence of female-headed households. The labor force participation rate of Dominican men (64 percent) and women (53.1 percent) is lower than that for the rest of the adult male (72.7 percent) and female (58.5 percent) population (Hernández and Rivera-Batiz 2003, 4). As Hernández and Rivera-Batiz explain,

> The comparatively high unemployment rates of Dominicans in
> New York City are connected to a painful long-term switch in the
> employment of the Dominican labor force from manufacturing to other
> sectors. In 1980, close to half of the Dominican workforce was employed
> in manufacturing. This declined to 25.7 percent in 1990 and to 12.4
> percent in 2000. . . . [Further,] the Dominican labor force is very young
> and mostly unskilled. Only 17.3 percent of Dominicans in the United
> States have managerial, professional and technical occupations, about
> half the proportion for the overall United States. As a result, the average
> earnings of Dominican men and women are substantially lower than
> those of other workers in the nation. (4)

In the United States, Dominicans are often incorporated into low-paying jobs in the secondary labor market, with important consequences for income (see Grasmuck and Pessar 1991; Guarnizo 1994; Itzigsohn 2009; Portes and Grosfoguel 1994). Finally, the prevalence of female-headed Dominican families with one adult income exacerbates poverty: "In 2000, as much as 38.2 percent of Dominicans in New York lived in this type of family, compared to 22.1 percent for the overall City. Close to half of Dominican female-headed families in New York City were poor, more than twice the poverty rate for other households" (Hernández and Rivera-Batiz

2003, 4). Gender discrimination in the labor market is to blame for some of this poverty. Indeed, while the majority of Dominicans living in the United States in 2000 were female (53.8 percent), those women earned on average 25 percent less than their male Dominican counterparts.[10]

These challenging economic conditions influence the social processes experienced by Luperón students and, as we show in Chapter 8, they limit the school's potential contribution to economic and social mobility.

Immigrating to Spanish-Speaking Nueva York

Another, related factor that has influenced the schooling and linguistic development of the Dominican youth in this study is the fact that many relocated to a Spanish-speaking community. In 2007, 47.6 percent of New Yorkers spoke a language other than English at home, and of those, 51 percent (1,865,922) of New Yorkers spoke Spanish (U.S. Census Bureau 2007).

Dominicans arrived in a city where the majority of Spanish speakers were Puerto Rican—U.S. citizens by virtue of the Jones Act of 1917. Although the proportion of Latinos who are Puerto Ricans in the city has decreased (from 80 percent in 1960 to 35 percent in 2007), Puerto Ricans remain the city's Latino majority (U.S. Census Bureau 2007). This has important implications for Spanish speakers in New York City, for the majority of Spanish-speaking New Yorkers have always been U.S. citizens and do not share with newer groups their status as immigrants.

Dominicans today make up 24 percent of New York Latinos, and they constitute the second-largest Latino group. As the number of Puerto Ricans declines, newer Latino groups have claimed a growing role in New York City alongside Dominicans. In fact, approximately three-quarters of New Latinos settle in just five states, and the majority settle in New York (Logan 2001, 7). According to the U.S. Census, in 2007, Dominicans were followed by Mexicans who made up 13 percent of New York Latinos, and they in turn were followed by Ecuadorians (7.79 percent), and then Colombians (4.25 percent). New York City's Latino population is highly diverse in national origin.

In New York, most immigrants have historically settled in segregated communities where others speak their language. Given the size of the Spanish-speaking community, it is possible for immigrants to live their entire lives in Spanish. People on the street, in stores, in clinics, in the supermarket—all speak Spanish. Signs are most often bilingual. Thus, for students who live in these contexts, Spanish is everywhere.

The majority of the students at Luperón live either in Washington Heights or the Bronx. Washington Heights is a large, predominantly Latino neighborhood in northern Manhattan that saw an influx of Cubans in the 1960s and, later, a flood of Dominicans. From 1980 to 1990, 78 percent of the immigrants who settled there were from the Dominican Republic; by 1990, nearly half of all residents in northern Manhattan were of Dominican descent (Linares 2005). Indeed, from 1990 to 2000 the Dominican population in Washington Heights and Inwood increased from 88,000 to nearly 117,000. While Dominicans formed 43 percent of the population of Washington Heights and Inwood in 1990, they constituted 53 percent of that population by 2005 (Fernández 2007). In 2000, the largest concentration of Dominicans outside of the Dominican Republic lived in Washington Heights (Duany 2003). These immigrant families were often struggling economically. From 1980 to 1990, the number of people receiving public assistance in Washington Heights and Inwood increased from 23 percent to 32 percent, while the number of families living below the poverty line rose from 24 percent to 28 percent (Linares 2005). In the early 1990s, Washington Heights led the city in homicides, had the largest concentration of teenagers, the most overcrowded schools, and one of the highest unemployment rates (García 1993; González 1992). However, the gentrification of the area in the 1990s, as whites pushed north in a crowded and expensive Manhattan housing market, forced many Dominican families into the cheaper housing stock of the Bronx, with a few heading across the river to New Jersey or up the river to Rockland County. According to the U.S. Census Bureau, in 2000 there were 644,705 Latinos living in the Bronx, making up nearly 50 percent of the population. Of this population, 242,320 lived below the poverty line, accounting for a significant majority of these cases. In 1999, the per capita income of Latinos in the Bronx was $10,475 (U.S. Census Bureau 2000). The number of Dominicans in the less expensive south Bronx increased from 133,000 foreign- and native-born in 2000 to 200,000 in 2005 (Hawkins 2007).

The sociolinguistic ecology in which immigrants live has important implications for their learning of a new language. International research has shown that greater support for the students' home language leads to higher long-term academic attainment (August and Shanahan 2006; Genesee et al. 2006; Lindholm-Leary 2001; Ramirez 1992; Thomas and

Collier 2002). August and Shanahan (2006) summarize the findings for the United States: "Language-minority children who are instructed in their first language, as well as English, perform better on English reading measures than students instructed only in English. This is the case at both secondary and elementary levels" (639).

This research finding is something that Luperón's Dominican educators, themselves having arrived in the United States as adolescents or young adults, understand deeply. The principal of Luperón, Juan Villar, described the home lives of students living in Washington Heights as "básicamente monolingüe, que todavía tiene lazos culturales y lingüísticos muy recientes y atados a comunidad" [basically monolingual, that still maintain cultural and linguistic ties to the community]. He continued, "No puede cortarse el cordón umbilical" [You can't cut the umbilical cord].[11] As we will see in Chapter 5, Luperón educators value the presence of Spanish and use the Spanish of the community as a tool to extend other language practices.

It is important to remember that though we are referring to students here as "newcomers," students do not arrive at the same time or in the same stage of development. In fact, new students arrive almost every day, as witnessed in our observations. Further, not all students are the age of ninth-graders. Some are older, although the school, understanding that unless students start in the ninth grade there is very little possibility that they will develop the complex literacy needed in order to graduate, encourages the parents to register them as ninth-graders. It is thus noteworthy that despite the greater homogeneity among these students with regards to English language proficiency, teachers have to contend every day with differences that are the result not only of individual acquisition, but also of different educational and immigration histories.

Indeed, though language is a clear commonality across these communities, Dominican students, like Dominican communities and neighborhoods in New York, are diverse. As Ahmed (2000) points out, the communities of immigrants that form in the United States are the result of multiple factors, mostly those associated with the economic, political, and social conditions in the United States rather than unifying features of the immigrants. Thus, communities that may seem homogeneous to "outsiders" are marked by different waves of Dominican migrants from different social classes and educational levels, and with variable regional or local sensibilities and histories.

In Washington Heights, Dominicans participate in complex webs of interconnected social networks that cross multiple and diverse organizations such as churches and schools, and incorporate various sets of regional and localized practices. Marte (2008) notes, in fact, that within the different forms of Dominican communities, there exist even smaller networks that claim a "Dominican" authenticity based on food production and preparation. Even though initial social links are often made when other Dominican families or acquaintances help newcomers attain employment (Grasmuck and Pessar 1991), these links bring together immigrants who likely would not have associated with each other prior to immigration. Ahmed (2000) posits that these communities are only possible in the receiving country, away from "home."

Immigrating to Schools in Nueva York

New York City schools have large immigrant populations. According to Schwartz (2005), in "1999–2000, roughly 16 percent of the city's elementary and middle school students were *foreign born*, with nearly one fifth—that is, nearly twenty thousand students—originating in the Dominican Republic. Another eighteen thousand hailed from Latin America, and roughly one fifth from the Caribbean and South America. Of course, there are also large groups of students that originate in China, the former Soviet Union, and many other countries around the world" (2; emphasis added). Fifty percent of new immigrant students in New York City arrive at the high school level, a period of adolescent development during which social and academic pressures are intense.

According to the New York State Education Department, the number of Latino students in New York City public schools rose from 39.4 percent during 2006–2007 to 39.6 percent during 2007–2008 and 39.8 percent during the 2008–2009 school year. Latinos are the largest minority in New York City public schools. In all, there were approximately 382,444 Latino students in grades K–12 during the 2008–2009 school year (NYS ED 2010). Stiefel, Schwartz, and Conger (2003) found that during the 1999–2000 school year, 29 percent of the students in New York City elementary and middle schools (approximately 192,037 students total) spoke Spanish at home. Furthermore, they noted that over two-thirds of New York City's so-called emergent bilinguals are Latino. A large portion of these Latinos are Dominican: in New York City in 2000, 111,553 children of Dominican descent were in the New York City public school system, constituting 10.4 percent of the student body and the largest single immigrant group (Hernández and Rivera-Batiz 2003, 4).

Though they make up a large proportion of New York City students, Latinos are not faring well educationally. In 2004, the New York City Department of Education found that Latino dropout rates were higher than those for all other groups in New York City public schools with the exception of the few American Indian students (De Jesús and Vásquez 2005). The implementation in 2000 of new New York State Regents requirements exacerbated the dropout rate for English language learners (Fine et al. 2007, 79). This is particularly significant since New York State has the third highest number of emergent bilinguals (after California and Texas). Finally, according to the Commission on Independent Colleges and Universities (2007), only a third of Latino New Yorkers earn high school diplomas—a rate lower than those of all other ethnic groups. Grade repetition increases the likelihood of students dropping out altogether: Fine et al. (2005) note that for high schoolers who repeat grades, the dropout rate rises to 40.1 percent by the seventh year.

High school completion rates for Latinos across the United States are low. According to the Education Resources Information Center (ERIC 2001), 63 percent of Latino students complete high school at a national level, as compared to 81 percent of black students and 90 percent of white students. The New York City Department of Education found that Latinos had a graduation rate of 53.4 percent in 2007, as compared to a 79 percent graduation rate for white students (NYC DOE 2008a). However, De Jesús and Vásquez (2005) warned that actual graduation numbers may be lower than those reported: they suggest that while the Department of Education in 2005 reported 46 percent of Latinos as graduating, only 33.4 percent of Latino graduates actually received a Regents-endorsed diploma, while 33.4 percent of Latino students had to enroll in a fifth year of high school (for additional critiques, see Fine et al. 2007, 2005).

Yet, even within the category of Latinos, there are important differences in the type of schooling received. Dominicans are relegated to underresourced and underperforming schools, resulting in part from residential segregation. One study found that Dominicans are one of the most segregated groups in the New York educational system. The authors reported, "The typical Dominican student attends a school where 96% of the students are poor. . . . Dominican immigrants go to school with students who are virtually all poor, virtually all black or Hispanic, and more likely to be LES [limited English skilled]. They also attend schools where test scores are significantly below average and where teachers are less experienced and less well educated compared to all other [immigrant] groups" (Ellen et al. 2002, 197). These findings were confirmed by Kasinitz et al. (2008), whose study of second-generation West Indian, South American, Chinese, Russian Jewish, and Dominican immigrant youth showed the significant comparative disadvantage of Dominicans in relation to residential segregation, school quality, and access to information about securing a good public education. No surprise, then, that in New York City the repetition rates for Dominicans are considerably higher than for the general Latino population, especially among male adolescents (Ellen et al. 2002; Rosenbaum and Cortina 2004).

In light of such information, it is surprising and encouraging to note that according to Hernández and Rivera-Batiz (2003), the educational situation of U.S.-born Dominicans has improved over time. They write:

> The Dominican second generation in the United States has educational indicators that suggest a remarkable acquisition of human capital over the last twenty years. This differs from the overall situation of U.S.-born Hispanics/Latinos, whose educational indicators are substantially worse than those for Dominicans. In 2000, close to 60 percent of all Dominicans born in the United States with 25 years of age or older had received some college education, with 21.9 percent completing a college education. By contrast, among U.S.-born Mexicans, only 13.3 percent had completed college, and 12.1 percent of U.S.-born Puerto Ricans had finished college. . . . The explosive increase of the educational attainment of U.S.-born Dominicans is reflected in the experience of Dominican New Yorkers. For U.S.-born Dominicans in New York, the proportion who attained some college education rose from 31.7 percent in 1980 to 42.8 percent in 1990, and to 55.1 percent in 2000. (3–4)

Perhaps this explains why Dominican families remain optimistic about the power of education: in one poll, an overwhelming 93 percent of Dominican students pointed to their schooling as the most important means of economic improvement for them and their families (Hernández and Rivera-Batiz 1997).

The students at Luperón have escaped the fate of attending under-resourced, underperforming public schools that so many other Dominican first- and second-generation youth face. Yet they are keenly aware of the poor educational conditions elsewhere. Many of their siblings and extended family members attend these schools, having arrived as younger children, having been born in the United States, having been denied admission to Luperón because of lack of space, or for other reasons. In fact, of the twenty students we followed over a four-year period, five had siblings at other schools. While they reported envying the more rapid development of English among their siblings, in general those we interviewed expressed their appreciation for their calmer and more academically rigorous education at Luperón.

But these adolescent newcomers at Luperón must also be understood within the context of the time in which they have immigrated. The students are greatly influenced by the specific sociohistorical, political, and economic conditions in which they live, as we discuss below. That is, not only is their schooling experience shaped by their emigration from the Dominican Republic and immigration to Nueva York, but also by the times in which their immigration took place.

Immigrating in the Twenty-First Century

The time period in which these youth are immigrating matters in key ways, including the effects of the transnational context of their lives, the international context of the school, and the awareness of English built through global popular culture, the Internet, and other means.

It is important to remember that Dominican immigrants are highly transnational (Guarnizo 1994, 1998; see also Georges 1990; Levitt 2001; Pita and Utakis 2002), typically retaining "strong cultural and economic links with their homeland even when they live in distant places over long periods of time" (Duany 1997, 198). The close proximity of the Dominican Republic to the United States and strong ethnic enclaves like Washington Heights in New York enable Dominicans to maintain social networks with family and friends in the Dominican Republic while living in the United States (Duany 1994; Grasmuck and Pessar 1991; Torres-Saillant and Hernández 1998; Pessar 1995). Many return home when they can, at least to visit, and remain deeply embedded in social and monetary economies back home.

The social worlds of these adolescent newcomers are not as Spanish-monolingual as they seem on the surface, and not as uniquely Dominican as they appear. Latino immigration to New York is quite diverse, and includes a growing stream of Mexican immigrants in particular (Smith

2006). During the years of our study, we saw the non-Dominican population of the school grow, as Mexicans, Ecuadorians, and Hondurans moved into Washington Heights. As we discuss in Chapter 5, the growing heterogeneity of Latin American national origins in the school had an important impact on the school and its way of organizing literacy instruction.

Yet another consequence of having immigrated in the twenty-first century has to do with the role of English. First, the greater popularity of English and its economic exchange value often motivates Dominican and other Latino parents to bring their adolescents to be schooled in the United States. Furthermore, as English continues to spread throughout the world (Graddol 2006; Phillipson 2003), some of the students coming from the Dominican Republic bring with them more previous knowledge of English. Schools in the Dominican Republic, even public schools, are increasingly teaching English, and middle-class students often have attended English language institutes after school and on weekends. And, in 2005, the Dominican Republic initiated an English-Spanish bilingual pilot project in thirty-four educational centers.[12]

English is also the language of pop culture in the world, and Dominican youth have made excellent use of burgeoning Internet access to expand their exposure to English. Many navigate English- as well as Spanish-language websites as they explore new social worlds and seek new information. Spanish-speaking teenagers flaunt their ability to follow songs in English and to rap bilingually. Latino stars such as Shakira are, like the teenagers themselves, constantly "crossing over"—that is, singing both in Spanish and English—and Latino youth take pride in their unique ability to cross over musically and linguistically.[13]

Once they arrive in the United States, Latino youth build on and extend these pop-English skills. They are avid television viewers, and besides watching the Spanish *novelas* that are so popular among teenagers, they often watch television in English, frequently using the SAP (Secondary Audio Programming) button to view a program in English with Spanish subtitles. They also switch between channels in the two languages and watch DVDs in one language with subtitles in the other. The students also increasingly use computers that function mostly in English—many have them at home. Even though their chatting with each other is most often in Spanish, they constantly access web pages in English. The radio is extremely popular in Latino homes, and besides the big Spanish-language stations of La Mega and La Kalle, many students report listening to *rock en inglés* [rock in English]. Like the characters in *In the Heights,* the youth at Luperón engage in linguistic and musical bricolage, constantly moving between idioms and musical styles as they consume symbolic resources that they engage in order to adopt and adapt hybrid identities.

The layered nature of immigration, in which some family members come before and others afterwards, also creates spaces for most of these adolescents to hear more English at home. Many of the adolescents have come to join mothers who had left them behind in the Dominican Republic when they were children, and thus many of the mothers speak more English than the adolescents themselves. They often have second families and younger children who speak English at home, providing opportunities for many of these newcomers to be exposed to English at home.[14]

Despite living in Spanish-speaking communities, students arrive at Luperón with some familiarity with English—even if it is limited receptive ability. While this ability serves as a valuable resource, it is not sufficient for the strong development of English oracy. Krashen (1981) has long held that students learn best when they receive comprehensible input—that is, messages that can be understood. The English of the Internet, popular music, cinema, and television might provide such comprehensible input. However, Krashen's comprehensive input hypothesis has been challenged by Swain's (1996) output hypothesis, insisting that language development occurs through output—that is, languaging productively, such as in speaking and writing. In addition, there is evidence that oral language serves as an important resource in literacy development. For example, August and Shanahan (2006) posit that oral language is most important in the development of text-level comprehension among language-minority students. Thus, as we describe in Chapter 5, Luperón has to work especially to develop the English oral abilities of its students.

Yet the historico-political context of relevance is not limited to these perhaps more celebrated elements of twenty-first-century transnationalism. As we explore in the following chapter, it is also extremely relevant that these students arrived during anti-bilingual times, in the period following the passage of NCLB.

3

Education Policy as Social Context

THE STUDY OF IMMIGRANT EDUCATION requires careful attention to the ways in which educational policies, made and remade at various levels over time, affect the daily work of schooling immigrant students. To understand schooling at Luperón demands an analysis of federal bilingual educational policy and NCLB legislation, as well as state and city policy responses, including the ways in which local organizations advocate for ethnic and linguistic minorities. It also requires that we consider the emergence of political support for the model of small schools. Federal policies circulate across multiple state, district, and school contexts and situations, shaping everyday practices (Levinson and Sutton 2001). Relevant policies must be studied "vertically"—that is, across time and across national, state, and local contexts, both in and outside of schools (Vavrus and Bartlett 2009). Such a vertical approach to policy study seeks to reveal "the ideologies, structures, and practices which are used to legitimate, effectuate, and reproduce an unequal division of power and resources (both material and immaterial) between groups which are defined on the basis of language" (Phillipson 1992, 47).

In this chapter, we consider interconnections between bilingual education policy in its disparate forms, the advent of accountability measures and how they got implemented at various levels, the small schools movement, and self-determination efforts by groups representing ethnic and linguistic minorities in New York. In Chapter 4, we examine how these various forces shaped Gregorio Luperón High School during its early decades, affording certain practices within the school even as they constrained instruction in other ways.

Immigrating during Anti-bilingual Times in the United States

Though bilingualism in the United States is not new, Spanish-English bilingualism has grown exponentially during the last decade as immigration from Latin America and the Caribbean increased. For example, in 2009, 48 percent of New Yorkers spoke a language other than English at home, and 24 percent spoke Spanish (U.S. Census Bureau 2009). The increase in Spanish-English bilingualism and immigration has provoked a backlash against ways of educating bilingually that had been used to educate immigrants since the civil rights era.

The modern era of bilingual education in the United States can be traced back to the Bilingual Education Act (1968) and *Lau v. Nichols* (1974). Title VII of the Elementary and Secondary Education Act (known for the title of section VII: The Bilingual Education Act) was passed for the first time in 1968. As a result, Congress put aside money for school districts that had large language-minority enrollments and wanted to start up bilingual education programs or create instructional material. The act was reauthorized with different provisions in 1974, 1978, 1984, 1988, and 1994, gradually increasing funding to English-only programs.

In *Lau v. Nichols* (414 U.S. 563, 39 L. Ed. 2d 1), the Supreme Court ruled in favor of the plaintiffs, Chinese American parents who had brought a judicial case against the San Francisco School Board on the grounds that their children were not receiving an equitable education. The court clearly ruled that "there is no equality of treatment merely by providing students with the same facilities, textbooks, teachers and curriculum; for students who do not understand English are effectively foreclosed from any meaningful education." But the Official English movement followed quickly. In 1981, Senator Samuel Hayakawa introduced the first constitutional amendment to make English the official language of the United States, and in 1983 he founded U.S. English, a group dedicated to passing legislation to make English the official language of the country. Since then, state after state has passed Official English laws, bringing the number of states with these laws to thirty by 2010 (Crawford 2004; García 2009a).

The most effective attack against bilingual education was spearheaded by a Silicon Valley software millionaire by the name of Ron Unz. In 1998, the state of California passed Proposition 227, which prohibits the use of native language instruction in teaching emergent bilinguals and mandates the use of Structured English Immersion (SEI) programs, where English is used as the sole language of instruction. In 2000, Arizona voters approved Proposition 203, which limited school services for emergent bilinguals to one-year SEI programs. And in 2002, Massachusetts voted to replace transitional bilingual education programs with SEI programs (Crawford 2004; García 2009a; García and Kleifgen 2010; García, Kleifgen, and Falchi 2008).

In the contemporary period, bilingual education, or what Crawford (2004) has called "the B-word" (35), has been gutted. References to bilingual education have been progressively silenced in the media, in federal and state education offices, and even in legislation. Bilingual education programs have given way to ESL programs. And the term *bilingual education* has been associated only with transitional bilingual programs, where the goal is to mainstream students (and cease support for the development of academic literacy in the home language) as soon as possible. In the United States, bilingual education programs that include two language groups who are learning each other's languages (so-called *two-way*) or one ethnolinguistic group with students who have different linguistic profiles and are learning two languages (a type of developmental bilingual education program) are now referred to as *dual language*. It is within this national context of attacks against the use of students' home languages in education, racism against Latinos, and linguicism against Spanish that Luperón operates. We explore the ways in which Luperón has handled this more antagonistic climate toward bilingualism in Chapter 4.

Immigrating at a Time of Changing Federal Educational Policies

The educational services for emergent bilinguals of Latino descent in New York City have been variably shaped by federal, state, regional, and district policies, regulations, and legal mandates. NCLB and its reverberations at state and local levels have resulted in systemic processes that aim to increase achievement for all students and increase accountability for all schools. Much emphasis has been placed on standardized statewide assessments as measures for learning. Federal policy, which is a particular form of decision making, has moved from functioning as an official tool to becoming an integral set of everyday practices as it circulates across multiple state, district, and school contexts and situations (Levinson and Sutton 2001).

The ways in which those services are delivered also reflect diverse interactions between the policies of federal, state, and local educational agencies, as well as more localized institutions and organizations, including but not limited to individual schools, tutoring and testing companies, and neighborhood organizations. As entities appropriate—interpret, adapt, and incorporate—policy according to their interests, histories, and aims, multiple negotiated versions of policy emerge (Koyama 2010).

While many federal policies have included assurances that English learners in New York City's public schools have access to and equity in the district's educational system, they have been interpreted and implemented variably across the multiple levels of governance and authority. They are most often developed at the institutional level and then enacted in "ways that are often disconnected to the constituents whose educational opportunities they are designed to enhance" (Quiroz 2001, 167). As Valenzuela et al. (2007) argue, there is evidence that NCLB is negatively affecting Latino youth. In fact, some aver that for emergent bilingual students, broadly sweeping, one-size-fits-all federal policies like NCLB use language to categorize, test, and discriminate against students much in the way policies formerly used race: such policies ignore income, culture, and other factors that affect English language learners' academic engagement and achievement (Gutiérrez and Jaramillo 2006; Monzó and Rueda 2009).

NCLB is the eighth reauthorization of the Elementary and Secondary Education Act (ESEA) of 1965, which was initially designed to "strengthen and improve educational quality and educational opportunities in the Nation's elementary and secondary schools." Title I of the act provides money to state education agencies to implement the ESEA through compensatory programs for children who were considered "deprived" or "disadvantaged" (Sizer 2004). This section of the ESEA constitutes the largest compensatory federal education program aimed at improving the educational opportunities of "disadvantaged" students. It provides resources to schools to improve learning for students deemed "at risk of educational failure." Ninety-six percent of the nation's highest-poverty schools (defined as those with 75 percent or more students eligible for the free and reduced-price lunch program) receive nearly half of the Title I funds.

With the passage of NCLB, the Bilingual Education Act (which had last been reauthorized under the Improving America's Schools Act [IASA] in 1994), was repealed and replaced with the English Language Acquisition, Language Enhancement, and Academic Achievement Act. This act required states to develop a single, uniform testing instrument for identifying and assessing all emergent bilingual students. Title I of NCLB requires the setting of academic standards and assessment of those standards for all students, including ELLs. Title III of NCLB, Language Instruction for Limited English Proficient and Immigrant Students, focuses on the acquisition of English skills. It requires states to adopt English language proficiency (ELP) standards and to administer assessments aligned to those standards.

While emergent bilinguals are a minority in the total population, they are an important demographic subgroup targeted by NCLB (Fetler 2008). The federal legislation, in theory, attempts to provide uniform school accountability measures to ensure that students are achieving their full academic potential; however, the legislation has done little to address resource inequities, shortages of teachers trained to serve emergent bilinguals, inadequate ELL curricula, and ineffective programs for Latino newcomers (Crawford 2004). The testing demands of NCLB have narrowed curriculum, promoted excessive test preparation, and abandoned programs that have over the long term proved successful for this substantial and growing sector of the public school population (Abedi 2004; Menken 2008). ELLs are often juggled between ESL classes and mainstream content instruction throughout the school day.

Under NCLB, the definition and identification of the so-called Limited English Proficient (LEP) subgroup and the measurement of its progress have proven to be problematic. NCLB bases its definition of an LEP student on lack of proficiency in English, as measured by state assessments. Once these students reach proficiency, as measured by tests, they are re-categorized, and their scores are no longer registered in the LEP category (Abedi 2004). As Crawford (2004) writes, "In other words, ELLs are *defined* by their low achievement level. When they have learned English, they exit the subgroup and their scores are no longer counted in the computation of adequate yearly progress (AYP). So it is not merely unrealistic—it is a mathematical impossibility—for the ELL subgroup to reach full proficiency, as required by NCLB" (3).

A student's success in acquiring English in essence reduces scores for the category. Acknowledging this fact, the U.S. Department of Education issued a non-regulatory guidance in 2007 that allows schools "to include 'former LEP' students within the LEP category in making AYP determinations for up to two years after the students no longer meet the State's definition for limited English proficient" (U.S. DOE 2007, 10).

Despite this improvement, many issues remain. It is important to understand the contradictions inherent in placing students in the LEP category because they are determined to lack proficiency on a test and then punishing schools when the same students, who have not yet exited the category, are found to lack proficiency on a test. When students do not test as proficient, the school's AYP is not met, and subsequently the school is considered to have missed a subgroup target. Missing any single target for two consecutive years places the school on a "needs improvement" list and opens it to sanctions. Schools serving the LEP population have little chance for success under NCLB. In an attempt to address this problem, federal non-regulatory guidance emitted in 2007 exempted newcomers from English language arts assessment for twelve months (U.S. DOE 2007, 10). But as Crawford (2008) points out, this measure is not logical: according to research, a year is simply not enough time to develop academic English (Hakuta, Butler, and Witt 2000; Collier and Thomas 1989).

Furthermore, the mobility of LEP students confounds efforts to measure progress. When a school experiences an influx of newcomers, its LEP subgroup's scores are likely to decrease. If several struggling students move away from that school, then the school will register an increase in test scores for the LEP category (Crawford 2004, 2008). The smaller the LEP subgroup, the larger the effect of such mobility appears to be (Abedi 2004). Such fluctuations are not measured as variations because of the mobility of the emergent bilinguals, but rather as concrete signs of progress toward or away from arbitrary AYP targets and state standards. These problems result when cohorts are measured cross-sectionally rather than longitudinally (H. Chu, personal communication, 2010). As Crawford (2004) notes,

> A fair, reasonable, and useful accountability system would track cohorts of students to gauge their long-term academic achievement. It would use multiple measures, including grades; graduation, promotion, and dropout rates; and alternative forms of assessment. It would be accountable to local parents and communities, not just to top-down directives. Finally, it would consider a school's "inputs" in serving ELLs, such as program design and teacher qualifications, rather than merely "outputs"—test scores alone. (6)

Unfortunately, such an accountability system seems highly unlikely under the current legislation.

There is also the issue of the validity of state tests given in English to emergent bilinguals. Hakuta and Beatty (2000) question the validity and reliability of English learners' scores on standardized English and mathematics exams that are designed for—and measured against—native English speakers; assessment tools cannot distinguish language mistakes from academic content errors. Even a provision of NCLB that allows states to test ELLs' content knowledge in their native language for up to three years does not mitigate the validity and reliability issues, as the tests are merely translated from English to Spanish without consideration of the incongruent difficulty in vocabulary (Abedi 2007a, 2007b; Crawford 2004; García and Kleifgen 2010). Native language tests are often not available, and they are obviously not appropriate for students taught primarily in English (Abedi 2007a; Crawford 2004).

Further, the exaggerated focus on testing risks exacerbating the exclusion of historically underserved racially and linguistically diverse populations. Kim and Sunderman (2005) show that group accountability targets place racially diverse schools or schools with large emergent bilingual populations at greater risk of failing AYPs. In fact, the academic progress and measured performance of emergent bilinguals, as a group, become critical to the school's overall performance. Some schools therefore avoid serving students categorized as LEP. For example, in their early years, charter schools and small high schools elected not to accept ELLs in an effort to maintain higher standardized test scores (Ravitch 2010). Further, as noted by Crawford (2008),

> the law does little to address the most formidable obstacles to [the] achievement [of ELLs]: resource inequities, critical shortages of teachers trained to serve ELLs, inadequate instructional materials, substandard school facilities, and poorly designed instructional programs. Meanwhile, its emphasis on short-term test results—backed up by punitive sanctions for schools—is narrowing the curriculum, encouraging excessive amounts of test preparation, undercutting best practices based on scientific research, demoralizing dedicated educators, and pressuring schools to abandon programs that have proven successful for ELLs over the long term. (2)

Notably, few federal resources are specifically legislated for immigrant students. One exception is the small amount of federal funding provided through the Emergency Immigrant Education Program to assist schools serving recent immigrants (that is, immigrants who have enrolled within the last three years). More generally, there is little in the way of policies or legislation specifying the provision of supplemental programs or resources for immigrant children per se.

Immigrating at a Time of Changing New York State Educational Policies

While NCLB represents an unprecedented expansion of federal power over public schools, it is the states, not federal agencies, that are responsible for adopting standards-based objectives and curricula, as well as developing testing, reporting, accountability, and sanction systems.[1] According to Sunderman and Orfield (2006), the demands placed on state agencies in order for them to comply with NCLB mandates are immense. Under NCLB, the state educational agency becomes the fulcrum between federal demands and local realities—and the tensions between the power and authority of the national, state, and district governing agencies are exacerbated. This is certainly the case with the provisions regarding Latino newcomers, many of whom are English learners.

Despite federal requirements for more uniform processes to identify and educate emergent bilinguals, language acquisition programs and policies have been defined and enacted more locally, and vary by state, district, and school as student populations change (Callahan et al. 2008; García and Kleifgen 2010). With the proportion of Latino newcomers increasing or becoming more concentrated in certain geographic areas, states and local educational agencies have been faced with addressing the growth. As a result, issues regarding emergent bilinguals, including enrollment, academic progress, definition, and methods of identification, have been found to vary dramatically at the state and local levels (Donley, Henderson, and Strand 1995; Kindler 2002; Mahoney and MacSwan 2005).

The Adequate Yearly Progress (AYP) requirements, which are the central mechanisms for improving school performances in NCLB, vary from state to state. For example, although 80 percent of state educational authorities make use of home language surveys to identify students initially as potential LEP (Kindler 2002), the different English proficiency assessments that are then given vary greatly. Some states use language proficiency tests, others employ achievement tests, and others use locally designed tests. These tests are sometimes commercially produced, and they can be either norm referenced or criterion referenced. Other states design their own tests (García and Kleifgen 2010). Similar to the initial English proficiency assessments, educational authorities vary in the kinds of assessments they give to reclassify students as English proficient or not. Some use oral proficiency tests, whereas others use assessments of classroom performance, literacy tests in English, achievement tests in English, and even teacher judgment (Zehler et al. 2003). Different states—and even different school districts within a state—employ varied criteria to classify students as emergent bilinguals. The result of these inconsistencies is that schools then "succeed" or "fail" based on differing definitions of who emergent bilingual students are and what these students know. Further, schools that meet high state accountability goals but do not meet targets for English learners fall into the same "failing" category as those who did not meet any targets (Novak and Fuller 2003).

Title III of NCLB requires states to hold their local educational agencies accountable for meeting annual measurable objectives (AMOs) for their emergent bilingual population. New York State has three AMOs for emergent bilinguals—(1) making adequate AYP, (2) making progress in English, and (3) attaining language proficiency. The New York State regulations governing the identification, program placement, and support services for LEP students are known as Commissioner's Regulations (CR) Part 154. Part 154 requires that all newly admitted students be given the revised Language Assessment Battery (LAB-R). Once identified as ELLs, students must be assessed annually with the New York State ESL Achievement Test (NYSESLAT). The NYSESLAT measures English listening, speaking, reading, and writing. In the spring of 2006, 192,425 K–12 students in New York State took the NYSESLAT.[2] In 2008, 82 percent of all students at Luperón were categorized as ELLs, according to the LAB-R. Thus, most students at Luperón need to be tested at the end of every academic year with the NYSESLAT in order to track their annual progress toward English acquisition. This adds to the heavy testing load that students at Luperón experience.

CR Part 154 also identifies the number of ESL units that schools must provide. High schools like Luperón must offer a minimum of three units (or classes) of ESL to those at the beginning levels, two units for those at the intermediate level, and one unit for the advanced level. These courses are mandated, in addition to any content-area class that may take place in

English. Consequently, this additional requirement has played a significant role in shaping the curriculum at Luperón.

On the basis of a district's Part 154 Comprehensive Plan, New York State provides aid for emergent bilingual students for up to six years. Title III funds are made available to all districts that have an approved CR Part 154 Comprehensive Plan. These funds can be used only for supplemental services such as after-school, summer, or weekend programs to increase English proficiency, and for professional development. Because the large majority of Luperón students have been classified as ELLs, the school has been able to organize a large number of supplemental offerings.

New York State has raised its educational standards by implementing high-stakes exams and requiring higher scores on Regents examination. Beginning in 2000, the state required all students to pass five content-based exams in order to graduate. The impact on ELLs was immediate: "The final dropout rate for ELLs one year after the implementation of the new Regents requirement was 50.4 percent, compared to a 32 percent dropout rate overall" (Fine et al. 2007, 79). Students entering ninth grade in 2002, 2003, and 2004 (those graduating during the years of our study) were required to pass examinations in Comprehensive English, Math A, Global History, U.S. History, and Science with a score of 65 in order to qualify for a Regents diploma or a score of 55 for a local diploma. Students entering after 2008 no longer had the option of a local diploma; this change is expected to affect immigrant students negatively (Avitia 2009; see also NYC DOE 2010b). These new requirements have forced Luperón to focus more intensively on test preparation in order to maintain four-year graduation rates of around 65 percent. (The five-year rate is even higher.) This graduation rate is no small accomplishment in a city where barely one-fourth of students denominated as ELLs graduate in four years, the graduation rate declined from 27 percent for the class of 2005 to 23 percent for the class of 2007, and only "one-tenth of ELL students in recent years have graduated with a Regents diploma" (Avitia 2009, 142).

While state testing requirements have shaped instruction at Luperón in important ways, the massive citywide restructuring experienced in New York City has also had significant consequences.

Immigrating at a Time of Changing
New York City Educational Policies

Educational policies in New York City have changed radically in the recent past, and the resulting policies have greatly affected schooling for immigrant Latino youth.

School governance in New York City was centrally controlled by local government officials until 1969. According to Ravitch (2000), "The highly centralized, highly professionalized educational system mandated by the Revised Charter of 1901 proved to be highly durable . . . [lasting] for almost seventy years with relatively minor changes" (67). Amid teacher strikes and a community uprising against the centralized Board of Education, Mayor John Lindsay relinquished control of the schools and transformed the top-heavy Board of Education, which had housed four thousand administrators who hired and assigned teachers, determined budgets, and mandated school curricula (Podair 2002).

As a result of the Decentralization Act of 1969, New York schools were governed from 1969 until 2002 by a central Board of Education with seven members: five appointed by the five borough presidents, and two appointed by the mayor. The board controlled high schools, selected the chancellor of schools, and oversaw budgets and educational policy. Thirty-two community school districts, each with its own elected board and superintendent, controlled elementary and middle schools (Ravitch 2009b). In 1974, during this period of community control, a landmark agreement was reached between the New York City Board of Education and ASPIRA of New York, which represented the parents of Spanish-speaking Puerto Rican children. The ASPIRA Consent Decree mandated the identification of Spanish-speaking students who were not proficient in English and required that they be instructed in a transitional bilingual education program. Consequently, bilingual education programs grew steadily in the city around this time (L. Reyes 2006).

In a radical departure from previous models of school governance, which had guaranteed parental and community participation to varying degrees, Mayor Michael Bloomberg assumed mayoral control of the schools in June 2002 (see Hemphill et al. 2009). The New York City Board of Education structure was replaced by the New York City Department of Education, led by former assistant attorney general Joel Klein. The community boards and the seven-member Board of Education were abolished. Instead, a toothless Panel for Educational Policy was formed, consisting of thirteen appointed members and the New York City chancellor. The mayor appoints eight members who serve at his pleasure, with the borough presidents appointing the remaining five.

In 2003, the New York City Department of Education began implementing a set of NCLB-guided reforms titled *Children First: A New Agenda for Public Education in New York City*. The plan reorganized the city's thirty-two community school districts into ten bureaucratic regions. Each region was headed by a regional superintendent, and under this person various local instructional superintendents supervised ten to twelve schools (Ravitch 2010, 72). The corporate model of centralized, hierarchical control evoked complaints from administrators and teachers about the micromanagement of classrooms (73). Further, the plan standardized curriculum and assessment, featuring a consistent focus on testing as measures of progress—and therefore generating an unfortunate level of test preparation.[3] During this period of standardization, and throughout the appropriation of the plan, reform activities and actions centered on three core principles—leadership, empowerment, and accountability—which centralized power. Though the mayor promised greater parental and community involvement, the elimination of local school boards and the central board (which had previously had a representative from each borough) made it difficult for parents to influence schooling, as did the mayor's and chancellor's unwillingness to consult the local community education councils. Nonetheless, the institution of a parent coordinator in each school did at least provide parents with a contact—if not always an advocate—within the school (Ravitch 2010).

The first phase of the city's comprehensive solution, the Children First reforms, received mixed reviews. In his 2007 State of the City address, Bloomberg insisted that the reforms brought "stability, accountability and standards to a school system where they were sorely lacking."[4] As evidence of the success of the Children First reforms, Bloomberg and Klein pointed to students' scores on state tests. Between 2004 and 2005, the percentage of elementary students scoring "advanced" or "proficient"—levels 4 and 3, respectively—in state math and English examinations increased in all grades except the eighth (Ravitch 2010, 87). ELLs and former ELLs, who together represent 25 percent of the public school student population, reportedly made substantial increases in English proficiency and mathematics. Between 2006 and 2009, the number of students across grades scoring at the lowest level became remarkably reduced. Education officials across the city and state lauded the improvements.

But claims that the tests measured increased learning are subject to debate. The independent, federal National Association of Educational Progress (NAEP) assessment showed that NYC students made no significant gains in reading or mathematics from 2003 to 2007, except in fourth-grade mathematics. Nor did the test show a reduced achievement gap. This discrepancy has at least two possible explanations: either the state tests were better aligned to the curriculum, as Bloomberg and Klein suggested, or, as critics claimed, schools were teaching to the test enough to produce a rise in test scores but not in actual learning, which might be measured by a distinct test like the NAEP (Ravitch 2010, 88). Further, the touted reduction from 2006 to 2009 in the number of students scoring at the lowest level (level 1) resulted directly from the state's decision to lower the bar and make it easier to score at level 2 (Ravitch 2010).

In reality, while Bloomberg and Klein presented improved test scores as evidence that greater knowledge and skills had been acquired over a particular period of time, the comparison of one year's tests to those of another do not necessarily show growth. Instead, comparing cross-sectional data—between the test scores of one year's fourth-graders with another's, for instance—quite likely holds schools accountable for "factors beyond their control, namely, random variations in test performance and change in the knowledge and skills that students bring to school [or the grade level] to begin with" (Kelly and Monczunski 2007, 279). Only longitudinal measures on vertically aligned tests can really demonstrate achievement across the years. With existing cross-sectional data, incremental increases and decreases in test scores from year to year reflect changes in the test, in test performance, and in the students taking the test, as well as shifts in instruction. However, the consequences of these shifts are high under NCLB and Children First.

Bloomberg and Klein also claimed that their reforms had radically reduced the achievement gap between African American and Latino students and their white and Asian peers. Their claim rested on improvements in the *proficiency rate*, or the percentages of students who exceed a test score determined to demonstrate proficiency. However,

> proficiency is a misleading and inaccurate way to measure achievement gaps. . . . Primarily, the problem is that we cannot differentiate between students who just made it over the proficiency bar and those who scored well above it. Proficiency rates can increase substantially by moving a small number of kids up a few points—just enough to clear the cut

score—or by shifting the cut score itself down. But African American and Hispanic students may still lag far behind their white and Asian peers even as their proficiency rates increase. (Jennings and Dorn 2008)

In contrast to proficiency rates, gaps in the scale scores of city students on state tests between 2003 and 2008 show a continued achievement gap in fourth-grade math and reading and eighth-grade math (ibid.). As Jennings and Pallas (2009) write, "In reality, the average African American and Hispanic student in New York City is as far behind his or her White or Asian peers as in January 2003 when the Children First reforms were announced. . . . What's worse, the achievement gap in mathematics in both fourth and eighth grades has grown by 12 percent and 22 percent, respectively" (31).

Mayor Bloomberg and Chancellor Klein also credited these reforms with a positive change in graduation rates, claiming that they increased from 49 percent in 2006 to 59 percent in 2009.[5] Yet graduation rates are notoriously malleable, depending on whether they include August graduates and those who earned GEDs, as well as whether they exclude students who took more than four years to graduate. Additionally, graduation rates are inflated when schools count students who left without a diploma as "discharges" rather than as dropouts: "While the city's reported four-year general education graduation rate was 62 percent for the Class of 2007, the graduation rate would have been 57.6 percent if students in the special education cohort were also included, 45.5 percent if all discharges were counted as dropouts, and 43.6 percent if students earning GEDs rather than high school diplomas were excluded" (Jennings and Haimson 2009, 81).

Critics point out that there is little to celebrate when at least 40 percent of New York's youth are failing to graduate. As Betsy Gotbaum, the city's public advocate, stated, "We can all agree that our on-time graduation rate is an embarrassment, if not a disaster" (2006). Numerous school staff and administrators likewise criticized the fact that nearly half of the city's students were being "left behind."

In 2006–2007, a second rather abrupt and confusing major reorganization was implemented. Klein abolished the ten regions established during the first phase of Children First and the direct supervision they had entailed. Principals became even more central figures, with each one mandated either to select a "support organization" that would gain supervisory control over his or her school, or to join the empowerment zone, where he or she would be free from supervision but held to greater accountability on the basis of test score results (Ravitch 2009a). Principals gained the power to spend funds redirected to their schools and to exert greater control over teacher recruitment, retention, and removal, becoming more accountable for their schools' successes. Luperón chose what eventually came to be called the Empowerment Schools Organization, which gave greater autonomy to its principal but required an increase in formative testing, as we discuss in Chapter 4.

Notably, educational spending rose dramatically during these reforms, shifting from $12.5 billion annually in 2002 to 21 billion in 2009; teacher salaries increased 43 percent (Haimson 2009, 10).

Also in 2007, the Department of Education launched a new accountability initiative that assigned schools progress report cards; the scores were based on annual changes in standardized test scores, emphasizing change, though they also reflected fairly unscientific ratings from teachers and parents; the measure effectively "focused the city's principals and teachers on test preparation, since test scores became the measure of whether a school would be praised or damned, and whether the principal and teachers would get a bonus and merit pay" (Ravitch 2009a, 4; see also Pallas and Jennings 2009).

The Children First reforms, following CR Part 154, required that each school submit a comprehensive language allocation policy (LAP) that outlined a systematic plan for providing emergent bilinguals with language development programs and curricula. Mirroring Part 154, LAPs were to delineate the basic requirements for ELL educational services. The school-specific policies focused on "ensuring" that emergent bilinguals acquired English skills and met state standards for each grade level. Schools were expected to identify ELLs and provide them with appropriate services. They were also required to select one of three program options for emergent bilinguals—(1) freestanding ESL, where instruction is all in English, (2) transitional bilingual education, in which two languages are used and instructional time in English increases as students gain proficiency, or (3) what New York City calls *dual language,* which can be either two-way bilingual education programs that integrate English proficient speakers (both bilingual and monolingual) with emergent bilinguals, or one-way developmental bilingual education programs that develop the two languages of a group of students (NYC DOE 2010a). Luperón's LAP identifies it as a transitional bilingual education program, although as we will suggest, Luperón's curriculum has unique characteristics that support bilingualism.

With the advent of Children First reforms in 2003, the NYC DOE Office of English Language Learners (renamed in 2010 as the Division of Students with Disabilities and English Language Learners) demonstrated a somewhat unusual (though not nearly strong enough) commitment to improve the schooling of emergent bilinguals in the face of national trends. Since 2003, the office has provided professional development for more than twenty thousand teachers, administrators, school staff, and parents. In addition, it has provided grants to support students with limited literacy in their home language and interrupted formal schooling (known in New York City as students with interrupted formal education, or SIFE), and to develop dual language bilingual programs. It has also generated major initiatives to create support networks and model solutions for schools striving to improve the academic achievement of emergent bilinguals. Luperón has received grants for its SIFE program and during our study was providing after-school and Saturday tutoring for students with low literacy in Spanish, as well as tutoring in Regents subjects and AP subjects for all.

As we explain in Chapters 4 and 5, these federal, state, and city reforms, as negotiated and enacted across diverse levels, form a significant structure of opportunities and constraints for the education of students at Luperón high school. In the following section, we explore one final, significant context that shapes the work of Luperón: the efflorescence of small schools in urban centers.

Immigrating at a Time of Changing New York City School Structures

A final key element of the policy context into which the youth of this study migrated concerns the expansion of small schools, in general and specifically the emergence of international schools in New York.

In the late 1990s, with significant funding from organizations such as the Bill and Melinda Gates Foundation and the Carnegie Corporation, urban schools around the country began rethinking the long trend toward large comprehensive high schools. In New York City, throughout the 1990s, the progressive small-schools movement helped open approximately seventy-five small high schools (Ravitch 2010, 82). In 2001–2002, with help from Carnegie, Bloomberg (as a new mayor) and his chancellor Joel Klein inaugurated the New Century High School Initiative, an ambitious campaign to replace the lowest-performing comprehensive high schools with smaller schools. In partnership with New Visions for Public Schools, an education reform organization, the city opened more than eighty new schools within the first seven years (Theroux 2007). The number of students enrolled in high schools with fewer than six hundred students grew from twenty-nine thousand in 2002 to eighty-five thousand in 2008 (Bloomfield 2009, 50). Various evaluations have heaped praise on the initiative. For example, examining fourteen of the new small schools, Huebner, Corbett, and Phillippo (2006) found high attendance, graduation, and college acceptance rates among the students.

However, the initiative has been critiqued for inadequate community partnerships, insufficient training for schools' advisory systems, high rates of turnover among teachers and administrators, and the ways in which the new small schools left older large schools with some of the hardest-to-teach students (Ancess and Allen 2006; Bloomfield 2009; Hemphill et al. 2009; Theroux 2007). The small schools themselves have been criticized for their unwillingness to develop strong programs for emergent bilingual students. In some instances, the draw of English dominant students to small schools has stranded students whose home language is not English in failing and closing high schools that have increasingly limited language support services, potentially exacerbating dropout rates among that vulnerable population (Advocates for Children of New York and Asian American Legal Defense and Education Fund 2009; Bloomfield 2009). These charges led the city in 2007 to require that new schools accept emergent bilinguals; however, advocacy groups charge that emergent bilinguals remain segregated, with 43 percent of them centralized in just 17 of the 233 small high schools in 2008 (Advocates for Children of New York and Asian American Legal Defense and Education Fund 2009).

Though established through different mechanisms and in an earlier period, Luperón has benefited from the favor shown to small schools. When, as we describe in Chapter 4, the school lacked support from some in its Region at the Department of Education, the fact that it was a small school serving Latino immigrant students undoubtedly helped it survive the criticism.

Further, Luperón shares many institutional similarities with a smaller but also popular reform: the emergence of *international high schools*. International schools are small high schools for newcomer immigrant youth. The original international schools purposely placed newly arrived, linguistically heterogeneous students in the same classrooms. Today there are two international high schools in New York City designed specifically for Spanish-speaking newcomers. Although the instruction by the teacher from the front of the room is in English, the classroom linguistic interactions include languages other than English both by the students and the teacher in small groups (see García, Flores, and Chu 2011).[6] Some of these international high schools employ dedicated teachers who are not only knowledgeable about second language acquisition and learning but also aware of, and responsive to, the issues that immigrant students face (see Fine et al. 2005, 2007; Sylvan and Romero 2002; Walqui 2000a). However, while international high schools respond to many of the specific needs of newcomer youth, they do not generally overtly support the development of the students' home languages.

Luperón is unique in that it is a *bilingual* high school that emerged from and continues to be supported by community activism. The concentration of Spanish-speaking newcomer immigrant youth made it possible for the founders of Luperón to organize a school specific to newcomer linguistic needs that uses the students' home language for content instruction while developing their English. In the next chapter, we trace the history of how such an unusual school emerged.

4

From Subtractive to Additive Schooling: The History of Gregorio Luperón High School

WHAT HAPPENS WHEN LATINO EDUCATORS identify the ways in which a school progressively dis-ables newcomer immigrant students by placing them in an unsafe environment, refusing to draw on their home language as a resource, denying them content-area instruction, and requiring them to learn English only—and then discover a provision in the system that will allow them to change the situation, and even support them as they act to do so? In short, what happens when a group of teachers, including immigrant teachers, reject subtractive schooling and strive to build a dynamic bilingual high school for Latino immigrants during a period of high-stakes testing, increased and diversified immigration, and the assimilation of Dominican families into low-wage work? What happens, in short, when educators form what Ancess (2003) called a "community of commitment"?

In this chapter, we recount the history of Gregorio Luperón High School, starting with its formation in 1993 and its opening in 1994 as a two-year transitional program. We discuss its conversion in 2001 to a four-year high school, its response to the 2004 New York City shift to mayoral control of schools and a regional structure, and finally its unification with the empowerment zone structure in 2006. In the course of describing these changes, we consider the cultural and political significance the school holds for its founders and many of its teachers. We analyze the significant social transformations that have influenced the school's development, including the growth of the school's student body and teaching corps, the national diversification of the student body, and the expansion of gangs and drug activity among peer networks in northern Manhattan and the south Bronx. We also examine carefully how city, state, and federal policies afford certain developments for the school and constrain others. Specifically, we question how these changes have affected the school's language education policies. Finally, we look at the meaning Luperón holds for parents, and the ways in which the school and parents work together to create a community.

The Beginning: To Live a Latino Dream

Understanding the emergence of Gregorio Luperón High School in the early 1990s necessitates a brief overview of the two immensely relevant contexts: the growing political power of Dominicans at that historical moment, and the general state of schooling for Latino immigrants in New York schools.

Relatively high levels of segregation in northern Manhattan allowed Dominicans to achieve greater control of neighborhood schools and, subsequently, political representation. A full 80 percent of the twenty-five thousand students attending elementary and middle schools in District 6 in the late 1980s were Dominican; the schools were miserably overcrowded and had some of the lowest reading scores in the city (Linares 1989, 78). According to Vélez (2007),

> By the early 1980s, Dominicans made up the majority of students in New York's Community School District 6 (in the Washington Heights neighborhood), at that time home to the city's most overcrowded schools. It was then that the Community Association of Progressive Dominicans confronted the school board and superintendent to demand bilingual education and other services for recently arrived immigrant families. The concerted efforts of community organizations, a parents' network throughout the district, and an aggressive voter registration drive led to greater Dominican representation on neighborhood school boards (and a majority in District 6). (136)

By the early 1990s, a group of educators formed the Dominican Association of Education Professionals in order to bring greater power to bear on the New York City Board of Education (Torres-Saillant and Hernández 1998, 85). Dominicans made important gains during this period in the opening of elementary and middle schools. A group of young people called Unión de Jóvenes Dominicanos [Union of Young Dominicans] began to pressure for improved high schools as well.

In New York City, political agitation in the 1980s for equal representation led to the 1991 redistricting that yielded a predominantly Dominican electoral district in upper Manhattan (Ricourt 2002). This shift produced the election of the first Dominican to the New York City Council, Guillermo Linares, and in 1996 the election of Dominican-born Adriano Espaillat to the New York State Assembly as northern Manhattan's representative for District 72 (Pessar and Graham 2001). Linares and Espaillat had, alongside other activists, helped organize the community to pressure for improved schools and more qualified teachers.

Dominicans began to use their newfound political power to remedy the deplorable conditions of New York City schools for Dominican children and youth. The shift in 1969 from mayoral control to a Board of Education and community school boards had not resulted in the desired changes toward educational quality. In his institutional analysis, Rogers (2008) noted that elected parents and community leaders weren't always effective:

> For example, the new powers of community school boards to select a superintendent and principals and to develop curricula were limited by concurrent powers of the chancellor. In addition, headquarters failed to play the supportive role needed to make decentralization work by inadequately training community school board members and district staff to take on new roles and ineffectively monitoring district and school operations. (x)

The community school boards and the central Board of Education also struggled with the general political economic conditions of the city in that era. After years of economic growth in the early 1980s, job growth in New York stopped abruptly in 1988, followed by a recession that caused job losses in nearly all major industrial sectors (Ehrenhalt 1993). The service industries, which had typically sustained economic downturns, were severely affected, with a significant percentage of job declines (Ehrenhalt 1993). Meanwhile, poverty rates soared.

These conditions resulted in abysmal schooling for many Latino immigrants. For example, George Washington High School was, at that time, a large high school with over four thousand students in Washington Heights to which most Dominican students were assigned.[1] In the late 1980s, the school experienced an astronomical dropout rate that hovered close to 50 percent.[2] There were also concerns about violence within and around the school, because "the police precinct which encompasses George Washington High School had the highest murder rate in New York City in 1989" (Siegel and Skelly 1992, 78). Community activists and Latino support organizations regularly appeared at community board meetings to protest the deplorable school conditions for Latino immigrant youth.

In 1992, the maverick schools chancellor Joseph Fernández announced a call for proposals to create new schools. Fernández was appalled by the circumstances of New York's schools. He hoped that smaller schools might reduce anonymity and restore a sense of community for some of the city's struggling immigrants (Fernández and Underwood 1993). Charged with being overly confrontational and too focused on a social agenda that included sex education and the distribution of condoms, Fernández was removed by the Board of Education in 1993. However, the new schools reform he had set in motion was to have important consequences.

In 1992, an assistant principal and several teachers at George Washington High School met to plan for the future. Disenchanted, upset, and angry over the poor education that their students were receiving, they took Fernández's call for proposals seriously and imagined what a school serving newly arrived Latino students and their community might look like. The group included Myrna Cubilete, the assistant principal; Juan Villar, a teacher and counselor; and Evaristo Espinal, a teacher. These educator-activists had helped organize community efforts to improve schooling for area youth. In a 2007 interview, Espinal described this group by saying, "Fuimos luchadores, pro-estudiantes, y pro-comunidad" [We were fighters, and we were for the students, and for the community]. The group was moved by the possibility of creating a school where youth from the community would be able to *superarse* [improve themselves]— a school in, of, and for the community. Espinal relayed, "Queríamos ser nosotros los artífices de ese cambio, y los motivadores" [We wanted to be the creators of that change, and the motivators]. Cubilete and Villar drafted a concept paper for the school that was then supported by the

Manhattan high school superintendent, Patricia Black, and other local politicians.

At the end of the process, seven faculty and one staff member from George Washington High School joined the new school. The group of educators included Dominicans, a Dominican Mexican, a Cuban, and a Puerto Rican; most of them lived in Washington Heights. Some of these original staff members had higher education degrees for which they were not licensed in the United States. For example, the science teacher had been a medical doctor before immigrating, a math teacher had been an engineer, and one of the staff members was licensed as a social worker in the Dominican Republic, although she was hired in the school system as a health aide.

What most of the new staff of the school had in common was a commitment to working with young people from a community with whom they shared many experiences as immigrants. One of them, history teacher Ydanis Rodríguez, explained his motivation:

> Compartir con un sector que era muy similar a lo que era Ydanis Rodríguez cuando llegue aquí—venir sin hablar inglés, de familia pobre. Servir a la comunidad de que yo soy parte y trabajar con un grupo de jóvenes de edad similar que yo llegué aquí.

> [To share with a population that was very similar to who Ydanis Rodriguez was when I first got here—getting here without speaking English, from a poor family. I wanted to serve the community that I'm part of and work with a group of young people who were the same age I was when I arrived here.][3]

During 1993–1994, with full funding from the New York City Board of Education, the faculty and staff of the future Gregorio Luperón Preparatory School worked at Choir Academy, planning what their school would look like. They attended workshops offered by the superintendent's office, which one founder reported were essential in forming the plan for the school. They visited other schools to study their models of education, and they met in working groups to make decisions about how to shape their school. Two schools were very influential in shaping Gregorio Luperón: LaGuardia International School, whose principal at the time was Eric Nadelstern, and Liberty High School, a temporary transitional program for newcomers that had a bilingual model of education.[4] The Luperón faculty spent months at each of the two schools, observing and learning how they worked with recently arrived immigrants.

At LaGuardia, the faculty witnessed an International School model that emphasized ESL across content areas, since its students came from many countries speaking twenty-seven languages. At that time, the school had negotiated a waiver so that its students wouldn't have to do the Regents exams that were required by New York State for high school graduation. Instead, LaGuardia used portfolio assessment. According to several founders, the model provided by LaGuardia and its principal, as well as their collaboration, were critical to the formation of the school. And yet the founders wanted something different: they wanted a bilingual high school for Latino newcomers, a rarity in the United States.

The chancellor had originally planned for the school to be modeled after Liberty High School, and gave it the name of Liberty II. As a transitional program, Liberty High School provided one to two years of schooling for newcomers before transferring them to four-year high schools. Liberty II would have a similar mission, although all its students would be Spanish-speaking newcomers.

After studying both models, the school staff decided to make bilingual education a priority. They believed that young new immigrants could not keep up with rigorous academic work in a language that they did not understand, and thus content courses had to be in Spanish. Two of the founding members of the school—Lissette Thompson and Héctor Holguín—had been medical doctors in the Dominican Republic; Espinal had been an engineer. They believed strongly in the importance of strong foundational content in science and math. And yet, in many high schools at the time, bilingual students were not offered science and advanced math courses because it was assumed that they would not be able to master the material. These teachers asserted that all students should be able to take content courses early. They claimed that if the young people had science and math in Spanish, they would acquire a solid understanding of the subjects that would then be transferred when they later studied the subject matter in English. Since the entire population of the school was going to be Spanish-speaking, they were in a position to offer content courses in Spanish.

The founding staff also believed that Spanish was an important resource that needed to be developed so that their student population would be fully bilingual. Their key idea was to build a solid ESL program and to encourage English language development, but to remain academically competitive by offering core courses in the content areas in Spanish.

Naming the School

Though Chancellor Joseph Fernández wished to name the school after an ongoing project, the founders decided that they wanted to choose their own name—one that communicated a sense of being Latino, and specifically of Dominican struggles. Even though the school was open to Spanish-speaking newcomers from any country, the site was in Washington Heights, a neighborhood with a large Dominican community (Hoffnung-Garskof 2008). The founding staff decided that it was important to give the school a name that was representative of the school population. Juan Villar first proposed the name "Minerva Mirabal," after one of the three brave Dominican sisters assassinated by Trujillo because of their strong political opposition to his dictatorship. But the Mirabal name was rejected after people from the community spoke to the founding principal and expressed their concerns about Minerva's association with Marxist ideology. Villar then proposed the name of Gregorio Luperón, a nineteenth-century founding father of the Dominican Republic. Villar explained to us his reasons for choosing the name:

> Yo creo que el mejor símbolo de la dominicanidad es Gregorio Luperón. Gregorio Luperón nunca levantó la espada en contra de un dominicano, nunca levantó la espada en contra de un haitiano. Gregorio Luperón se reveló en contra de la potencia que dominaba su país. Se enfrentó a los soldados españoles, los derrotó, y fue el único líder dominicano que murió teniendo amigos que hablaban en inglés, francés—que eran cubanos, puertorriqueños.

> [I think that the best symbol of Dominicanness is Gregorio Luperón. Gregorio Luperón never raised his sword against another Dominican, he never raised his sword against a Haitian. Gregorio Luperón rebelled against the power that controlled his country. He faced Spanish soldiers, he defeated them, and he was the only Dominican leader who died having friends who spoke English, French—who were Cubans, Puerto Ricans, Jamaicans.]

For Villar and the other founding members, Luperón was an important symbol of not only Dominicanness but also solidarity with Haiti and the Caribbean and, more broadly, with Latin America. In addition, Luperón was a black Dominican, confronting the members of the Dominican school community with their own racial identity as Latinos of color. The figure of Luperón also became a reminder of the prevailing existence of racism against Haitians by some Dominicans back home, and the racism that the Dominican students experience in the United States. Thus, Luperón served to mobilize students against racism.

The School Opens Its Doors

Gregorio Luperón Preparatory High School opened its doors to students in September 1994 as part of the New York City Alternative Schools district and as a transitional program for Spanish-speaking newcomers where students would stay for one to two years before transferring to a four-year high school. That year, the *New York Times* reported that Latino students had the highest dropout rate of all NYC students—25.2 percent, compared to 9.4 percent for Asians, 12.3 percent for white students, and 18.9 percent for students of African descent (Newman 1994). Luperón was a school aimed precisely at stemming the high dropout rates for immigrant Latinos.

When the staff of the school walked into their assigned space, a converted warehouse with few windows on 181st Street in Washington Heights from which they eventually operated for fifteen years, the site was still being remodeled.[5] "We had to sweep it, clean it, paint it," reported Villar. Another founder added, "Our first meeting was held in this room [where the interview was being conducted], full of school materials and dust from the construction. . . . We went from room to room, cleaning up." Nevertheless, the staff decided that they were going to begin anyway. They cleaned up some of the rooms and got old furniture from a school that was being restructured.

The first child to register, in October 1994, was a Dominican girl, Elba Duarte, who coincidentally bore the last name of the nineteenth-century Dominican patriot who is considered the father of the homeland, Juan Pablo Duarte. That first year, 1994–1995, the school enrolled 122 students. Staff members recalled telling students and parents that if they were going to be part of the school, they had to work hand-in-hand with them to get their building ready. Almost every day, new students came to enroll in the school. During the first few years, everyone who worked at the school had to fulfill multiple tasks, regardless of his or her job description: "Se hacía de todo, lo que fuera" [We did everything, whatever].

Besides its director, the school employed two science teachers, two math teachers, two social studies teachers, four ESL teachers, and one physical education teacher that first year. There was also an office worker, a payroll secretary, a health aide, a custodian, and other support staff.[6]

The philosophy of the teachers and staff was that they wanted to provide the students with a holistic education that was culturally and linguistically appropriate for Spanish-speaking newcomers to the United States. They took the students on neighborhood walks and to the public library to get new borrowing cards, and they took field trips to museums and cultural organizations. To enrich the curriculum, the school worked with Hispanic organizations such as Repertorio Español and the Puerto Rican Traveling Theatre.

After one year, according to the original design, students who were proficient enough in English and had the sufficient number of academic credits were transferred to four-year high schools. Students who did not have enough credits and had limited English proficiency were to stay for another year. One founder described it thus:

> Era una escuela transicional, un año supuestamente. . . . Completaban créditos y avanzaban mucho en inglés. Si no pasaban los créditos, los dejábamos un año más. . . . Cuando llegamos aquí, teníamos el programa claro, como Liberty. Designamos un programa de noveno, desde el primer día se le daba ciencia. Diferencia al principio, les dábamos ciencia, y veníamos con visión clara. A todo el mundo se le daba ciencia. En ese primer año, los estudiantes se fueron perfectamente, otros se quedaron, los que tenían deficiencias académicas, y muchos de ellos se quedaron aquí dos años. No pasaban el inglés.

> [It was a transitional school of one year, supposedly. . . . They would complete credits and advance a lot in English. If they didn't complete the credits, we'd leave them in the school for another year. . . . When we arrived here (in this building), we had the program clearly designed, like Liberty. We designed a ninth-grade program, but from the first day

we gave them science instruction. The difference was that we gave them science instruction, and we came with a clear vision. Everyone was given science instruction. In that first year, some students did well, others who had academic deficiencies stayed behind, and many of them stayed for two years. They didn't pass English.]

Staff members reported that during those early years, many schools actually requested students from Luperón because even though the students sometimes had limited proficiency in English, they had solid academic skills.

The founder and first director of the school, Myrna Cubilete, had started the school with the understanding that she would retire after five years. During the process of creating the school, she trained some of the original staff members to run the school, making clear her desire that one of them would be ready to replace her upon her retirement. Juan Villar, who had been the project's assistant director and a co-founder of the school, went back to graduate school during those early years to get his administrative credentials.

After the founding principal retired in 1999, the New York City Board of Education hired as principal a Puerto Rican woman who had been an assistant principal at Liberty High School. When she passed away in 2000, Villar became principal.

Los pioneros: Poniendo su piedrecita

Fifteen years after the founding of the school, eleven of the original staff members (five staffers, five teachers, and the principal)—*los pioneros*—remained at the school.[7] We interviewed ten of them over the course of our research. From these pioneers, all Dominicans, we got a sense of how they built the school one *piedrecita* [small stone] at a time, and how those plans had to be adjusted as times changed. The image of collaboratively contributing small stones to build a school in, of, and for the community to which they themselves belonged was given to us by a staff member who said, "Uno puso su piedrecita porque salieron de aquí. Si no nos hubieran llevado de la manito, no hubiéramos llegado." [Everyone put their little stone because they came out of here. If they (the leadership) had not taken us by the hand, we wouldn't have made it.]

Despite the many times that the *piedrecitas* turned to *piedras en el camino* [obstacles on the road], and the many struggles that the school community has had, the pioneros remain committed to the dream of building a school of, in, and for the community. Their interviews revealed how their life experiences shaped their early commitment to the school, and their continuing dedication during the more complicated—and occasionally disillusioning—period of change.

The process of developing a school and sustaining it during radically transformative changes in New York City was described primarily as a sustained act of hope and love by the pioneros. The clarion motivation for the pioneros was hope in the improvement of their community and the opportunities for their children. In telling us the story of the dream, one of them told us, "Estábamos muy ilusionados, con los muchachitos que estaban perdidos, no hablaban el idioma, pero tenían ilusiones de hacer carrera." [We were very hopeful, with the youngsters who were lost, who didn't speak the language, but who were hopeful of having a career.] The determination among the pioneros that not knowing English should not lead to academic failure motivated them to start the school. These newly arrived students wanted careers and wanted to be professionals, but the school system was simply not teaching them because they spoke only Spanish. It is interesting to note that the motivation of the pioneros was not just to have individual students succeed but "trabajar haciendo gente" [to work at building community (lit., people)]. The pioneros were moved not just by a goal of getting individual students to succeed in school, but by a desire to build the community. In this regard, one of them told us that the task was "balancear el progreso individual unido con el esfuerzo colectivo" [to balance the individual success of students with the collective effort] in order to improve the community. A teacher summarized this hope:

> Ilusión. El deseo de ver su gente superándose o dejar de ser estadística negativa con los latinos, especialmente con los recién llegados. Si los padres no pueden, por lo menos los hijos que puedan ser vehículo de romper ese círculo en la familia de la miseria.

> [Hope. The desire to see your people improving or not being the negative statistic of Latinos, especially among those who have recently arrived. If the parents can't, at least their children can be a vehicle to break that family circle of misery.]

When these pioneros spoke about Luperón, they frequently expressed their love for the school, which represented their community and, of course, their children. Their affection was so palpable that often in their interviews they humanized the school as a person they would physically embrace. A secretary told us, "Siempre uno abraza la Luperón, pero porque es de uno" [We always embrace Luperón because it is ours].

A symbiosis between the school, the children, and themselves as adults working at the school was frequently expressed among the pioneros. For them, the school is *la comunidad de uno* [their community]; the youth are immigrants just as the teachers once were; the youth struggle with the new language and culture just as the adults once did. One of the teachers told us that by working with these students, he is regularly reminded of when he arrived in New York City: "Me recordé cuando yo llegué aquí como estos muchos recién llegados como yo, teenager." [I remembered, when I arrived here, just as these newcomers, as a teenager.] Their personal experiences motivate them to help the students beyond what is required. A staff member explained that helping those who struggle as she did when she arrived made her feel good: "Me gusta ayudar y bregar como cuando tú llegaste. Uno se siente bien." [I like to help and to struggle, just as when you arrived. You feel good.] The school provides a familiar context to students who arrive "nuevecitos en una tierra extraña" [very new in a strange land]. The pride the pioneers took in the success of the students was palpable. More than one conveyed the following:

> Son muy respuetuosos, muy cariñosos. . . . Me encuentro con
> ellos en el vecindario. Vivo aquí. Nos encontramos por ahí, en el
> supermercado, y son muy cariñosos. Son muchachitos de la comunidad
> de uno también. . . . Cada vez que se gradúa un grupo siento mucha
> satisfacción, cada vez que se gradúan.

> [These students are respectful, they are very loving. . . . I meet up with
> them sometimes in the neighborhood. I live here. I see them, and they
> are very loving. They are the children of my community. . . . Every time
> a group of them graduates, I feel a deep satisfaction, every time they
> graduate.]

Just like their newcomer students, the pioneros spoke little or no English when they arrived in the United States. The pioneros serve as models of how to become professionals in an English-speaking world. Some teachers felt that their Spanish accents when speaking English could actually encourage students to try to speak English:

Ellos ven que yo tengo dificultad en inglés; tengo mi acento. Ellos ven mi energía de hablar en inglés, y a mí me parece que se han motivado: *Si H. tiene su acento, si algunas veces dice palabras no bien pronunciadas, entonces, ¿por qué yo no lo voy a hacer?*

[They see that I have difficulty in English; I have my accent. They see my effort in speaking English, and I think that they become motivated: *If H. has his accent, if sometimes he says words that aren't well pronounced, why then can't I do it?*]

The school serves as the community of the pioneros in more than one sense: most of the pioneros lived in Washington Heights originally, and many still did at the time of our study. One of the teachers explained, in English, "Many of us used to live or still live in this community. It's not like we're from another place. When I go to the supermarket, three kids from Luperón work there."

The school has been experienced by many pioneers as a family. A secretary told us, "Aquí uno no piensa en los sueldos; se piensa de los muchachitos, de la comunidad de uno; de que el personal pueda ayudar." [Here, you don't think about salaries; you think about the young people, of one's community; of how the personnel can help.] This motivation for work seems to be best summarized in what could be the motto for the pioneros, expressed by another of the secretaries: "Todo por nuestra comunidad y por nuestros muchachos" [Everything for our community and for our children].

Though the focus has been on caring for the adolescents, the pioneers have also established important mutual support relationships. "A uno lo cuidan" [They take care of you], said one of the staff members. When one of the pioneras who worked in the office during our study was first hired, she did not have a high school diploma, did not speak English, and had never worked outside of the home. But she was deeply committed to the community and the children. She was hired as support staff and, while there, was encouraged to get her high school equivalency diploma. She related her experience:

Me ayudaron muchísimo. Yo me sentí muy bien con ellos. Me dieron la oportunidad que yo nunca había trabajado. . . . Yo saqué el GED; iba a las clases en la Washington. Aquí M. me daba la oportunidad de que yo estudiara las lecciones.

[They helped me a lot. I felt really good with them. They gave me the opportunity since I had never worked. . . . I got the GED; I went to classes at George Washington. Here, M. gave me the opportunity to study my lessons.]

As in a family, the school is the home: "Todos nos sentíamos como en la casa, en familia" [We felt as at home, as a family]. But, the pioneers stressed, it's a Caribbean home, where the doors are always open. This image of open doors emerged frequently in the staff's talk about the school. One told us:

Our doors are open. We can assist people in ways you can't imagine. Our valedictorian last year had problems with her green card; without it, she couldn't get a scholarship. You wouldn't believe what the principal did to help her get her green card before graduation. We have a student having financial difficulties this year. People pitch in to help them. If a parent comes with a problem, something nothing to do with education, and we can be of service, we're willing to do that. Or a referral. We are open to work with any agency in or outside of the community.

This feeling of being at home—*en casa*—led one of the staff members to express her joy in getting up to come to work:

Me sigo levantando con ganas de venir a trabajar para acá. Es como que ésta es mi casa, yo no sé. Desde que yo comienzo a subir los escalones, yo voy tarareando. Yo no me imagino estar en ningún otro sitio. Ésta es mi casa.

[I wake up wanting to come to work here. This is like my home, I don't know. As soon as I start going up the steps, I start humming. I can't imagine being in another place. This is my home.]

And because they feel at home, these teachers and staff members work well beyond what is required of them because, as one of them said, they have to "stretch their hand" a bit more—go the extra mile—in order to make the difference [Estirar un poquito más la mano de lo que le dicen a uno, go the extra mile para hacer la diferencia].

These relationships require immense amounts of trust, which emerged as another theme in our conversations with the pioneros. Clearly the pioneros at George Washington High School didn't trust the central Board of Education to do well for the Dominican students who were newly arrived and didn't speak English. Referencing their guiding vision in the founding of Luperón, one explained: "¿Qué me ilusionó? Íbamos a tener nosotros ahora el poder para decidir qué necesitaban nuestros estudiantes. A diferencia de la Washington donde otros eran los jefes, aquí íbamos a ser nuestros propios jefes." [What did I hope for? We would have the power to decide what our students needed. Instead of at GWHS where others were the bosses, here we would be our own bosses.] A different teacher told us that her main motivation for leaving George Washington was "saber que la escuela estaba en manos de alguien que creía en los estudiantes no como número, sino como seres humanos" [to know that the (new) school would be in the hands of people who believed in the students not as numbers but as human beings].

That trust continued to operate during our observations, for the most part. The teachers often reported that "aquí no hay que estar vigilando a nadie" [here there is no need to watch anyone], because everyone in the school felt responsible for improvement. Another reason why they don't need to be watched is that, in a small school, "no hay dónde esconderse" [it is impossible to hide]. The pioneros, and especially the staff, also expressed deep levels of trust in the principal, Juan Villar, whom they affectionately call "Juanchi." One of them explained, "Tenemos a Juanchi como principal, y esperamos que dure mucho aquí. Tiene muchas buenas relaciones con los padres y maestros." [We have Juanchi as principal, and we hope he lasts here a long time. He has good relationships with parents and teachers.] Prior to becoming an administrator, Villar had been a teacher and a counselor, and his teachers generally felt that he understood and shared their concerns. As an immigrant who came to the United States after completing high school in the Dominican Republic, Villar understood not only the teachers' struggles but also those of the students. Despite the changes that have affected some of the new teachers differently from the pioneros, Villar has remained a central figure in the school—always present, sometimes controversial, and fully committed to his students and community. We will return to this discussion below.

In its early years, while functioning as a two-year preparatory school, Luperón received accolades from the community it served. As one pioneer stated,

> Desde el primer año impactamos con los muchachos que nos tocaron, al extremo que venían y regresaban para decirnos que se habían hecho profesionales. Nos demonstraban que uno no estaba arando en el desierto. Que ellos la recibían, en un grado bastante alto.

> [From the first year, we influenced a lot of the kids who studied with us. Some came back to tell us that they'd become professionals. That showed us that we were not working in vain. They performed well with what they got here.]

Among certain circles, they were celebrated. The teacher continued, "El fruto de ese éxito, comenzó a tener fama: una escuela de inmigrantes, con alto porcentaje de asistencia, bajo porcentaje de violencia, prácticamente inexistente; empezamos a destacarnos." [The fruit of that success is that we started to become known: a school for immigrants, with a high rate of attendance, low incidence of violence, it was practically nonexistent; we started to get known.]

While struggling to get established, Luperón avoided some of the more intense challenges that were yet to come. The small faculty shared an intense social and political commitment to the school. The student body, too, remained small and ethnically homogeneous, creating a strong sense of solidarity. Situated as it was in the Alternative Schools district, Luperón received relatively little scrutiny from the educational hierarchy; as one of the founders said, "We were invisible because we were so good." As a transitional program, it was not required to administer the demanding, high-stakes New York State graduation tests known as the Regents exams (though the faculty has chosen to administer them since the school's inception). Faculty members were concerned about the future of their students. On completion of the program, most of the students continued their education at schools such as Martin Luther King Jr. High School, Manhattan Center, Hostos-Lincoln Academy, and DeWitt Clinton High School. But, like many of the city's high schools, some of these schools were plagued by low enrollment, high dropout rates, and high levels of violence. For example, MLK Jr. was charged by Advocates for Children with illegally discharging students not making adequate progress toward graduation; it was closed permanently after a horrific shooting and sexual assault in the late 1990s and the shooting of two students on school grounds in 2002. As such, many worried that Luperón was preparing its students for success, only to launch them into difficult and sometimes impossible educational circumstances.

Growing Pains: Becoming a Four-Year High School

During the first few years of the school's existence, there was a healthy debate regarding the future of Luperón when a proposal to shift it into a four-year school emerged. On the one hand, a handful of teachers—including both pioneers and newcomers, and Latinos and non-Latinos—worried that the shift to a four-year school would have negative repercussions. First, they worried that it would unduly segregate students and limit their English acquisition. As one pioneer explained:

> Yo me opuse desde un principio a ser una escuela de cuatro años. Eso me hizo cuestionar el proyecto. Porque yo no era partidario de una escuela de cuatro años, mayormente dominicanos. Estamos en Washington Heights. Y entonces yo me opuse porque yo visualizaba iba a haber problemas por esa vía debido a limitaciones por el inglés, los problemas que puedan venir por académicos de los recién llegados. [Pero la idea] era algo indetenible, y hubo que dar para adelante. Una parte no estaba de acuerdo. Siempre yo creí que el proyecto de dos años iba a tener mejor resultados, y después otro high school habría mayor contacto con el inglés y mayor contacto con otras culturas. Pero bueno, aquí estamos.

> [I opposed the idea of becoming a four-year school from the beginning. It made me question the project. Because I wasn't supportive of the idea of a four-year school, mostly for Dominicans, all in Washington Heights. I was opposed because I thought there would be problems due to the limitations of English, the academic problems the recently arrived youth would have. . . . (But the idea) was unstoppable, and it had to move forward. One part didn't agree. I always believed in the two-year model, that it would have better results, and after two years in another school they would have more contact with English and with other cultures. But here we are.]

Those opposing the shift worried that concentrating youth in Washington Heights would reduce their cultural and linguistic integration in New York. One ESL teacher described the school at that time as a "cocoon," and worried that students would feel less need to develop their English if they didn't face the eventuality of "going to Planet America" after two years. "We thought it would be a ghetto. Let's send them out, broaden their horizons," she explained. However, the majority were concerned that all their hard work with these youth was being lost once the students transferred: too many of them were dropping out, and even those who stayed in school were too often tracked into low-yield sheltered content courses.

In 2001, after much debate, the school became a four-year high school in the Alternative Schools district. Because of its particular emphasis on science and math for all students, its name was changed from Gregorio Luperón Preparatory High School to Gregorio Luperón High School for Science and Mathematics. This change left Luperón subject to many changes, such as no longer being exempt from administering the New York State Regents exams required for high school graduation.

Furthermore, this localized shift coincided with a landmark reversal of management structures for New York City schools. In 2002, when Mayor Bloomberg was given control of the school system, the community school boards that had been in place for decades were abolished. This radical move unsettled many community leaders, because it stripped them of their sense of political participation in local schools. At the same time, the federal NCLB legislation was signed into law, instituting a period of intensified high-stakes assessment. As we describe in the next two sections, these changes, plus more general political economic and migratory shifts, have had significant consequences for Luperón.

Restructuring: Joining Region 10

In 2003, Bloomberg reorganized school districts into ten geographical regions, and Luperón was placed in Region 10. This reorganization, which occurred at the beginning of our study, inaugurated a difficult period for Luperón. Region administrators came frequently to the school, criticizing the fact that many Luperón students required five years rather than four to complete the exams necessary for a Regents diploma. Faculty and staff complained that the regional administrators clearly had no idea of the school, its history, or its mission. As one faculty member said, the Region

> wants a yes man. They don't want any questions. . . . The Region cares about paper and numbers, not stories and people. . . . We're teaching kids. We care about them. We have a wonderful faculty—experienced, caring, dedicated. But that doesn't seem to matter. The system hasn't given us the credit we deserve for the work we've done. We could have done a better job, in terms of percentages [of pass rates on tests]. But compared to other schools, we've done a good job.

Moreover, teachers felt they were under surveillance; they worried that the observers were trying to catch them making a mistake. Teachers told us often during informal observations how brusque or even rude Region observers were when they came to the school. One teacher decried the "politics of the bulletin board," in which Region observers came into schools to see if the appropriate content was hanging on hallway bulletin boards, and into classrooms just to see if the "do now" assignment that high school students do when they first walk into a classroom was written on the board. It was all "micromanagement, que muchas veces quieren llevar a principales a ser CEO y no educadores que valoren el desarrollo de los estudiantes" [micromanagement, and often they wanted principals to be CEOs, not educators who value the development of students]. Another teacher concurred, stating that a representative from the Region's office would come, "and the only thing he would say was, 'Why is that paper there?'" During an observation we conducted, one teacher was furious with the constant interruptions from visiting Region folks; she said that they "come randomly, frequently, and they are cold, rude, and uncomfortable while they are here. They pass judgment after only sitting in on a class for a few minutes." One of the assistant principals at the time jokingly threatened to lock Region observers in a closet on their next visit.

But the jokes belied a more serious issue: some powerful figures in the Region seemed displeased with Luperón. They were demanding that Luperón improve its English Regents pass rate. Further, though Luperón was succeeding at graduating most of its students within a five-year window, consonant with the five to seven years required to develop academic competence in a second language (Cummins 1981a, 1981b), the Region wanted Luperón to increase its four-year graduation rate significantly. "It's all about the numbers," said one assistant principal at the time. Rumors that the Region wanted to close the school only eased when a particularly unpleasant administrator was transferred to a new position.

Growth and Specialization of Faculty and Administration

The school experienced many fundamental changes simultaneously. When the school shifted into a four-year high school, the faculty grew considerably, introducing people who had not shared the original sociopolitical vision of or commitment to the school. The faculty expanded from eleven members in 1994 to twenty-three teachers in 2003–2004 and twenty-seven in 2006–2007. In the process, some of the earliest members of the school community came to feel that the clear original mission had become somewhat diffused. Greater professionalization and division of labor have influenced the school; there are more specialized personnel and tasks are more person-specific. One staff member explained:

> Antes los estudiantes venían deprimidos, y traían problemas de la casa —económico, sentimental—les hemos buscado solución, pero eran mucho por esos años. Entraban llorando, "Yo quiero que tú me oigas." "Yo quiero esto." Pero ahora, lo referí al psicólogo. Ya no se puede hacer.

> [Before, when students came in depressed, bringing problems from home—economic ones, romantic ones—we found solutions, but it was a lot during those years. They used to come in crying, "I want you to listen to me." "I want this." But now, I refer them to a psychologist. We can't do that anymore.]

The family atmosphere has shifted as the school has hired more teachers with diverse backgrounds who do not share the same immigration histories and might not have the same community commitment. One staff member noted the change:

> Cuando comenzamos éramos como una familia, los muchachos, el personal, era como tan unido, una familia. . . . Estamos ahora en un sistema dónde no se puede seguir eso. Le ponen límites a ello. Ya no es como comenzamos. . . . . Veo las personas nuevas que vienen. No se sienten como nosotros. Otra gente va llegando y no es igual.

[When we started we were a family, the youngsters, the personnel, we were so close, a family. . . . Now we're in a system where one cannot continue that. They put limits on that. Now it is not as when we started. . . . I see the new people who come; they don't feel like we do. Other people arrive and it isn't the same.]

Several of the pioneros sensed a lack of interest among the new teachers and staff who did not identify as much with the mission of the school (and often did not stay more than a year or two). As one of the founding teachers said, "Hay que elevar el nivel de ownership" [We have to raise the level of ownership]. But others felt that, overall, the teaching staff was committed to the school's mission of serving immigrant youth. As one explained,

Algunos se han ido, otros han venido. En algunos hay un actitud de desinterés, no se identifican tanto con la misión. Pero Villar siempre ha tenido, me parece a mí, bien claro qué tipo de personal él quiere para la escuela, y qué tipo de maestro él tiene para sus estudiantes, siempre debe demonstrar su interés por los estudiantes y su bienestar. Hay algunos más expresivos, otros más distantes, pero la mayoría en el momento decisivo estamos ahí.

[Some teachers have gone, others have come. Some are uninterested, or don't identify as fully with the mission of the school. But, in my opinion, Villar has always been clear about what kind of people he wants for the school, what kind of teacher he wants for his students, they should always demonstrate interest for students and their well-being. Some are more expressive, others more distant, but the majority, when it comes down to it, we are there.]

This sense of commitment was not limited to the teachers. The year that Luperón graduated its first class, one of the women working in the kitchen saved her money and purchased a class ring.

The expansion of the faculty also brought the occasional difference of opinion over language education. Some of the new English teachers who were themselves not immigrants felt that the school should be using more English across the curriculum. "I just worry about these kids," said one teacher, "I mean, how are they going to make it once they leave here?" Another weighed in, "Three periods a day is just not enough for these kids. It would be different if they were getting lots of English outside the school, but they aren't." Others who had been there longer tended to see the value of teaching academic literacy in Spanish, though they admitted that it had taken them awhile to come to this conclusion.

Other challenges emerged. The school's growth in size and professionalization, and the increasing demands for accountability, resulted in more bureaucratization, with the addition of three assistant principals: one for administration, another for math and science, and another one for English, Spanish, and social studies. During the period of our study, there was significant turnover among assistant principals from year to year before the staffing finally stabilized in 2007. Approval by assistant principals is now required for many decisions. Some teachers have expressed resentment over the hierarchy that resulted from expansion and specialization. Although some teachers welcomed the initiatives of the new assistant principals, others found them to be an obstacle and chafed at the social distance of their beloved principal. A staff member lamented how changes had resulted in less flexibility: "Antes tú tenías una idea, la compartías con Villar o con Myrna; si era factible la aprobaba, y uno la ponía a trabajar. Ahora hay más limitaciones." [Before, when you had an idea, you shared it with Villar or with Myrna; if it was feasible, you put it to work. Now there are more limitations.] Some teachers felt that the sudden expansion to three assistant principals was unnecessary, and that instead the school needed more teachers. However, others noted the advantages of having more assistant principals, specifically to help teachers obtain important information. One said,

> En cuanto a la parte académica, el peso caía más sobre el maestro, y obtener información correcta de beneficio de estudiantes y la escuela. En los Regentes cuando comenzamos a entrar en el mundo, pudo haber sido catastrófico. Hoy día, el maestro se dedica más a la parte académica y [los administradores] buscan material de apoyo. Definitivamente que sí es bueno, . . . los administradores aquí trabajan muy de cerca con nosotros, y buscan la solución al problema que se presenta, en el salón de clase o escuela. Hay más apoyo.

> [As for the academic part, the responsibility fell heavily on the teacher to obtain the correct information to benefit students and the school. When we started giving the Regents, it could have been catastrophic. Today,

the teacher is more focused on the academic part and administrators seek support materials. It's definitely good . . . the administrators here work closely with us, and seek solutions to problems that arise in the classroom or the school. There's more support.]

Several of the assistant principals hired during the time of our study spoke no Spanish, and a few Dominican teachers admitted feeling that this lack of bilingualism influenced how they saw them. As one teacher said, "A veces uno discrimina a la inversa" [Sometimes we reverse discriminate]. In 2007, the school managed to hire assistant principals who understood and shared the vision for the school. One, a Latina, had experiential knowledge of the struggle for Latino education; the other, of Indian heritage, worked to acquire enough Spanish to engage in jocular teasing with the principal, faculty, and students, and she took a study tour of the Dominican Republic to understand students' cultural, social, and academic experiences.

In summary, the expansion, diversification, and specialization of faculty and administration occasioned by the shift to a four-year school introduced cultural and procedural changes that proved challenging. And yet, it also taught the faculty, staff, and students to value diversity, to trust others, and to question their own prejudices.

Growth and Diversification of Student Body

At the same time, the student population was changing quite radically. Over the course of three years, as the school moved to a four-year model, the number of students more than doubled. The Dominican student population continually grew more diverse in terms of class background and origin: in 2003, the Dominican Republic was experiencing a major economic crisis due to the collapse of major banks, which spurred even higher levels of immigration, especially among Dominicans from more rural areas (Amnesty International 2004; Loucky, Armstrong, and Estrada 2006). Teachers reported receiving more and more students with interrupted formal education (SIFE), and students who were not adequately prepared to enter high school; many of these students had low levels of Spanish-language literacy because of inadequate schooling in the Dominican Republic (2003–2004). One of the founding teachers explained that these students with limited Spanish literacy, now so dominant in their classes, are "la retranca en la calle—se tiene que reducir la velocidad" [the break in the street—you have to reduce your speed]. This population, a product of new immigration, is more prevalent today than a decade ago; their presence in school requires more intensive educational attention than Luperón is usually able to provide.

In this same period, Latino immigration to northern Manhattan continued to diversify, with Mexican and Central American newcomers appearing in greater numbers. According to the U.S. Census of 2000, the population of Mexican immigrants in New York City rose to 180,000, but considering that a significant number of these immigrants are undocumented, Smith (2001) argues that the total population may be as high as 300,000. In 2006, New York State was home to 207,828 Central American immigrants, or 10 percent of the total Central American population who immigrate to the United States (Migration Policy Institute 2006). In 2004, a founding teacher told us, "There are more nationalities now. That makes us a stronger community of learners, more accepting of one another. Now, only 60–70 percent of the students are Dominican. Immigration from Mexico to the East Coast has exploded. When I moved into this neighborhood, there were very few Mexican students."

Across the street from the school, Dominican businesses were being replaced by *taquerías*. From his time during the early years of the four-year school, a former administrator of Luperón observed that Mexican and South American students felt somewhat isolated at the school, but not to the point of feeling alienated: "The Mexican students tend to hang out together and the South American students tend to hang out with each other." In an effort to promote interaction among students of different backgrounds while ensuring their safety, the school initiated an after-school program and invited students from area schools to attend. While this diversification brought many advantages, it also contributed, for some members of the school community, to a diminishing sense of cultural cohesion. We turn to this topic later in this book.

Teachers noted cultural shifts among Latino youth as well, with young people becoming more worldly and bolder, and having more sexual and drug experiences than in previous decades. In 2007, a support staff member noted that the youth were becoming "más atrevidos, más sueltos, más libres. Latinoamérica va cambiando también. Se encuentra de todo. Pero básicamente los nenes son respetuosos y muy buenos. Siempre hay uno que otro, el fresco, el cabeza duro." [more bold, more free. Latin America is changing too. You find everything. But basically they are respectful and good kids. There's always one who's cheeky or hard-headed.] One of the teachers explained:

> Ya no hay la inocencia que había antes. Tienen mucho mundo callejero. Lo de gangas es nuevo, y vienen con esas experiencias desde allá, desde la República, El Salvador, desde México. Hay muchas niñas que tienen más horas de vuelo que una azafata de American. Tienen más mundo.

> [There's no longer the innocence that there was before. They're more streetwise. The gangs are new, and they come with that experience from there, from the Dominican Republic, Salvador, Mexico. There are many girls who have more flying time than an American Airlines flight attendant. They are more worldly.]

The teacher's reference to "flying time" indicated not only the transnational movement of girls between the Dominican Republic and the United States, it also suggested a frequency of sexual experiences for young women.

The rapid increase of youth gang activity in the 2000s also influenced the student body at Luperón. Two of the more active groups specifically targeted Dominican immigrants for recruitment: Dominicans Don't Play (DDP) and the Trinitarios. The Trinitarios reportedly formed within the state prison system (including at Rikers Island) in order to protect its members from the Latin Kings and the Bloods; it "broadened onto the streets of New York where members' 'ability to conduct narcotics trafficking were facilitated by their ties to the Dominican Republic,' according to a federal official" (Baker 2009). The DDP and the Trinitarios heavily sought members in and around Manhattan high schools, where in 2007 and 2008 gang-related attacks, several youth were injured and one was killed. Both gangs were involved in drug trafficking in Washington Heights; on March 10, 2009, nearly forty members of the Trinitarios were arrested in a raid.[8] This increase in gang activity affected the students, and especially the boys. Some boys were worried about their transit to and from school, while others found the gangs exciting and attractive. Faculty and staff remarked on the dangers of these activities for their students. One pionero reported:

Lo único en todo ese tiempo que yo puedo pensar y me da tristeza, y eso viene siendo en los últimos dos o tres años que se está presentando eso. De la cuestión de las gangas. Es tan rápido, porque eso no se daba. Me da tristeza de que la escuela vaya a cambiar mucho por eso. De que los otros muchachos se vayan a contaminar con eso. Me da mucha tristeza saber que muchos de ellos van a parar a la cárcel, dejan la escuela, se convierten en otra cosa. . . . Están en venta de droga, cosas ilegales, quizás la atracción pueda ser el dinero, la presión de que si tú no lo haces, hacemos cualquier cosa. Son varones mayormente, las muchachas porque están ligadas con los muchachos.

[The only thing in my whole time here that makes me sad, and this has been in the past two or three years, is the issue of gangs. It happened so fast; we didn't have this problem before. It makes me sad that the school has had to change a lot because of this. Because some boys are contaminated by this. It makes me really sad to know that many of these youth are going to go to jail, they leave school, they've become something else. . . . They get involved in selling drugs, illegal stuff, maybe it's the lure of money, or they're told that if they don't do it, the others will do something to them. They are mostly boys; the girls get involved only because they are connected to the boys.]

These changes among the student body, and cultural swings among Latino youth, paralleled a shift in control over admissions at Luperón. Whereas the school was originally allowed to do its own screening, the Region took over that responsibility post-reorganization. When one teacher was asked what she wished for the future, she said,

Que la superintendencia no nos limite. Antes nosotros hacíamos nuestro propio screening, anunciábamos la apertura de admisiones, y hacíamos exámenes. La Región impuso su autoridad y empezaron a mandar estudiantes. No tenemos control sobre quién admitimos. Vía superintendencia, muchos de esos muchachos están entrando aquí.

[That the superintendents don't limit us. Before, we did our own screening, we announced the opening of admissions, and we did the exams. The Region imposed its authority and started to send us students. We don't have control over who we admit. Through the superintendent, many (underprepared students) are coming into the school.]

The changing student body—with more students who are poorly prepared and coming from Latin American countries other than the Dominican Republic—has proven challenging. The higher accountability measures imposed by NCLB pose a challenge for all newcomers, but they are especially challenging for those who have low literacy in Spanish. Second, with a diversifying student body, the Dominican teachers (and principal) cannot always depend on a shared cultural background in order to build close relationships with students and devise ways of helping them learn.

Changing School Context

According to faculty at Luperón, the mandated focus on accountability that came with the transition to a four-year school forced the school to lose its flexibility and become more regulated. One staff member explained the change of tone at the school:

> Con todos los cambios con la cuestión del departamento de educación, la escuela ha cambiado un poco el tono. El trato que los maestros tienen que tener con los muchachos. Es todo reglas. El tono ha cambiado un poco. . . . Todos los cambios, hay más cambios, más cambios, más cambios. En el trabajo ha habido cambios, más de presión, porque para ellos everything is accountability, más bajo la presión de que hay que hacer más papeleo, más por la raya. Antes eran más flexibles. Ahora hay que tener más cuidado, porque ya no es así.

> [With all the changes with the Department of Education, the school has changed its tone. The relationship that teachers have to have with the youngsters. It is all rules. The tone has changed some. . . . All the changes, there are more changes, more changes, more changes. The work has changed, more pressure, because now for them everything is accountability, there is more pressure that one has to do more paperwork, it is all more by the rule. Before they were more flexible. Now you have to be more careful, because it is no longer that way.]

It is interesting to note that as the student population at Luperón grew more heterogeneous, policies made assessment more homogeneous; that is, as ethnic and social differences have increased in New York City, the educational policies resulting from NCLB expect sameness more than ever. Nevertheless, the school has slowly (albeit not perfectly) adapted to the new rules. Luperón principal Juan Villar described the adjustments while complaining about the homogenization of assessment expectations:

> We're in the process of unlearning everything we have learned to see if we can make the most adequate transition, eso es bien difícil. Estamos teniendo mucha resistencia tanto de los maestros viejos, como de los nuevos, por razones distintas. Los viejos porque piensan que de alguna manera lo que ellos hacen genuinamente representa lo mejor para las necesidades de los estudiantes. . . . Los [maestros] jóvenes expresan su resistencia no a las nuevas cosas que piden y a las modificaciones, pero al timing, y al hecho de que todos son metidos en un saco y evaluados con la misma medida, y no hay diferencias para medir a los niños americanos cuando llegan a la edad de catorce, y los que vienen de México a los catorce años.

> [We're in the process of unlearning everything we have learned to see if we can make the most adequate transition, and that's very difficult. We're having a lot of resistance from the old teachers, as well as the new teachers, for different reasons. The old ones because they think that what they do in some way represents the best for the students' needs. . . . The young ones show their resistance not to the new things that are required or to the modifications, but to the timing, and to the fact that everyone is treated the same and measured with the same measurement—(the same test for U.S.-born) American children when they turn fourteen, and those who come from Mexico at age fourteen.]

The pressures of accountability and testing, along with the expansion of the school, brought important cultural changes. The sense of shared political commitment and hope that characterized the first decade was, according to some, replaced by an emphasis on accountability and numbers. "Now the computer can track us," said one of the founding teachers, and "todo es número" [it's all numbers]. One of the staff members regretted that they have had to turn down many students who had completed ninth or tenth grade outside the United States and wished to join their corresponding grade level at Luperón. Because of the stiffer graduation requirements, they would never be able to graduate; instead, their only option was to begin high school again, in order to buy themselves the necessary time to develop academic English. This staff member sadly said, "Casualmente cuando vienen en el grado 11 o el 12, les tenemos que explicar que no van a graduarse aquí—primero, por el idioma y también porque tienen exámenes que son en inglés." [As a matter of fact, when they come in grades 11 or 12, we have to explain to them that they won't be able to graduate from here—first, because of the language, and also because they have to pass exams in English.]

In short, within a period of five years, Luperón expanded and diversified its faculty and student bodies and experienced enormous changes in its school culture while struggling to adjust its curriculum and pedagogy to the newly imposed, high-stakes exams. As we describe in the next section, the school was also adjusting to rapid changes at city hall.

Empowerment? How Bloomberg's Reforms Have Affected Luperón

In 2005, in an effort to reduce bureaucracy while increasing accountability, Mayor Bloomberg and Schools Chancellor Klein experimented with the formation of *autonomous schools* (later Empowerment schools) that were outside the control of the Regions. By 2007, they dissolved the Region structure, replacing them with four coalitions of schools organized as Learning Support Organization Networks. The Empowerment Support Organization that Luperón joined was one of those networks. Administrators of schools in the Empowerment Support Organizations gained broad authority over budgets as well as programming, curriculum, and professional development; in turn, they agreed to implement periodic assessments that were meant to yield formative data on students' learning (as measured, obviously, by standardized tests), which in turn would help teachers target their instruction. Luperón became an Empowerment school in 2006, a year before schools were mandated to join Learning Support Organizations.[9] In this section, we question to what extent Luperón has become "empowered" by this most recent organizational restructuring.

Luperón's realignment, which occurred late in our study, yielded one highly significant outcome. As a result of joining the empowerment zone, the school was required to evaluate students every six weeks. They could either choose to develop their own assessments, which would be very time-consuming and had to be completed quickly, or they could select a private, for-profit company to provide the assessments. Given those constraints, Luperón elected in the first year to use materials from Princeton Review. Teachers were meant to collect the data regularly and adjust instruction accordingly. Yet these tests were in English, designed for native speakers of English, and completely inappropriate for Luperón students. As Villar complained, "We have to do evaluations of our kids using an instrument developed for a population that has nothing to do with our kids."

These periodic assessments were only the latest in a parade of tests that the students were being asked to take. Teachers and students started expressing a strong sense of test overload. Interviewed during a month of concentrated testing (April 2007), one administrator said, "There's no communication between the people who are asking to test these kids. NYSESLAT, AP exams, ELA [English language arts] everything in May, plus periodic assessment, and the end of the marking period."

The intensification of testing particularly affected English and math, the two content areas highlighted on the accountability reports. As Villar explained:

> We've had to reorganize the school. We have to erase what we have
> learned; not to forget it, but deactivate it and learn new things. The
> structure we have, the manner of organizing has to change. We are
> paying attention to conversations between departments. We are forming
> different committees across departments; we are encouraging visits
> between teachers. There's a huge emphasis on English because that is
> the hardest part for us. We need to understand what is demanded of the
> English teachers.

As it turned out, the conversations across departments have served them well, with students doing increasingly better on Regents exams, especially on the English Language Arts Regents. The faculty first jointly analyzed the English Language Arts Regents during one of the professional development sessions that Bartlett and García held for the Luperón staff the first year of our study. Through such discussions, Luperón faculty members have learned to build collaboratively on the same academic language and literacy skills across disciplines and languages.

Our school-based observations noted an increase in test preparation, including talk about test strategies, as of 2007. And the faculty and administration were seeking tools specific to test preparation. For example, in late 2007 one teacher told us, "Ahora mismo va a llegar un programa buenísimo que vamos a trabajar con unos controles de la computadora, preguntas de Regentes, qué porciento tenemos buenos y nos va a decir dónde estamos fuertes, diagnosticar" [Soon a great new computer-based program will arrive that has Regents questions, shows us what percent of the questions we do well, it will tell us where we are strong, it's a diagnostic]. The pressure to improve test scores resulted in more time being spent on test preparation, for better or for worse.

And yet, our school-based observations also note that there was an increased sense of professionalism during this time. Administrators learned how to make important decisions that affected their school's financial existence. They learned to track student data and to provide professional development to support the teachers. Teachers became more knowledgeable about their students as they looked at results together.

After one year of using the Princeton Review materials, the faculty at Luperón opted to design their own periodic assessments. These DYO (Design Your Own) assessments proved to be more relevant for Luperón students, and teachers reported that the results were more reliable and more useful. Further, the requirement for periodic assessments was reduced to twice a year, thus easing the testing burden.

Because of Luperón's history and its commitment to the community, the increased attention to test scores did not destroy its collaborative spirit, its social mission, or the critical pedagogy of care teachers had developed for their students. In fact, while administrators and teachers were becoming attentive to test scores, along with the rest of the nation's schools, the Luperón community was simultaneously engaged in a social and political battle for its survival: fighting for a new school building.

Fighting for, and Getting, a New School

During this time of significant accommodations to the strictures of Regents exams and the requirements of the empowerment school model, the Luperón administration, faculty, students, and parents were also engaged in a political battle. The school facility, originally designed to house a transitional program of no more than 250 students, was absolutely insufficient for the school that Luperón had become. Packed with more than

350 students, the former warehouse had only twenty-one classrooms, few windows, no gym or athletic fields, no auditorium, and no science laboratories. The cafeteria was so small that it could accommodate only a fourth of the student body at any single moment, requiring administrators to spread lunch over four shifts. The overcrowded hallways and stairwells made transit between classes difficult and, during the time of our study, necessitated frequent fire drills to ensure that students could escape the building in the event of an emergency. The faulty air conditioning and heating left rooms steamy and uncomfortable many days in the school year.

From its earliest days as a four-year school, Luperón teachers had begun to organize students and parents to agitate for a more appropriate site. They circulated petitions and held regular protests at the school. During the first few years, the Department of Education offered Luperón a few other locations. Two were outside Washington Heights; faculty and staff felt strongly that leaving the Heights would weaken their strong connection to the Dominican community. The students, parents, and faculty remained adamant and continued to pressure the city for a new building in the Heights. Finally, they persuaded Schools Chancellor Joel Klein himself to come to their school, in what was considered a public relations coup. One teacher noted the importance of getting a new school building:

> El cambio más reciente, y lo más importante, es el edificio nuevo
> que se logró. No por la administración de la ciudad que amaneció y
> decidió darnos una escuela. Fue un proceso de lucha en que padres
> y un 50 percent de los estudiantes de esta escuela. Los estudiantes y
> los padres fueron a una audiencia pública en que estaba el Canciller,
> y convencieron a Klein que venga. El visitó la escuela. Tuvimos que
> recurrir a hacer demostraciones, frente a la escuela. Hicimos una
> campaña recopilando miles de firmas, en la comunidad. Los estudiantes
> aquí fueron el 70 percent los que contribuyeron a esa lucha. Una
> coalición incluía a los padres, a los estudiantes, a los profesores, y
> que recibió apoyo del community board de esta área, y personas de la
> comunidad a causa de la escuela.

> [The most recent and most important change is the new building that
> we achieved. It wasn't that the city administration one day woke up
> and decided to give us a school. It was a process of struggle involving
> parents and 50 percent of the students of this school. The students and

their parents went to a public hearing attended by the chancellor, and they convinced Klein to come to the school. He visited the school. We had to resort to demonstrations in front of the school. We had a petition campaign, getting thousands of signatures, in the community. The students here were 70 percent of the support for that fight. The coalition included parents, students, teachers, and got support from the community board and community people on behalf of the school.]

Thanks to this groundswell of support, in 2005 Bloomberg announced that the city would spend $41 million to construct a new high school for Luperón. Even with committed funding, finding an appropriate site for the building within Washington Heights proved difficult, as some local power brokers cast the teenaged students as potential problems. When school supporters found a felicitous site that offered access to public parks and community institutions, local politicians—including a well-known Latino figure—blocked the move. With consistent community pressure, however, a suitable location was eventually found. Located at 165th Street and Amsterdam Avenue, the new facilities include a library, gym, auditorium, science labs, music and art room, kitchen, cafeteria, and wireless Internet access. The project was completed in time for the opening of the 2008–2009 school year.

It is critical to note the paramount role that family members played in asserting the demands for a new school building. Although the 2007 reorganization has been highly criticized for not giving parents and communities a voice, Luperón's parents have continued to be at the center of Luperón's life. We now turn to examining the value that Luperón has for families, as well as the important roles that families play for Luperón.

Parents and Community

The presence of parents in a New York City high school, and especially of immigrant parents who do not speak English, is not common. Many parents are undocumented and afraid to enter a high school where a photo ID has to be shown to a security agent working for the New York City police department at the front door and where the sign-in sheet includes the names and addresses of those visiting. Nevertheless, parents do show up at Luperón. Sometimes they are visiting the parent coordinator, Kenyi Ogando, but most of the time they are visiting the principal himself, Juan

Villar, who continues to act as a counselor not only to students but also their families. At other times, they are attending the many events for parents that the PTA puts together, or the monthly parent meetings, which take place in the evening and in Spanish.

We start first by reporting on the interviews that we conducted in 2007 with twenty-six family members—all mothers, except for one. Although the meetings were originally planned as focus groups, we learned quickly that the women arrived as their schedules allowed, after work and often exhausted. Thus, we interviewed them as they came—some singly, some in groups. Many of the women were working as home attendants or in factories, but there was one who was employed in a travel agency, and another who was working as an accountant. Two were attending a community college in the south Bronx, and only two were unemployed. At the time of our interviews, some were undocumented, but most had come to the United States with family reunification visas and held green cards. Although the majority were poor, one of the mothers had earned a college degree in accounting in the Dominican Republic; she was retired, and mentioned her desire to have her children learn English as motivation for her immigration. All but three of the women interviewed were Dominican. Two mothers were from Honduras and were speakers of Garifuna as well as Spanish. The one aunt we interviewed, who had custody of her nephew, was from Mexico. Our conversations with these parents and guardians revealed them to be strong women, struggling to challenge the odds that surrounded them—inadequate housing, little English, poor or no work, distant families, nonworking marriages, detached stepfamilies, and sometimes difficult teenagers. Here we present their views regarding the school, as expressed during these interviews, before turning to the topic of parental participation.

A School for the Family: Parents Speak Out

Our conversations with the mothers and the aunt revealed the important role that Luperón plays for many families. The women considered the school to be an important resource in the process of adjusting to a new country and in feeling at home and secure. In addition, the women placed immense amounts of faith in the education and the English-language teaching that their children were getting at Luperón. In what follows, we develop the four ways in which the women perceived Luperón: the school as *familia*, the school as *seguridad,* the school as key to a better education, and the school as a way to learn English.

School as *Familia*

Many mothers communicated their sense that Luperón provides a space in which they feel secure and in good company. They stated that Luperón, a school for immigrants like themselves who feel alienated, helps parents and students feel more secure. One mother explained:

> Como ésta es una escuela para inmigrantes, cuando los padres vienen por primera vez, por eso se sienten con tanta confianza con la escuela. Tú aquí sientes seguridad. . . . Tú te sientes como si tú estuvieras en tu país.

> [Since this is a school for immigrants, when parents come for the first time, that's why they feel so much at home in the school. You feel secure here. . . . You feel as if you were in your own country.]

This feeling of being "at home" or in a family, expressed poignantly by the pioneros, was echoed by many of the mothers. One of the mothers stated that, at Luperón, "El niño no es un número" [the child is not a number]. And, she added, "Es muy familiar la escuela" [The school is very family-like].

The women described how the Spanish used at the school and the shared sense of culture created a feeling of belonging. Speaking of the human warmth that she felt in the school, and of the help that she had received, another mother says:

> Me gusta como el calor humano. No sé si es porque hablamos el mismo idioma. Nos entendemos bien; cómo tratan los profesores a los estudiantes, como si fuera una familia. Nos ayudamos de ambas partes.

> [I like the human warmth. I don't know if it is because we speak the same language. We understand each other well; how the teachers treat the students, as if we were all a family. We help each other on both sides.]

The symbiosis between teachers and students that the pioneros spoke about was also discussed by the women, who felt connected to the teachers and their children as a family. But the support is mutual—"de ambas partes." Parents support the school because the school helps their children and the broader community. For this mother, the school was like a family that spoke her language. This symbiotic collaboration created a sense of well-being and peace to which the mothers often referred, in phrases such as *Nos sentimos bien* [we feel good] and *aquí estás con paz* [here, it's peaceful].

Many mothers narrated situations in which school personnel had partnered with parents and gone well beyond the usual boundaries set between school and home in order to support the development and well-being of immigrant adolescents. For example, one mother recounted her difficulties with her son, whom she had originally left in the Dominican Republic at the age of five when she went to the United States to work. Her son resented having been taken from his grandmother and his father in the Dominican Republic at the age of fourteen to find her remarried and with a new family.[10] The son was angry, and his mother felt desperate. In Luperón, and especially in its principal, Juan Villar, the mother found help at a critical moment. She said:

> Encontré que todos hablaban mi idioma. Yo creo que entré a mi casa. Me presentaron a un principal. Yo encontré que no es de oficina, que es de los pasillos, de las aulas, de la calle, la cafetería. Te da su número de celular, que contesta el teléfono a cualquier hora del día o de la noche. Siempre dice que si es su estudiante es su hijo. Que no es por el dinero, que lo lleva dentro. . . . La Luperón es lo que me da tranquilidad. Juan Villar le abrió la puerta; le daba agua de beber. . . . Villar dijo, "Yo nunca le cerraré las puertas. A. es mi hijo también." . . . Villar es el que me da fuerza.

> [I found that everyone spoke my language. I felt like I was entering my own house (lit., I think I came into my house.) They introduced me to the principal. I found that he is not an office-based principal—that he is in the hallways, in the classrooms, in the street, in the cafeteria. He gives you his cell phone number, and he answers the phone at any time of the day or night. He always says that if (a person) is his student, he or she is his child. That it is not because of the money, but that he has it all inside him. . . . Luperón is what gives me peace. Juan Villar opened the door for him; he gave him water to drink. . . . Villar said, "I will never close my doors to him. A. is also my son." . . . Villar is the one who gives me strength.]

The women expressed deep appreciation for the school and repeatedly referred to it as a blessing and a gift. Referring to the school, one of the mothers told us, "Como inmigrante dominicana, esto es una bendición de Dios porque cuando usted llega aquí recibe este regalo, pues es una bendición" [As a Dominican immigrant, this is a blessing from God because when you arrive here, you receive this gift, so this is a blessing]. Sadly, few Latino families have articulated such feelings about their children's schools, but we found these expressions to be fairly common among the parents we interviewed.

School as *Seguridad*

The school also offers these parents a security that other city schools do not offer. Many mothers told us that they bring their children to Luperón in part to keep them safe. One told us, "Aquí los muchachos no pelean; no hay drogas. En otras escuelas llegan con armas." [Here the students don't fight; there are no drugs. In other schools, they bring arms.] Indeed, during our four years of close observation at the school, fights were infrequent, they rarely occurred inside the school building, and when they occurred they were dealt with directly and immediately by the principal. Youth who started fights several times were counseled extensively by the administration and told that if they continued to create problems, they would be encouraged to seek another school. The school developed a peer mediator system to defuse conflict. Somehow, the close attention and cultural pressure seemed to work, for the most part: two assistant principals we interviewed, who had both served elsewhere, marveled at how rarely fighting occurred at the school.

Some mothers sent their youth to Luperón because they were simply afraid for the lives of their children in what they considered a dangerous city, or what more than one called "una selva de cemento" [a cement jungle]. One mother spoke honestly of her fear that her child would be killed and of the protection that Luperón offered him:

> Y nosotros venimos con miedo, y que te persiguen. Uno vive con un poquito de miedo. . . . Quiero garantizar su vida, la seguridad de mi hijo. Yo no quiero que me lo lleven a una escuela en que le dieron una puñalada. Ahora mismo lo que veo garantizado es la vida de A., y cuando llega aquí, aquí no anda cortando clases. Aquí hasta el que limpia le dice lo que le tenga que decir.

[And we come afraid, and that they're following you. You live with a certain fear. . . . I want to guarantee his life. My son's safety. I don't want to have him taken to a school where they will stab him. Right now I see that his life is guaranteed, and when he gets here, here he doesn't cut class. Here even the janitor tells him what he has to tell him.]

While the federal government and the city system are concerned with numbers and tests, this mother's central concern was the safety of her son and his life. She passionately believed that Luperón kept her son safe, away from danger, and in school. Indeed, while observing our focal students more intensively, we noticed that teachers and other staff paid careful attention to students who were not where they were supposed to be, and sometimes could specify in which class a student should be at that moment. The teachers we interviewed were keenly aware of the importance parents placed on order and security. One teacher explained:

La primera ventaja de esta escuela es la seguridad. En otras escuelas hay mucha violencia. Los padres cuando vienen aquí, hay orden y disciplina. Ven la dedicación de los maestros. Los padres lo dicen y lo saben, el compromiso que hay. Los administradores hacen su trabajo de forma mecánica, esta administración lo lleva mucho más allá, tienen inversión humana, más allá de administrativo, compromiso con el futuro de estos jóvenes.

[The main advantage of this school is security. In other schools there are high levels of violence. When parents come here, they see order and discipline. They see the dedication of the teachers. The parents talk and know about the commitment that exists. Some administrators do their work mechanically. Our administration takes it much further, invests in humans, has a commitment to the future of these youth.]

Parents were also duly concerned about the underlying threat of gang activity in northern Manhattan. Several of the mothers were reassured by the school's attention to this threat, including a system of checking students' *pulseritas* [bracelets] for gang signs. This was also the subject of many parent meetings and is discussed below. The mothers gained confidence in learning that the principal "no es de oficina . . . es de la calle" [he's not of the office . . . he's of the street]. They told us that Villar paid careful attention to discussions among students about these topics and regularly kept abreast of activities outside the school. Villar and his teachers were often seen talking to students outside of the school building, on corners, at fast-food restaurants, and in the gasoline stations of the neighborhood. Villar himself was not hesitant to scold the youth when he felt it necessary. One day at school we overheard a student boasting that outside of school he could do as he wished. Villar retorted in a patient but firm manner: "If an accident happened and you were killed, would people not say that you were a Luperón student?" The student said, "I guess so." "Then," said Villar, "how could you say that I can't care for you if you're outside of the school grounds, when even if you're dead, you're considered my student?" The mothers found such attitudes on the part of faculty and staff to be reassuring, even though they knew that a school alone could not guarantee the safety of their children at all times.

School as Key to a Better Education
The parents of these immigrant youth had generally made tremendous sacrifices to bring their children to the United States in order to be better educated. Sometimes education, and especially education in English, had been their only motivation to immigrate, especially because quality education at the secondary level in the Dominican Republic was scarce, and good private high schools had gotten costly. The mothers viewed high school and college degrees from the United States as passports to a better future. For them, Luperón offered them the promise of a good education for their children.

Mother after mother told us about coming to the United States so that their children would receive a better education:

> Vine para que mis hijos tengan una educación más amplia que la que hay en nuestro país. Un joven graduado de allá, casi no le sirve de muchas cosas.
> [I came so that my children would have a more encompassing education than the one there is in our country. To graduate from there, it really doesn't do them much good.]

> Cuando el niño estudia aquí, el diploma aquí es mundial y le vale en cualquier parte. Hay mucho futuro para los jóvenes.

[When the child studies here, the diploma here is a world diploma, and it is worth something anywhere. There is much future for the youngsters.]

La educación es super mejor aquí.
[Education is super better here.]

El país de nosotros es subdesarrollado, y tiene poco incentivo. Los maestros luchan con los brazos. Aquí te le dan computadoras.
[Our country is underdeveloped, and it gives you little incentive. Teachers there fight with their arms (because they have no equipment, and must rely only on themselves). Here they give them computers.]

While everyone else in the United States was speaking the language of NCLB and wringing his or her hands over the achievement gap, these mothers stated confidently that the education their children received at Luperón was far better than what they would have received in the Dominican Republic or Honduras. Like Ogbu's voluntary migrants, the parents' dual frame of reference helped them to appreciate schooling at Luperón (see Ogbu and Simons 1998). But they were specific about the site: as many mothers explained, the education at Luperón was not typical of the education received by most immigrants in the city.

In this promise of success, Luperón played a most important role for these parents. The mothers described the school as *lo máximo* [the best] and *una escuela especial* [a special school], one with teachers who speak their language and a Dominican principal who is, for them, *crema y nata* [the cream of the crop] and *brillante* [brilliant]. They averred that at this school their children would *superarse* [advance] by studying, learning trades, pursuing careers, and becoming professionals. One mother who held two jobs as a home attendant expressed the following hope for her daughter:

Que se haga professional. Que elija su carrera. Lo que le guste. Que se supere, que yo con lo que trabajo, y lo poco que me falta vivir, basta. Ellos están empezando. . . . Que se supere, para que no sea una más. Que no tenga que ir a una factoría.

[To become a professional. To choose her career. Whatever she likes. To improve, because with the work I do, and the little that I have left to live, it's enough. They're starting out. . . . To improve herself, so that she's not just one more. That she won't have to go to a factory.]

The mothers expressed awareness of the changes that were being made in the curriculum and the rigorous requirements that their children had to meet. They were grateful for this academic rigor and for the efforts that Luperón was exerting to help their children learn. One of them told us, "Yo siento que los están preparando más. Les están exigiendo más. Más tutoría; cuando están flojos los están ayudando más." [I think they're preparing them more. They're requiring more. There's more tutoring; when they're weak, they're helping them more.]

School as a Way to Learn English
The issue of learning English was paramount for these mothers. Many stated explicitly that leaving the Dominican Republic was a sacrifice that they had made to provide their children a chance to become educated in English. What is interesting for us is that despite the struggles of these students with English proficiency, all but two of the women we interviewed seemed very pleased with their children's English development and the school's role in teaching English.

The ways in which parents talked about their youths' English development were revealing. "En inglés va bien" [in English she's doing well], one told us. "Ya está en el nivel 2 de inglés" [she's already in the second level]. From the school's perspective, level 2 English is not sufficient to make adequate progress, and they work furiously to help students advance so they can pass the English Regents, but for this mother, a nonspeaker of English, being in level 2 showed progress and suggested that her daughter was doing well. Another mother expressed her happiness that her daughter, who had arrived two years prior to our interview, was already speaking English. Her manner of expressing that sentiment revealed the mismatches between her expectations and those of the school and society at large in the development of her child's English. In telling us that her daughter already speaks English, she said, "Ya lo coge" [She already gets it]. As we know, "getting it" is not the same as performing in the academic English necessary to graduate from high school. But whereas this is a source of worry for the school whose students have to meet Adequate Yearly Progress (AYP) targets imposed by NCLB, the daughter's burgeoning conversational skills were a source of pride for the mother. The same can be said of the mother who had been in the United States for a while and who told us about her newly arrived son:

> Está aprendiendo inglés bastante. En el corto tiempo, ha avanzado mucho. Entiende mucho inglés y lo habla, conmigo, con los otros niños que nacieron aquí, que saben. Puede ver televisión en inglés. Se desenvuelve bien en inglés.
>
> [He is learning a lot of English. In the short time, he has made a lot of progress. He understands English and speaks it, with me, with the other children who were born here, who know. He can watch television in English. He gets along.]

This mother was also very pleased with her son's progress. She seemed to have an understanding that English development takes time, and she was delighted that for the moment he could speak with her younger English-speaking children, as well as follow television in English. The language needed to understand television programs has little to do with the de-contextualized academic language needed for school. Yet, knowing that her son has a life outside of school and that his involvement there has important consequences for his self-esteem, his happiness, and his sense of adequacy and fulfillment, the mother was pleased that he could "get along." Her concerns for her son's *educación* exceeded the more narrow conceptualization of education prevalent in the United States (Valenzuela 1999a; Valdés 1996).

Most of the mothers we interviewed did not speak English. In one of the small-group interviews, one mother said, "No hablo ni papa de inglés" [I don't speak a bit of English], to which another one quickly replied, "Ni papa, ni yuca," a common retort for expressing absence: neither potato nor yucca—nothing. The mothers who understood how difficult it is to develop English language proficiency were proud of the progress their children were making. They understood the difficulties in acquiring English, but they were confident that their children would learn it. Referring to the English of the students at Luperón, one of the mothers told us with aplomb, "Es un idioma nuevo, una vida nueva, pero lo aprenden" [It is a new language, a new life, but they learn it].

Yet, the mothers perceived significant challenges. They worried that the youth heard too little English. The families were all living in Spanish-speaking communities where Spanish, and not English, is heard. Even the mother who had a college degree and was bilingual complained that only Dominican Spanish with a cibaeño accent was heard in the mall where she worked in the pharmacy.[11] She practiced her English only with the suppliers: "Estoy trabajando en contabilidad, en un centro commercial que tienen farmacia. Es muy latino. Hablan más cibaeño que otra cosa. Estoy practicando el inglés con los surtidores." [I am working in accounting, in a shopping center that has a pharmacy. It's very Latino. People speak more cibaeño than anything.]

Because they were surrounded by Spanish during most of their extracurricular time, the youth of Luperón relied more on the school itself to provide them with a context in which to learn and practice English. Some mothers felt that more could be done to support these efforts. Several argued that too much Spanish was spoken at Luperón. Another said that more subjects should be taught in English. Some said that the youth were reading and writing English better than they could speak it, because they didn't get enough practice speaking English. And yet, the mothers as a whole seemed to feel that, as they struggled with the adaptation of their children to a new culture, a new language, and a new school system, English development was important but second to maintaining ties with family, language, and culture. As one of them said, "El idioma de uno es el primero y el inglés lo lleva de segundo." [One's language is first, and English is carried as second.] Thus, these mothers were happy and satisfied as they watched their children develop as English speakers. They understood that since English is second, it would take time to develop. But they were confident that English would come, and they supported Luperón in its efforts.

Families for a School: Parent Meetings

While the school offered the families much support, it did so while requiring the families' cooperation. The school has at various times offered parents classes in GED, ESL, citizenship, floral arrangement, and other topics, sometimes in cooperation with other agencies in the community. One of the things that the school requires is that families attend its monthly meetings. On average, between seventy-five and one hundred parents attend these meetings, which are held in Spanish. Although the principal and the parent coordinator attend every meeting, the meetings are run by the president of the PTA, a mother. The tone is familiar and inviting; the Spanish used is informal. At every meeting we observed, the messages were the same: "Esto es un trabajo de dos" [This is work for two] and "Nosotros aquí en la escuela y Uds. como padres" [We here in the school and you as parents].

At one meeting, the parent president started by announcing a parent dinner and encouraging those in attendance to bring a dish. But she added, "Si es muy costoso, le damos el dinerito pa' que lo haga" [If it's too expensive, we'll give you a little money so that you can do it]. All parents were invited, and money was not an obstacle because what was important was that they attend: "Lo más importante es la presencia de Uds." [The most important thing is your presence.]

During a January 2007 meeting, the parent coordinator, Kenyi Ogando, a Dominican herself, started out by saying, "Ante que todo, feliz año nuevo. Todavía no pasó la Vieja Belén." [Before everything else, Happy New Year! The Vieja Belén hasn't come yet.] Those of us who were Spanish-speaking but non-Dominicans looked at each other—who, when, or what was the Vieja Belén? As someone quickly explained to us, the folk figure is an old woman who brings simple gifts to poor Dominican children on the Sunday that falls three weeks after Three Kings Day. Using such cultural and linguistic hooks, the parent coordinator effectively related to poor Dominican families. Following that beginning, Kenyi announced the new ESL classes and citizenship classes for adults that were being given jointly with United Neighborhood Centers of America, a community agency. Then she told them about upcoming final exams and the Regents. While informing them, she also gave them advice, lovingly telling them that "sus hijos ya tenían que haber estado en su casa. Reposando." [Your children should already be at home, resting.] Finally, she reviewed graduation requirements and the number of credits that students are required to complete in order to be promoted.

At another parent meeting in 2007, the principal also spoke, communicating not only the results of the Regents and the final exams, but also about a recent incident during lunch when five seniors got drunk outside the school building. Strikingly, the principal indicated that the poor judgment and actions of the individuals reflected on the entire school community. After reporting how the school had successfully finished the first term academically in terms of AYPs, the principal then said, "En plano de reputación terminamos muy mal." [In terms of reputation, we ended the semester very poorly.] The parallels he drew between the health of the school community, the behavior of its students, and students' academic achievements revealed how this school is different from others. The principal and school staff care about their students as human beings, not just as academic beings. And beyond the individuals, they care about the community itself. The principal continued that the students' drunkenness reflected the "vergüenza de ellos mismos, de sus compañeros, y el récord de la escuela" [shame not only to themselves, but also to their classmates, and to the school]. At Luperón, community building is prized, and such community building requires the support of peers and families.

After announcements, parent meetings always turned to difficult topics about which parents needed more information. At one meeting, a Latino officer from the neighboring police precinct talked to parents in Spanish about the Trinitarios, the Latin Kings, the Crips, and the Bloods; he told them where these gangs operate, and he explained their signs. At another meeting, Luperón's social worker reinforced the danger of gangs who were preying on newcomer immigrants. AIDS was another important topic, covered when a Latino doctor from the Interamerican College of Physicians and Surgeons came to speak.

The topics covered are sensitive; addressing these issues well requires cultural sensitivity and solid information. Villar, who prior to becoming a principal worked as a school counselor, has extensive expertise in some of these subjects, and he shares it openly with the parents. Without blaming students or parents, he reminds parents that the immigration experience is traumatic, and that New York City is not "la tierra prometida" [the promised land] but a hostile environment. He reminds them of the difficult situations in which their children live—in crowded quarters with little privacy, with new family and in new family arrangements, with a new language, in a rigorous and demanding school. As he speaks honestly with the parents, he reassures them of the school's commitment to this partnership. As Villar stated, "Mi motivo es ayudar en el proceso de abrir más el diálogo con los padres, madres y estudiantes. Mantener la integridad de esta escuela, y asegurar que no caiga como otras escuelas." [My motive is to help in the process of opening more dialogue with fathers, mothers, and students. To maintain the integrity of this school, and ensure that it doesn't fail as other schools have.]

The topics often initiated intense and poignant discussions among the parents. At one meeting, one of them stood up and said, "Nosotros contribuimos de que se críen delincuentes—o por descuido o porque vivimos aglomerados en una selva de cemento que es New York." [We contribute to their delinquency either because of negligence—or because we live piled up in this cement jungle that is New York.] A long discussion ensued, with parents reassuring each other that they're doing the best they can, and that what's important is to work with the school.

One senses during these meetings that the school staff members and the parents are not in different camps. In fact, they need each other. The parents need the school to help them and their children. The school needs the parents to help educate the children, build a school with integrity, and uplift the community. The relationship between parents and school is continually reinforced as one that's two-sided—parents perceive the school in terms of its work for the families; educators perceive the families in terms of their work for the school.

Conclusion

Through the historical process detailed in this chapter, the educators at Luperón have succeeded in forming what Ancess (2003) calls a "community of commitment." Ancess explored various critical features of such communities in three high schools, including "human scale school size," "caring relationships," "close working proximity of teachers who collaborate," and "strong, nurturing, and shared leadership," among others (1–56). In this chapter, we have demonstrated the importance as well of a committed community and families who are responsible for the school (and to whom the educators are responsible). Furthermore, using a sociocultural analysis of policy as practice, we have shown how federal, state, and local policies and politics have alternately threatened and made possible the survival of the community of commitment at Luperón.

In the next chapter, we examine more specifically the language policies and pedagogies implemented at Luperón, and their role in forming this community of commitment in Washington Heights.

5

Languaging at Luperón

As we sat in Jakob Clausen's windowless English 6 classroom on the third floor of the converted warehouse that housed Luperón in 2005, we asked him about the window panes made of construction paper that we saw displayed on the wall. He described how, early in the year, he asked students to construct their own windows with four panes—language, culture, family and community, and future. He explained that these four elements were the core of his pedagogy and the school's philosophy. Immigrant students, he explained, often complain of feeling *tranca'o* [locked up and trapped] in New York City (see Chapter 6).[1] The school's task is to help them open those windows—to provide the air, space, and freedom the students need to grow, but always building on who they already are and their existing viewpoints. We asked Clausen, "What role does English and Spanish instruction play in that task?" "English is critical," Clausen explained, "but you can't teach them English without drawing upon Spanish." He elucidated:

> I threw that [English-only teaching] away. I think [bilingualism] is important. My understanding about language learning and cultural aspects has been deepened here. These adolescents have been taken from their community, often under adverse family conditions; they meet parents with new families; their parents are now divorced; [they're coming] with an idealized view of America. If you took their language away too, it would be terribly detrimental. The metaphor of drowning is one I can understand.[2] I think of that when I look at these students. I try to think of their situation. They have to have their oxygen, their language.

In this chapter, we consider the language use and language education approach employed at Luperón and what it can teach us about educating immigrant youth more broadly. In New York City, programs for English learners can be only of three types—(1) ESL, (2) transitional bilingual education, or (3) dual language bilingual education. Because Luperón uses Spanish in teaching content, the program at Luperón cannot be considered ESL. As a high school for Latino newcomers where students stay until they graduate, Luperón is not strictly a transitional bilingual education program since students do not "exit" to "mainstream" classes. Nor is Luperón a dual language bilingual program, since only Latino emergent bilingual students attend this school.

Luperón is unique: it does not follow any norm as defined by the New York City Department of Education. One teacher described what she perceived: "There are only four programs [in the DOE]: transitional, dual language, gifted and talented, and SIFE. Ours doesn't fit." The language education model being used at Luperón is distinct. Luperón isn't exactly an international school either, since it doesn't belong to the Internationals network and content is taught in the students' home language. Luperón is a small school, but it predates the celebrated small schools supported with Gates or Carnegie money. Luperón's unique nature has kept it in a category by itself, making it relatively unknown. In some ways this anonymity has shielded the school.

In García and Bartlett (2007), we referred to the type of bilingual education program that Luperón follows as a *speech community model*. As we said in Chapter 1, Luperón's language education approach is consonant with the complex theory of applied linguistics described by Larsen-Freeman and Cameron (2008). As we will see, Luperón's language practices follow those of the school community—those of the students, the teachers, and the school leaders—rather than being externally imposed. As do all schools in New York City, Luperón has a written language allocation policy. Yet, in practice, Luperón's language policy is negotiated every minute as a sense-making mechanism by teachers and students.

The school does not categorize newcomers simply as "limited English proficient," as the federal government does, or as "English language learners," as recent literature and scholarship describe them. Rather, they are adolescents for whom bilingualism in both academic English and academic Spanish is emerging and will, no doubt, emerge. Thus, Luperón extends Spanish and develops its academic use by incorporating it meaningfully to teach content that is needed, as we will see, to graduate from high school. At the same time, the school opens up bilingual spaces within content classes taught in both Spanish and English, building on hybrid practices, in order to develop academic language in both English and Spanish. Following García (2009a), we refer to this use of bilingual or multiple discursive practices in learning and teaching as *translanguaging*. Finally, the school develops the kind of languaging in English and Spanish needed for the high-stakes Regents exams the students must pass in order to graduate. Before we consider those practices in detail, we review here the empirical evidence as well as the theoretical constructs that provide Luperón the impetus to extend Spanish, to develop the languaging practices of tests both in English and Spanish, and to use translanguaging practices to develop academic English as well as to empower students and teachers to participate in these multiple discursive practices.

Evidence and Theories

Research Evidence

Luperón's attention to the development of Spanish for emergent bilinguals is consonant with the empirical evidence around the world that shows near consensus among researchers that greater support for a student's home language, and academic development in that language, is "positively related to higher long-term academic attainment" (Ferguson 2006, 48). In the United States, the research conducted by Ramírez (1992), Thomas and Collier (1997, 2002) and Lindholm-Leary (2001) supports this finding, although these four studies were conducted with elementary-grade students. Thomas and Collier (1997) state, "The first predictor of long-term school success is cognitively complex on-grade level academic instruction through students' first language for as long as possible (at least through grade 5 or 6) and cognitively complex on-grade level academic instruction through the second language (English) for part of the day" (15).

Both Thomas and Collier (2002) and Lindholm-Leary (2001) suggest that a 90:10 model of instruction—a program where *initially* 90 percent of the instruction is in the students' first language and moves gradually to a 50:50 arrangement—is more efficient in helping students reach grade-level achievement in their second language than a 50:50 model, where 50 percent of the instruction initially is in the student's home language and 50 percent is in the additional language. Luperón not only uses Spanish in cognitively complex rigorous subject instruction but also does so tenaciously during the first years of the students' school experience.

In their synthesis of the research evidence in the education of emergent bilinguals, Genesee et al. (2006) repeat that students enrolled in educational programs that provide extended instruction in their home language through late-exit bilingual education programs outperform students who receive only short-term instruction through their home language. They also found that bilingual proficiency and biliteracy are positively related to academic achievement in both languages. Other meta-analyses of the literature have repeatedly shown that emergent bilinguals who are in bilingual education programs where content is taught in their home language, even if these programs are transitional in nature and students eventually exit into mainstream classes, outperform those in English-only programs on tests of academic achievement (Krashen, Rolstad, and MacSwan 2007; Rolstad, Mahoney, and Glass 2005; Slavin and Cheung 2005). Likewise, the National Literacy Panel on Language Minority Children and Youth concluded that bilingual education approaches in which the child's home language is used are more effective in teaching children to read than are English-only approaches (August and Shanahan 2006). August and Shanahan (2006) summarize these findings for the United States by saying, "Language-minority children who are instructed in their first language, as well as English, perform better on English reading measures than students instructed only in English. *This is the case at both secondary and elementary levels*" (639; emphasis added). Luperón's language education policy is consonant with all these research findings; Luperón's students do better in English reading because they receive challenging academic instruction in Spanish. However, as we will see, the role of Spanish at Luperón has much to do with the value of the home language practices for the community, the parents, and the students, and not solely with how it supports the development of English.

Theoretical Constructs

To support its emphasis on the development of Spanish, its flexible use of both languages in translanguaging, and its attention to the development of the academic language of the tests, Luperón's practices are substantiated by a number of theoretical constructs. We introduce these theories before turning to a fuller description of Luperón's practices.

Linguistic Interdependence and Common Underlying Proficiency

Cummins (1979, 1981a, 1981b) first posited that the acquisition of an additional language relies on the ways in which the emergent bilinguals' home language bolsters the process. Cummins (2008, 38) called this theory *linguistic interdependence*: "To the extent that instruction in Lx [one language] is effective in promoting proficiency in Lx [that language], transfer of this proficiency to Ly [the additional language] will occur provided there is adequate exposure to Ly." A related theoretical construct is that of *common underlying proficiency* (Cummins 1979, 1981b), which posits that knowledge and abilities acquired in one language are potentially available for the development of another. Researchers have consistently found that there is a cross-linguistic relationship between students' home and additional languages (Riches and Genesee 2006). This is particularly the case for literacy. Theories of linguistic interdependence are at the core of Luperón's Spanish language practices to extend English, but as we will see in the following section, Spanish language practices also have much to do with extending Spanish academic language and literacies.

Academic Language and Literacy

The ways in which people language—their languaging—is clearly very different from standardized academic language, which has "deliberately and artificially imposed characteristics" (Romaine 1994, 84). When communicating with people we know, either orally or in writing, languaging is most often supported by cues that have little to do with language itself—gestures, repeating, providing examples. This is what Cummins calls *contextualized language,* which is used for *basic interpersonal communication skills* (BICS) (Cummins 1981a and b). The completion of school tasks, and especially assessment tasks, requires not only a different set of language abilities but also different languaging. To engage in most schoolwork, students must be able to language with little or no extralinguistic support with what Cummins calls the *decontextualized language* required for *cognitive academic language proficiency* (CALP). Cummins posits that whereas BICS can be developed in one to three years, it takes *five to seven years* to develop the academic abstract languaging needed for CALP (1979, 1981a and b, 2000).

Street (1984, 1996, 2005) has proposed that literacy is not a monolithic construct made up of a discrete set of skills; rather, literacy practices vary in key ways according to different sociocultural contexts, and they are influenced by social, cultural, political, and economic factors (Bartlett

2010; García, Bartlett, and Kleifgen 2007; Kenner 2000, 2004; Martin-Jones and Jones 2000; Gutiérrez and Orellana 2006). What counts as literacy, and which literacy practices are considered appropriate, varies situationally and relationally. Thus, a student who has gone to school in the Dominican Republic for many years has experienced a way of communicating "in and around writing" (Hornberger 1990) that is profoundly different from what is expected in the United States, and at Luperón specifically. It is not simply that English differs from Spanish; rather, the "languaging," or the language and literacy practices in which students engage, vary in the two societies and the two school systems.

Studies comparing literacy practices in the Dominican Republic and the United States help to illuminate these critical differences. In her insightful study of the literacy practices of a young Dominican immigrant (given the pseudonym Yanira), Rubinstein-Ávila (2007) outlines the important sociocultural differences in languaging faced by Yanira. The Bible and the Catholic Church played key roles in Yanira's early literacy socialization (for similar data on young Latinos in the United States, see Farr and Barajas 2005; Mercado 2005a, 2005b; Zentella 2005); combined with her early experiences in school, this socialization led Yanira to associate good reading with oral performances, "such as reading out loud from the stage of a church and performing in school plays" (Rubinstein-Ávila 2007, 595). Yet this sort of oral competency in reading was rarely requested or rewarded in her American middle school. In relation to writing, Yanira remarked significant contrasts between textual structures and sociopedagogical expectations related to writing in Spanish and English.[3] She reported that while teachers in Santo Domingo expected students to copy notes from the board and memorize them, her teachers in the United States often asked her for reports that used various resources (e.g., the textbook, the Internet) and included, in some situations, her own opinion. "So," she said, "even if I understand the English, I still sometimes don't know how to complete it [the assignment]" (584). As Rubinstein-Ávila concludes, Yanira "faced the pressures of learning a new language and developing academic skills in the new language but also was expected to gain awareness of the particular kinds of literacy practices and knowledge that were valued in her adoptive society" (585). Yanira experienced frustration along with a "shift between her feelings of competence in a known and familiar environment (the Dominican Republic) and her confusion toward the new, seemingly more dynamic, complex, and not at all transparent literacy demands in the U.S. context" (585). Indeed, "what counts as literacy in particular communities is by no means universal, neutral, static, or necessarily empowering" (586).

The expressive tradition and expository writing so common in the United States is difficult for students from places "where the central focus is either the text or the teacher as the central authority and source of information" (Watkins-Goffman and Cummings 1997, 438). Expectations about argumentation and structure vary among cultural contexts; writing in Spanish is often less direct (or some might say more subtle) than the argumentation that predominates in American academic literacies (Watkins-Goffman and Cummings 1997).

One must be careful not to overgeneralize, especially given how context-specific literacy practices can be. However, based on these studies and the reflections of reading and writing in the Dominican Republic offered by the students in our study, it is clear that the general approach to literacy practices in public schools in the Dominican Republic requires copying the words, reading a few words carefully, and decoding them (for a similar description, see O. García 2001). Students noted a much greater emphasis in U.S. schools on the development and expression of personal opinion. Reading was different in their New York school as well: students have greater choice of books in the United States, and teachers expect much more independent reading than the students normally did in their previous schools. Students living in a poor country, where texts are expensive, are not exposed to reading multiple texts and are generally not expected to consult the Internet or other sources as they might be in New York. Finally, the literacy practices required for forms of assessment varies radically in the Dominican Republic and the United States. In general, while Dominican exams greatly emphasize content and specific recounting of factual information, U.S. forms of assessment such as the English Regents exam are designed to probe the application of writing modes to material that might not have been previously seen (Grant 2001; Menken 2008).

These sociocultural differences in literacy and assessment practices have important implications for educating immigrant students, for despite all the evidence regarding the transfer of skills from one language to another (e.g., Cummins 1981b, 1991, 2000; Carson et al. 1990; Gabriele et al. 2009), the lack of convergence in literacy practices between the two societies leaves many Dominican students unable to apply what they know about reading, writing, and testing in Spanish to tasks in English. In order for transfer from Spanish to English to occur, students either need the languages to feature similar literacy practices, or they need to be taught new genres and textual expectations more explicitly (August and Shanahan 2006). Many Dominican students can decode and copy, but these skills will not help them pass the complex standardized exams required to graduate from high school, even when those are written in Spanish. Thus, to educate these students appropriately, and for any transfer of literacy practices to occur, they have to *develop academic literacy practices in Spanish* that are similar to academic English literacy practices in U.S. schools, or they need to receive explicit instruction in different writing conventions and opportunities to practice them. This is perhaps one of the most misunderstood aspects of the education of emergent bilinguals.

Academic Language, Academic Literacy, and Adolescents

One of the most salient issues in educating newcomer adolescents has to do with the development of the complex English literacy practices in which they must engage. Elementary school children born in the United States and raised in Spanish-speaking homes usually come into school with some receptive ability in English—a result of watching television and having lived for five years in an English-speaking society, even if their exposure to that society has been minimal. Elementary school children "language" to communicate simpler ideas than adolescents. Their literacy practices use more contextualized language.[4] The English language and literacy development of adolescents is, by contrast, a more complex and demanding task.

Research has shown that older students can make quick progress and that they are neither less successful nor less efficient in acquiring an additional language than children (Singleton 2001). But for adolescents who have been schooled in societies with very different languaging practices, the development of academic English is difficult. The academic English language skills that they need are increasingly complex and build on foundational decontextualized language skills that the literature tells us take from five to seven years to develop (Cummins 1991; Hakuta, Butler, and Wit 2000). Adolescent newcomers, therefore, not only have greater languaging demands but also less time to develop necessary complex literacy practices.

As high school students, the newcomers at Luperón do not have five to seven years to develop their English. They must take and pass the English Regents exam in order to graduate from high school. Thus, they must be innovative in order both to develop the academic literacy in English that they will need in the technological world of the twenty-first century and to pass the exams that will enable them to graduate. Educators of newcomer adolescents must make use of the students' languaging in Spanish and the oracy they're developing in English as they work to help students build complex academic literacy practices in English.

Dynamic Bilingualism and Translanguaging

As we said in Chapter 1, scholars of bilingualism have long argued that bilinguals are not two monolinguals in one and that their communicative needs are different (Grosjean 1985, 1989; Valdés 2005). By proposing the concept of *multicompetence,* Cook (2002) argues that the lives and minds of second language speakers are different because they hold knowledge of two languages in a single mind. Likewise, Herdina and Jessner (2002) propose that bilinguals have two or more dynamically interdependent language systems whose interactions create new structures that are not found in monolingual systems.

To capture the complexity of bilingualism, García (2009a) has proposed a model of *dynamic bilingualism* in which the multiple language practices of bilinguals are considered in interrelationship. Second language teaching and learning usually rests on a monoglossic ideology, by which monolingualism is the ideal and bilingualism is conceived as two balanced wheels of a bicycle. Monoglossic ideologies of bilingualism treat each of the child's languages as separate and whole and view the two languages as bounded autonomous systems. García (2009a) has proposed that bilingualism is *not linear* as in the additive and subtractive models of bilingualism proposed by Lambert (1974), where a second language is merely added or a first one subtracted. Instead, especially in the twenty-first century, bilingualism is *dynamic* in that there is no such thing as two separate autonomous languages but rather language practices that are complex and interrelated. Bilingualism does not result in either the two balanced wheels of a bicycle (as the additive bilingual model purports) or the single wheel of a unicycle (as the subtractive bilingual model suggests). Instead, bilingualism is like an all-terrain-vehicle with individuals using it to adapt to both the ridges and craters of communication in uneven terrains. Like a banyan tree, bilingualism is complex, as it adapts to the soil in which it grows (see García 2009a). Dynamic bilingualism rejects the linear conceptions of traditional second language acquisition (SLA) models; instead, it emphasizes how the languages of bilinguals interact dialogically (Dworin 2003; Moll and Dworin 1996; Valdés 2004).

As we demonstrate later in this chapter, Luperón adopts such a dynamic bilingual approach.

Further, a dynamic bilingual approach takes into consideration the different and varying language practices for distinct purposes that are the result of the different contexts in which languaging develops and functions. Dynamic bilingualism does not emphasize a static conception of learning in order to approach "native-like proficiency," which is itself a political construct (see Canagarajah 1999; Kramsch 1997). Instead, dynamic bilingualism employs a practice approach to bilingualism. That is, it does not emphasize "having" English or "being" a speaker (or reader, or writer) of English and Spanish; instead, this ecological approach accentuates *using* languages to negotiate situations (García 2009a; Larsen-Freeman and Cameron 2008; van Lier 2000; on "being" literate versus "doing" literacy, see Bartlett 2007). In this view, students do not "have" languages. Instead, language is learned through its use in specific social contexts over the course of a lifetime.

Luperón uses the students' emergent bilingualism and languaging practices flexibly, promoting their ability to use the two languages to varying degrees and for distinct purposes. Educating for dynamic bilingualism builds on the complex and multiple language practices of students to develop new language practices in both academic English and academic Spanish. García (2009a) has referred to the process by which students and teachers engage in complex multiple language practices to make sense of the learning and the teaching by the name of *translanguaging*. Research all over the world is showing how translanguaging practices, if properly understood and suitably applied in schools, can in fact enhance cognitive, language, and literacy abilities (Gajo 2007; Heller and Martin-Jones 2001; Lewis 2008; Wei 2009; Martin-Jones and Saxena 1996; Serra 2007).

Macroacquisition

Brutt-Griffler (2004) has studied the English language acquisition of entire societies that have adopted English as an additional language. *Macroacquisition*, the term she uses to refer to this acquisition process, is different from individual SLA in that it is a social practice, and thus, as she says, "the embodiment of the process of language spread and change, or language change through its spread" (138). Unlike individual SLA where the focus is the ultimate attainment of being like a "native speaker" (although this concept is highly contested—see, for example, Kramsch 1997, 2009), successful macroacquisition results in language spread that is always accompanied by language change, as new speakers and users of the language appropriate language practices. This is the case, for example, of societies like Singapore, where Singapore English has spread throughout the entire population. In the macroacquisition process, the language being acquired is transformed since the language practices people engage in vary distinctly according to different social, national, geographical, and historical contexts. But communities of speakers who acquire a language as their own, adapting it to their own social needs and practices, cannot be said to speak that language "with errors." As Brutt-Griffler (2004) indicates, "Any language is the linguistic expression of the speech community that speaks it" (129).

At Luperón, students are engaged in a process of macroacquisition, with the entire community of speakers moving developmentally toward more complex uses of both English and Spanish. At the same time, Luperón teachers understand that macroacquisition means that the students' English has distinct characteristics as bilingual speech. It is not that English is acquired with the features of monolingual "native speakers" by developing English, the community turns from being a Spanish monolingual one to a bilingual one. Likewise, its Spanish shows features of language use in contact with another language. Yet, by accepting this process of macroacquisition of a bilingual community, teachers help students to negotiate their language practices in ways that enable them to do well in high-stakes exams taken in academic English.

Practices

The theoretical constructs we have described give support to the language practices at Luperón, which we outline here. The emphasis on extending Spanish has to do with the important role that the home language has in both language and cognitive development, as well as the conviction that languages are interdependent and that there is a common underlying proficiency; the understanding of the complexity of academic language and literacy use as social practices; the acknowledgment that adolescent language and literacy practices are different from those of young children; and the awareness that the decontextualized language of assessments in the United States, such as the Regents exams, differs from other uses of Spanish with which students might be familiar.

The translanguaging pedagogy for developing English skills has much to do with the understanding of the dynamics of bilingualism and the interdependence of language practices; the knowledge that successful macroacquisition of English will always be accompanied by language change; and the awareness of the decontextualized language of English-medium assessments like the English Regents test.

We now turn to each of these two practices separately.

Extending Spanish

The numerous bilingual and biliterate teachers on the faculty of Luperón have pragmatic knowledge of language learning processes, even the ones whose other language is Hindi or Russian rather than Spanish. The Dominican educators have lived the process of becoming Spanish-English bilinguals. In fact, in interviews they often referred to the fact that Luperón's immigrant students are just like they were, and as they continue to be—members of Spanish-speaking communities and families. These educators appreciate the value of Spanish and bilingualism. The teachers who started out as monolingual English speakers or bilingual in other languages have quickly developed some Spanish-English bilingual ability, understanding messages and even using Spanish phrases in their English speech.

Students come to Luperón with a broad range of academic literacy in Spanish. For students with low Spanish literacy, strong Spanish literacy instruction is provided. Those who have literacy challenges in Spanish are identified and retained in the early levels of Spanish class in order to provide them with more time to practice basic Spanish literacy.

At a group meeting in 2005, we heard the principal express his support for the teaching of Spanish as the students' mother tongue:

> La enseñanza del español en Gregorio Luperón debe responder a los cánones de la enseñanza del español como lengua materna. Esto quiere decir compartir nuestra literatura latinoamericana y española; nuestros autores; nuestros modos de escribir, pensar, y hablar.

> [The teaching of Spanish at Gregorio Luperón should respond to the canons of the teaching of Spanish as a native language. This means to share our Latin American and Spanish literature; our authors; our ways of writing, thinking, and speaking.]

But over the years, there has been less emphasis in Spanish language and literature instruction for students other than those who enter with low literacy. Some see this as an abandonment of Spanish, for the need to have students perform well in the English Regents has necessitated changes in curriculum. However, some of the content Regents Exams needed to graduate are also given in Spanish.[5] To graduate from high school with a Regents diploma, students must pass exams in Math, Science, U.S. History and Government, Global History (all available in Spanish), in addition to an English Language Arts exam. And this in itself has meant that Spanish continues to occupy an important place in the Luperón curriculum, as teachers have had to extend the ways in which students use Spanish so that they can attain the academic Spanish literacy needed to take challenging exams in Science, Math, and Social Studies. In a twist of fortunes, the fact that the content Regents are now translated, and that they count toward high school graduation, has meant that Luperón has paid even more attention to Spanish, albeit of a different kind. Unlike other high schools that abandoned the use of Spanish in bilingual education when faced with the challenge of the English Regents, Luperón has strengthened its academic use of Spanish. In the early years, Spanish at Luperón was used as the medium of instruction only because students didn't speak English and needed to be educated, or because it was the topic of the Spanish language arts class. Now, Spanish is used as a medium of instruction not only with those who are emergent bilinguals but also with fluent bilinguals. Little by little, Spanish has expanded from the domain of the Spanish language arts class, to which Spanish is often relegated in high schools, or the class for English language learners to being one of the languages of education for all. Thus, Spanish has lost its "remedial" quality, and it has taken its place alongside English as an equal partner in instruction—especially in assessment. The status of Spanish has been raised among both students and faculty. Spanish is no longer a support structure, a scaffold, or a remedial tool. Spanish is in itself the structure of learning and knowledge-building, and the language of the high-stakes tests—a language that counts.

Spanish continues to play an important role in helping students progress in content areas while they are securing a firm foundation in English. The decision to incorporate Spanish is particularly important for those students who have not experienced quality education before arriving in New York, since their content-area knowledge tends to be quite weak. These students face significant challenges in adapting to school culture and attaining appropriate levels of content knowledge for their grade. As one assistant principal told us, "These kids are asked to produce just like someone who has had a basic education, first to eighth grade, all in the United States, all in English. They need other resources in this rich country, rich city, in order to do that." She recognized that the use of the students' home language at school is one such resource—rather than a detriment—to promoting achievement: "One of the girls who graduated [in the first graduating class] started here in the [basic Spanish] literacy program. She passed six Regents, and now she's at Bronx Community College." School success is therefore bolstered as students are given the home language support they need.

Spanish is also used at Luperón in academic ways that are often beyond those used in schools in the Dominican Republic. There is a subtle and important difference between just using Spanish to teach content when students do not speak English, and using Spanish in important academic domains, which include high-stakes testing. Whereas the goal of the first use of Spanish is the understanding of content, the objective of its second use is education itself. Thus, a language of education must enjoy full privileges and assume important academic functions for which academic Spanish is needed. This distinct goal for Spanish has had an impact on the academic distinct use of Spanish at Luperón, as we discuss here.

In Dominican high schools, little attention is paid to Spanish oral development, but research has repeatedly shown the interrelationship of oracy and literacy (August and Shanahan 2006). Many content-area classes at Luperón incorporate group work, pair work, and class discussions to promote Spanish oral development: a history teacher asked students to debate the causes of underdevelopment in their native countries; an English teacher asked Dominican students to compare the treatment of Jews in Germany prior to World War II to the treatment of Haitians in the Dominican Republic, which generated heated discussions; in a Living Environment class, pairs of students discussed the importance of biodiversity; and a U.S. history teacher asked students to compare the use of propaganda in the 1800 elections to the race between Fernando Ferrer and Michael Bloomberg. In describing the differences between the teaching at Luperón and in the Dominican Republic, students frequently point to the oral discussions as one of the defining characteristics. Perhaps one of them in a focus group said it most poignantly: "Como lo que hace X en clase, uno se expresa más; es más hablar que copiar" [Like what X does in class, you express yourself more; it is more speaking than copying]. Unlike in the Dominican Republic where copying from the book was a prevalent practice, students are now expected to use Spanish to discuss ideas, engage with historical and scientific concepts, and to imagine a new world.

Spanish writing at Luperón is not limited to personal essays, which were the kinds of essays most prevalently assigned in the Dominican Republic and used in their current Spanish language arts classes. Instead, students' skills are strengthened through assignments that involve discussing sophisticated topics in their U.S. and global history and science courses. Students are asked not only to write thematic essays based on a historical or scientific topic in Spanish but also to analyze many primary documents and write integrated argumentative essays. Additionally, in science, students write up experiments, define hypotheses, and identify variables and data.

Reading literature is a very different experience from reading about science, social studies, or math. Although reading literature in Spanish is still emphasized at Luperón, and as we will see also important in the preparation for the English Regents, the students' Spanish reading now includes social and scientific knowledge. The documents that the Regents contain are written by journalists, scientists, historians, politicians, and lawyers. In addition to narratives, students are expected to read graphs, tables, maps, and scientific diagrams, all in Spanish. As such, Luperón students develop advanced content-specific academic vocabulary that they use with ease. The Spanish heard in classrooms at Luperón is not solely that of the home and the neighborhood, it is now that which is spoken in high schools and universities all over Latin America and Spain. This has a profound effect on the attitudes of these students, as they perceive themselves as educated Spanish speakers.

And yet, content teachers teaching in Spanish are doing more than what is done in Latin America or Spain, for their teaching practices reflect educational and cultural norms in the United States, as well as the learning processes and ways of demonstrating knowledge that are important in the United States. Thus, the Spanish language use in these classrooms is adapted to the exigencies of academic language in the United States. For example, the members of the faculty across disciplines frequently use graphic organizers to help students visualize concepts, and they have students produce their own graphic organizers to check understanding. In a Living Environment classroom we observed, students made semantic maps of sexual reproduction, using key vocabulary terms; other classrooms displayed student-produced posters, written in Spanish, showing the process of meiosis and literary elements. The geometry teacher, in particular, used diagrams to teach concepts.

The faculty also teach content-area vocabulary in Spanish directly and systematically, focusing on both meaning and form (Lapkin and Swain 1996). They help students draw on contextual and background knowledge across curricular areas and disciplines. Across the disciplines, several teachers keep word walls to display key vocabulary.

The pedagogy used in all content-classes combine process-interactive approaches with explicit teaching, consonant with research in the United States. The teachers are constantly encouraging higher levels of thinking, speaking, reading, and writing. They engage the students in brainstorming and in discussion. At the same time, they emphasize direct teaching of Spanish language structures and discourse for specific subject-topics. Clearly, teachers are aware that they are not only teaching new content, but also developing the Spanish language and discourse associated with the discipline.

The development of Spanish is also related to two other ways in which Luperón students succeed. The Spanish Language Regents is not one of the Regents required for a basic Regents diploma, but a foreign language Regents is required for an advanced Regents diploma.[6] The access to the advanced Regents diploma is thus facilitated by the attention Luperón pays to the development of academic Spanish. Also important in this regard is the availability of Advanced Placement (AP) courses in Spanish. Many students opt for AP Spanish as a way to show their advanced knowledge of academic Spanish.

For Spanish to take this important role at Luperón, it is immensely helpful that many of the teachers are themselves Dominican immigrants. These teachers often see themselves mirrored in the youth they teach; they have a strong commitment to the instruction of these youth as a means of advancing the entire ethnic community. Further, one teacher suggested to us that in his opinion, Dominican teachers are more demanding of these students. He explained:

> Los vemos de otro punto de vista. Ellos los ven desde un punto de vista romántico, muchos alumnos que son más motivados. . . . Nosotros los conocemos a un nivel profundo, nosotros los vemos completamente. . . . Nosotros tenemos un punto de vista más real, los conocemos. Los vemos con sus virtudes y sus deficiencias para poderlos ayudar.

[We see them from another point of view. The (English speaking teachers) see them more romantically, especially the motivated ones. . . . We know them more deeply, see them more fully. . . . We have a more realistic point of view. We know them. We see their virtues and their deficiencies, in order to be able to help them.]

The Dominican teachers made frequent use of their shared cultural background with the majority of students in order to pique their interests or keep them engaged. A math teacher referenced Dominican baseball leagues and statistics; a history teacher compared the American and Dominican processes of independence; the health teacher referenced high rates of teen pregnancy in the Dominican Republic; the physical education teacher taught *merengue, bachata,* and *salsa* dancing in the cramped classroom space available. Two administrators playfully fanned the flames among students in an argument over the best city in the Dominican Republic. These common cultural references made Dominican students feel at home.

Another way in which Spanish is supported through cultural understandings is the presence of Latin American literature in the curriculum for the Spanish language arts class. Students read classical Latin American authors such as the Dominican Juan Bosch, as well as Jorge Luis Borges, Rubén Darío, Gabriel García Márquez, José Martí, Gabriela Mistral, and Pablo Neruda, and classical authors from Spain such as Lope de Vega. Sometimes they read, in translation into Spanish, works of well-known Latino U.S. authors. Most important among these is Dominican Pulitzer Prize winner Junot Díaz, who has visited Luperón and with whom they feel a tight connection. They also read works by Dominican American Julia Alvarez, Puerto Rican Esmeralda Santiago, and Chicana Sandra Cisneros.

Spanish in Luperón is also the language of identity and there is much metalinguistic discussion among students about Dominican Spanish. We observed one Spanish literacy class during which the students discussed varieties of Spanish and the value of each:

El mejor español lo hablan en España. Nosotros venimos de esa lengua. Ellos dicen *esperanza* con "z."
[The best Spanish is spoken in Spain. We come from that language. They say *esperanza* with a "z" sound.]

Nosotros no pronunciamos nada. El español dominicano es macheteado.
[We don't pronounce anything. Dominican Spanish is cut with a
machete.]

Todos los españoles son correctos; son tradiciones; son tu idioma. Pa'
otro país el español es malo, para uno es el mejor.
[All Spanishes are correct; they are traditions; they are your language.
For one country your Spanish is bad, for another it's the best.]

El mejor español es el dominicano, depende de qué parte. Yo soy de
Santiago y los cibaeños dicen la "i," pero tú no lo dices; depende de
dónde se venga. Depende de qué familia se venga.
[The best Spanish is Dominican, but it depends where you're from. I am
from Santiago and the cibaeños speak with the "i," but you don't say it
that way; it depends on where you're from. It depends on the family one
is from.]

Yo creo depende de la educación de padres, de la escuela. Los capitaleños
hablan con la "l." Hay muchos lugares que tienen diferente habla. Eso
nos caracteriza a nosotros, como caracteriza a los españoles hablar con la
"z." Por ejemplo, decimos *libreta* en vez de *cuaderno*. Su acento es único;
no todos venimos de un mismo sitio. No somos iguales.
[I think it depends on the parent's education, on the school.
Dominicans from the capital speak with the "l." There are many places
where they speak differently. That characterizes us, as Spaniards are
characterized by speaking with a "z." For example, we say *libreta* instead
of *cuaderno*. Your accent is yours and unique. We don't all come from
the same place. We're not the same.]

The teacher then asked the students to think about Mexican Spanish. The
students immediately became defensive: "A mí me da lo mismo que sea
mexicano. Yo hablo con ellos normal." [It's the same for me that they're
Mexican. I speak with them normally.] One of them is proud of the different ways of saying things that the Dominican students have learned from
their Mexican classmates: "Conocemos como le dicen ellos de diferentes
formas. Por ejemplo, *tú quieres cenar ahora*, ellos dicen *ahorita mismo*."
[We learned how they say things in different ways. For example, for "do
you want to eat now," they say, "right now."]
But in the difference between the *ahora* and the *ahorita* lies a tale. For

these dialectal differences sometimes cause miscommunication. One of the students shared that "los mexicanos a veces no nos entienden" [sometimes the Mexicans don't understand us]. This was precisely our experience on a day when we were interviewing mothers. One of our research assistants was Mexican, and she welcomed the tired mothers who came to our small-group interviews after work. Diligent and respectful, the research assistant told the Dominican mothers to sit down and that we would be with them *ahorita*, which for her meant "right away," but which in Dominican Spanish means "in a little while." Before we knew it, we almost had a revolution in our hands, with mothers demanding that they be taken care of *now*!

Although we didn't experience any type of miscommunication in the classroom because of different varieties of Spanish, we did witness students making fun of Mexican students and referring to them in mocking ways as *ándele güey* [come on, guys] and *órale* [let's go]—common Mexican expressions. One of the Mexican students talked about the many differences with Dominican students, despite the fact that they make him feel at home:

> Yo me siento bien con los dominicanos. Las diferencias son muchísimas. Los dominicanos hablan y en vez de hablar, gritan. Y los mexicanos, no, hablamos un poquito bajito; rara vez que hablamos recio. Y otro, su vocabulario. Hay palabras que no les entiendo.
>
> [I feel fine with Dominicans. There are many differences. Dominicans talk, and instead of talking, they scream. And Mexicans don't, we speak quite low; very few times do we raise our voice. And another difference, their vocabulary. There are words that I don't understand.]

Clearly the original Dominican educators have had to extend their understandings to other Latin American contexts that they may not know. Additionally, they have to work diligently in order to promote sociolinguistic understandings of variation among students. However, even as it has been extended from being just Dominican Spanish to Latin American Spanish, in this school the Spanish language has not lost its sense of connection to students and of identity with a group. Both teachers and students frequently refer to the bonding nature of Spanish, and Spanish is clearly accompanied by an academic value and function that is deeply respected. This academic value comes not only because it is the language of education and high-stakes tests, but also because it facilitates the development of academic English, a topic to which we now turn.

Translanguaging

That the status of Spanish is high at Luperón is something that everyone recognizes. At the same time, there is continued tension between the elevated status of Spanish and the urgency of acquiring advanced skills in the dominant language, English. Although it is possible to graduate having taken four Regents exams in Spanish, students must also pass the English Regents exam. The English Regents is a six-hour two-day examination.[7] As García and Menken (2006) and Menken (2008) have shown, these tests require students to display high levels of academic-register English. The English Regents provides four overall tasks: listening (listen to a passage and then write an essay and answer multiple-choice questions based on the passage); reading (read a text and corresponding graphic; write a persuasive essay and answer multiple-choice questions, using both documents); literature (read two different passages from differing genres of literature, answer multiple-choice questions and write an essay that ties both texts together around a set theme); and "critical lens" (read an often abstract quotation; write an essay based on two works of literature that must be used to agree or disagree with the quotation). The English Regents requires a total of four essays, difficult for emergent bilinguals who generally "develop receptive skills more rapidly than the productive skills needed to write an essay in academic English" (Menken 2008, 69; see also Cummins 1992; García and Menken 2006). Further, many items on the English Regents are not context-embedded and offer no visual support. They too-frequently make historical or cultural references likely to be unfamiliar to immigrant Latinos, and they employ sophisticated vocabulary more appropriate to the students with eleven years of U.S. schooling, for whom the test was originally designed, than for the immigrant students taking it (Menken 2008). The discourse structures of the examination are difficult for any emergent bilingual.

It is then the tension between the higher status of Spanish combined with the urgency of the dominance of English that propels much of the translanguaging pedagogy that we observe at Luperón. As the pressure for high pass rates on the English Regents built, and the cut-off scores were raised, the school began to emphasize the need to teach English across the curriculum. An ESL teacher described the changes:

> I came to Luperón in its fourth year, and I've seen it metamorphose. It was a cocoon. Most of the kids just spoke Spanish. English class was the only time they heard English. It was a contrived situation. It's not like that anymore. The announcements are now bilingual; the teachers themselves are changing. . . . Now the kids want it, they speak English amongst themselves. . . . And the teachers see we've got to speak English. . . . It has evolved.

In its early years as a four-year high school, Luperón still conserved some characteristics of the cocoon, following what many believed was the best way of educating adolescent language-minority students. Spanish was the dominant language in the curriculum and of a rigorous education. ESL was taught by specialized teachers. Both languages were strictly separated, in what Cummins (2008) calls "two solitudes." The idea was to be educated rigorously in Spanish only during subject matter instruction and in Spanish-language literacy classes that were taught as a mother tongue. In ESL classes, only English was to be used. But as the words of Clausen and the ESL teacher quoted at the beginning of this chapter elucidate, bilingualism is at the center of all teaching done in the school.

The school engages teachers and students in translanguaging practices, by which actors use multiple languages to make sense of new content and the teaching and learning process. Although sometimes translanguaging occurs unplanned, many teachers' pedagogical practices intentionally and flexibly employ the two languages to promote bilingualism and biliteracy. At Luperón, translanguaging emerges as educators teaching subject matter in Spanish draw on their students' oral and literacy abilities to introduce English slowly. Translanguaging also occurs as English emerges during ESL lessons, both by students and teachers who are bilingual. Translanguaging pedagogies are particularly important for newcomer adolescent youth because they build on students' strengths (Zentella 2005). They also reduce the risk of alienation at school by incorporating languaging and cultural references familiar to newcomer youth.

Bilingual education programs that have monolingualism as a goal encourage language mixing in ways that lead to language shift. However, bilingual education programs that develop bilingualism not as two autonomous and separable language systems but rather as functionally and dynamically interrelated can support the mutual development of both languages (García 2009a). It is possible to alternate and blend language practices for effective learning to take place and to normalize bilingualism without functional separation. This is what Luperón is trying to accomplish, as it experiments with language and pedagogical practices that builds on cross-linguistic relationships in order to enhance transfer.

This translanguaging was evident in our observations and our interviews with both students and teachers. The students recognize this well. Describing an ESL class, a student told us during a focus group, "Ellos hablan los dos idiomas. Hablan en inglés. Lo que no entiendes, preguntan, y lo traducen." [They speak both languages. They speak in English. What you don't understand, you ask, and they translate it for you.] After trying to explain the use of English and Spanish, another student said, "Aquí enseñan inglés de poquito." [Here they teach you English bit by bit.] Yet another student explained this pedagogy, commenting that it was much better than that at his old school: "Es mejor, los maestros la mayoría hablan, ellos lo explican en español, y así se va aprendiendo más." [It's better, most teachers speak it; they do the explanation in Spanish, and that way you're learning more.]

Translanguaging into English in Spanish-Content Classes

That the urgency of English for the English Regents is what is propelling the translanguaging in Spanish-content classes was communicated to us in 2007 by one of the pioneer science teachers, who said, "We need to speak more English with students. I've started speaking in English in class. . . . I've been talking with the assistant principal, who says we need to speak more English with the students. I've decided that in the fall, I'll start completely in English, and informally too I'm going to speak English."

Some see this increased use of translanguaging as a danger—a possible loss of the spaces that were formerly occupied by Spanish. For example, the principal told us:

Miramos con tristeza y preocupación, cada día más desplazar el español. Hemos tenido que eliminar la instrucción de español a muchos niños. No hubo oposición de ningún nivel. Estamos mirando la clase de español y obligándonos a llevar a estudiantes a hablar inglés. Estamos perdiendo nuestra herencia lingüística y cultural.

[We look with sadness and worry at the daily reduction of Spanish. We've had to eliminate Spanish instruction for many students. There was no opposition at any level. We're looking at the Spanish class and requiring the students to speak English. We're losing our linguistic and cultural heritage.]

And yet, others see this as an opportunity—a possibility of creating bilingual spaces that are more relevant to the students in the school—in both Spanish and English classes.

The subject-matter instruction in Spanish that we observed often contained elements from English, even from the very first day of school for the recently arrived newcomers. For example, one math teacher writes the city-mandated "aim" (or learning objective) and "do now" (opening task to get students focused immediately) prompts on the board in English. We observed him having one student read them aloud in English, and then asking two others to translate them into Spanish and then explain the triangle inequality theory. Another math teacher regularly writes his "do now" and "aim" in both Spanish and English. One day, students were discussing "side angle side congruency." The teacher explained the rule in Spanish, and then wrote it on the board in English and had students read the rule in chorus: "We can test congruency of two triangles by measuring their sides and angles. If one triangle has two sides equal and the included angle equal to another triangle, then the two triangles are congruent."

A social studies teacher explained his translanguaging approach by telling us, "The class is officially in Spanish, the exam is in Spanish, but I'm infusing as much English as possible." He later observed, "Translating is fun. I don't do this every day. But it is to encourage them." Beyond providing a context to deepen dialogue and thus conceptual information, translation can be a pedagogical technique to spur English language acquisition. While translation has fallen into disfavor in the field of second language teaching as communicative approaches have gained prominence, at Luperón, where the goal is not oral communication but academic proficiency, translation remains an important pedagogical strategy.

Ironically, it is the unavailability of advanced content-area texts in Spanish that has spurred translanguaging pedagogical strategies at Luperón. As Spanish-language textbook publishers lost the California market after the passage of Proposition 227, fewer Spanish-language texts have been produced, especially for high school students at advanced levels.

Thus, teachers often have texts in English with which they teach in Spanish. Extending the ways in which Latin American countries use English language texts in secondary and higher education while teaching in Spanish only, the school builds on translation from the English of the textbooks to the Spanish of the classroom as a way to make sense of the academic material presented in the text. The need to use English texts and to translate them into Spanish creates a dialogic context, which spurs rich conversation and dialogue. This translation practice sometimes engages teacher and students in important metalinguistic talk and cross-cultural reflections, important for adolescent newcomers to make sense of their languages and cultures.

Because textbooks are so often in English, the use of dictionaries, glossaries, and manual translators is evident in almost all classrooms. And whenever available, Google Translate functions as a companion to these students.

Some content teachers align the Spanish academic language use with that of the English academic language needed to pass the English Regents. For example, in Spanish language arts classes, students learn key concepts for literary analysis—important for the English Regents—and read literature that they can then use to answer the literary interpretation question. And teachers of advanced Spanish have them practice some of the tasks required of the English Regents. Content teachers have also become aware of reading strategies that students need across languages, including, for example, what to do to make sense of unfamiliar vocabulary. We observed that this strategy is practiced often in Spanish content classrooms.

In an advanced science class, the teacher uses translanguaging as his pedagogy of choice. One day, the teacher had his class meet in the computer lab, where the instructions and material were in English. The textbook was also in English. The "topic" and the "do now" written on the blackboard were translanguaged:

Topic: What causes earthquakes?
Do now: Las letras *a*, *b*, *c* y *d* son las ubicaciones de los epicentros a lo largo de una línea de oeste a este en la superficie. La profundidad relativa de cada terremoto está indicada. . . . ¿En qué parte del interior de la tierra ocurrió el terremoto que se encuentra debajo del epicentro *d*? [The letters *a*, *b*, *c*, and *d* stand for the sites of the epicenters in a line that goes from west to east on the surface. The

relative depth of each earthquake is indicated. . . . In what interior surface of the earth did the earthquake that is underneath the *d* epicenter occur?]

After a while, the teacher gave an explanation in Spanish of the "do now," as he reviewed the students' answers. He then asked the students to turn to the computer program where, he explained, they were going to learn about earthquakes. All the material was presented on the screens in English:

Teacher: Hit the bar [the space bar on the keyboard to advance].
   Vamos con el foco. ¿Quién me puede leer lo que dice el foco, en inglés? [Let's go to the focus. Who can read what the focus says, in English?]
Student 1: [*reading*] Energy is released according to whether the focus is on the earth.
Teacher: La energía está relacionada con el foco y la manera en que viaja en todas las direcciones. [Energy is related to the focus and the manner in which it travels in all directions.] Hit the bar again. Who wants to read in English?
Student 2: The place underground where the break occurs is the focus of the earthquake.
Teacher: What does it say?
Student 2: En el lugar debajo de la tierra donde la rotura ocurre en el foco, donde ocurre la rotura es el foco del terremoto. [The place under the earth where the rupture occurs is the focus or center of the earthquake.]
Teacher: ¿Cómo podemos observarlo?, ¿qué representa la línea? [How can we observe it? What does the line represent?]
Student 3: Una falla. [A fault.]
Teacher: Una falla, donde el terreno bajó y donde empieza todo, se llama foco. El epicentro es la parte encima del foco. Repitan lo que dice en inglés. [A fault, where the earth fell and everything began, it's called the focus. The epicenter is the part above the focus. Repeat what it says in English.]
Students: The epicenter is the top of the focus.
Teacher: Lo básico, el foco es donde se rompe, y el epicentro es otra cosa. Ahora bien, puedo continuar. [The basic thing is, the focus

is where the earth split, and the epicenter is another thing. Good.
Now you can continue.] Hit the bar. Now, read the summary
together.
Students: An earthquake is any vibrating, shaking, or rapid motion of
the earth's crust.

The class continued this way for the next forty-five minutes. By translanguaging, the teacher not only ensured that students learned the content of the science lesson, but also encouraged the learning of specialized
vocabulary and phrases in English and the comprehension of the written text. The students repeated in English and read in English, while the
teacher provided explanations in Spanish that ensured that they understood the material.

Such translanguaging was common across the curriculum. The following shows an exchange between the social studies teacher and students
of a social studies class with level 2 ESL students. In this class, the students were using a U.S. history book that had been translated into Spanish. Nevertheless, by using a translanguaging pedagogy, this teacher en-
deavored to give students some exposure to oral English. Whereas in the
science class, the teacher was exposing the students to a written text in
English, in this class, the teacher raised oral questions in English, attempting to get students to listen to academic content in English and to speak
in English. His efforts were not as successful as in the first case:

Teacher: How was the constitution of the United States constructed?
[*silence*] Cómo se construyó la constitución de Estados Unidos?
Student 1: The constitution was perforated, I think you say? Actually, I
don't know.
Teacher: You don't know? Vámonos a la pregunta 5 [Let's go to question
5], number 5. Let's summarize that in English ¿Quién puede
decirnos estos nombres en inglés? [Who can tell us these names in
English?] Who's the current secretary of state?
Student 2: Condoleezza Rice.
T: Condoleezza Rice is Asesora de Seguridad Nacional—National
Security Advisor, not secretary of state. Ella no es miembra del
gabinete del presidente. [She's not a member of the president's
cabinet.] El National Security Council is like an independent board,
no responde a nadie [it doesn't answer to anyone]. (2003)

During this exchange, the teacher, bilingual himself, tried not only to teach the students about the U.S. government but also to introduce terms that the students will need. He did so not directly, but by using both languages flexibly and in ways that allowed the students to hear and acquire English government vocabulary in the context of Spanish and to expand their conceptual understandings. For example, in the last sentence of the exchange, the teacher used the Spanish "no responde a nadie" to expand the idea of an independent board. That is, he did not translate "independent board" for "junta independiente," but instead encoded the conceptual understanding in Spanish. In that way, students were doing much more than acquiring English terms; they were developing knowledge and understandings that otherwise would be lost to them.

In another session of the same class, the teacher and students got into a heated discussion on how to translate the term *district court*, which students had been translating as *cortes districtoriales*. The teacher said:

No sé cual es el equivalente. No creo que lo haya en México y Santo Domingo. *Cortes districtoriales* no está bien dicho. Circuit courts— cortes de circuitos y apelaciones.

[I don't know what the equivalent is. I don't think there is one in Mexico and Santo Domingo. *Cortes districtoriales* is not the right way of saying it. Circuit courts —court of circuits and appeals.]

As students and teachers appropriate English language skills and a U.S. Latino identity, bilingualism becomes an important part of their language practices. Despite the attention paid to Spanish at the school, the more academic Spanish of the students is increasingly used alongside English in ways that mark the bilingual identities that these students are constructing for themselves. The teachers respond to the changing linguistic and cultural landscape of students in the school—no longer solely monolingual Spanish-speakers, no longer Dominicans from the island. Teachers develop a sense of teaching U.S. Dominican emergent bilinguals, who in order to graduate as educated U.S. Latinos, must become fully bilingual, proficient in English but also in Spanish. Thus, their teaching adapts to the changing context, now not fully Spanish monolingual but increasingly sharing space with English.

But the space that Luperón constructs is neither about Spanish only nor about pushing Spanish out. Rather, following an ecological approach (Haugen 1972; Mühlhäusler 1996), the language practices of Luperón teachers adapt to those of the emergent bilinguals who are moving along a developmental continuum that is not solely about one language or the other, but simultaneously about both. And so, we look now to what happens in spaces that are supposed to be in English, but where Spanish also plays a sense-making role.

Translanguaging into Spanish in English Classes

The opening up of bilingual spaces also occurs in the English part of the instruction. Because most of the ESL teachers are bilingual or have some degree of passive understanding of Spanish, Spanish is often used to support instruction in English. "I try to control myself and not use too much Spanish," one of the ESL teachers told us, "but I can't help it." This view expressed by the ESL teacher on the use of Spanish in teaching English reflects early thinking, which originated in Canada, that a "mixing" approach produced weaker academic results than a "separation" approach (Cummins and Swain 1986). What was called "concurrent translation," which consisted of random code-switching, was discouraged (Jacobson and Faltis 1990). Cook (2001), for example, points out that "recent methods do not so much forbid the L1 as ignore its existence altogether" (404). But in recent years, as we said before, the research evidence has shown that translanguaging can in fact enhance cognitive, language, and literacy skills (Creese and Blackledge 2010; Ferguson 2003; Gajo 2007; García 2009a; Heller and Martin-Jones 2001; Lewis 2008; Wei 2009; Martin-Jones and Saxena 1996; Serra 2007). Martin-Jones and Saxena (1996) have established that translanguaging is not necessarily bad, and that it is how language is used, and by whom, that shapes the students' perceived value of the two languages in a bilingual classroom. Gutiérrez and her colleagues (1999) have suggested that the "commingling of and contradictions among different linguistic codes and registers" offer significant resources for learning (289). Cummins (2007) also shows the importance of translation for SLA and quotes two newcomer students engaged in producing bilingual identity texts. One student says, "When I allowed to use Hebrew, it helps me understand English I thinking in" (13). The other one continues, "I think better and write more in English when I use Urdu because I can see in Urdu what I want to say in English." Cummins concludes by saying, "When students' L1 is invoked as a cognitive and linguistic resource through bilingual instructional strategies, it can function as a stepping stone to scaffold more accomplished performance in the L2" (14).

In ESL classes at Luperón, English teachers encourage students to draw on their Spanish while writing in English. We observed one teacher telling students as they wrote stories, "If you don't know a word in English, write it in Spanish. You can always get the English word later."

The majority of the early-level ESL teachers spoke Spanish fluently, allowing them to facilitate this process. Below, we demonstrate how three different early-level ESL teachers translanguaged in order to ensure that their students were understanding content and instructions.

In a second-year ESL classroom, teacher #1 primarily addresses the students in English. She addresses specific comments and phrases to students she feels are not understanding. Though she addresses them in English, students respond primarily in Spanish. Their task today is to write a "friendly letter" in English, incorporating adverbs of frequency. E. is writing at his desk. When the teacher passes the first time, he has only one sentence; she makes no remark. She returns after eight minutes have passed and asks him, "Cuáles son los adverbios?" He responds, "Never" and "sometimes" (in English). She says, "Y 'always'; 'usually' también" [And "always"; "usually," also]. E. begins to include the adverbs in the letter and asks [another student] for help, in English, for how to use "usually."

Teacher #2 is reviewing vocabulary in an ESL 2 class. She regularly shifts between English and Spanish.

Teacher: "Blush": When you get red, como de vergüenza [like you feel ashamed], when you get red. Ponerse rojo en la cara [to get red in the face]. "Laugh," "reírse," when you make noise when you are happy. How do you say "suddenly" in Spanish?

Students: "De repente."

Teacher: "Nearly"?

Student: "Cerca."

Teacher: No, "near" is "cerca." "Nearly" is "casi"—"almost." "Shy"? [*silence*] What you all are not. "Tímido." . . . "Slowly"? [*silence*] What is "slowly"? "Lentamente," the opposite of "fast."

In first-level ESL, teacher #3 is working on a reading activity that also has students reviewing vocabulary and practicing present continuous.

Teacher: Who is writing this postcard? Pamela, ¿qué quiere decir "who"?

Student: "Quién."

Teacher: Look at the postcard. ¿Qué quiere decir 'where'? Where is London? What language do they speak in England? What is Susan doing in London? Is she working?

Student: She's writing the letter. She's on vacation.

Teacher: Yes, she's on vacation. With whom?

Student: George.

Teacher: Who's George? She's on vacation with her husband and her children. Where are they staying? [*The teacher looks at the paper with a new student who just joined the class and comments,* "Yo sé que todo es nuevo para usted" (I know that all this is new for you).] Pamela, just point when I'm talking. Where are they staying? What is staying? [*silence*] "Quedando."

Student: At the Grand Hotel. They are at the Grand Hotel.

Teacher: What kind of hotel is it?

Student: Beautiful.

Teacher: What is beautiful and large?

Student: The room.

Teacher: What is Susan doing right now? She's watching TV and wait, José, and writing a postcard.

Student: [*under her breath*] "Ta viendo la televisión y escribiendo."

Teacher: Where is George and where are her students? Do you understand? More or less? . . . Okay, now let's read. Let's pronounce it together first and then you read. Listen, repeat. Look, listen, read, think about it. Are we ready? [*reads text aloud*] Dear reader, . . . I'm writing to you from London, England. From London, England. I'm on vacation with George and the children and we're having a very good time. The weather here is warm and sunny. How's the weather at home? How's at home in Los Angeles? We're staying. We're staying. We're staying at the Grand Hotel. Our rooms are very large and beautiful. Our rooms are very large and beautiful. Right now. Right now. I'm at the hotel watching TV and writing postcards. George and the children are at the London zoo. How are you? What are you doing? See you soon. See you soon. What is "soon"?

Student: "Te veo pronto."

The class reads the text once again. Then the students are assigned a writing task: to write a postcard to someone back home.

As shown in these excerpts, the teachers use Spanish to check comprehension, explain directions, and offer direct translations. The frequent peppering of the conversation with Spanish seems to keep the students engaged as they listen for requests of translations, to which they often answer chorally. These words are then added to their vocabularies as the students copy the words in English while attending to their Spanish meanings.

Further, these teachers enthusiastically identified cognates (and warned of false cognates) whenever possible. One ESL teacher explained, "I use cognates to make the students aware of how many words they already know in English, and to draw parallels to show that English and Spanish grammar are similar, to make connections. . . . I use Spanish as a tool to get them back on task when they're distracted. I use it for humor, for making parallels." This teacher had a bright green COGNATE poster hanging in her classroom; every time a cognate emerged in class, she would call out, "What is that an example of?," and her students would shout, in chorus, "A cognate!" But cognates were not the domain only of the English teachers; all content-area teachers flagged them when possible.

Yet the use of Spanish oral proficiency to develop English oral proficiency is not limited to these kinds of activities. In upper-level English classes, students were encouraged to try out their burgeoning English to express complex ideas, but they were also allowed to explain points of view in Spanish. For example, in a level 5 ESL class, students were reading *The Outsiders*. In the course of this lesson, the teacher taught concepts such as flashbacks and analogies. Toward the end of the class, he guided a discussion of gangs and whether (as a character in the book posits) there is such a thing as a "fair fight." While the teacher encouraged students to try their answers in English, he assured them that they could explain in Spanish if they preferred. This decision ensured that no student was barred from participating, while targeting the development of the same skills in the students regardless of what language they chose. A surprising number of the students gave their answers in English.

In our observations across the early years of the study, we noticed that teachers who were not bilingual were much more likely to experience discipline problems from students. When we asked students about this during our third annual interview, they confirmed this observation. A translanguaging pedagogy helped maintain student interest and further their learning.

The use of Spanish was an efficient way to contextualize for the students the academic decontextualized English language. As Walqui

(2000b) says, the issue of decontextualized language is "especially acute in the reading of textbooks. Secondary school textbooks are usually linear, dry, and dense, with few illustrations" (1). The use of contextualized language greatly facilitates the acquisition of academic language and literacy for emergent bilinguals.

To contextualize the English texts further, Luperón faculty also made extensive use of graphic organizers, visual texts, and technology. For example, in an early-level English class we observed, students were required to write stories comparing themselves to a brother, sister, or friend. After one student read a model, the teacher used a T-chart to compare the two characters. Then the teacher instructed students in writing on the board: "Make your own chart; organize your thoughts, write the main idea; write the paragraph."

As previously mentioned, teachers made good use of word walls and other visual displays of vocabulary. One particular ESL teacher who taught levels 1 and 2 made lists of new words every time the class read a new story. Each word was listed in a sentence and underlined, so that the students could see it used in context. The lists, on large sheets of paper, were then hung on the walls for future reference. By late March, there were so many all around the room that it seemed like she would have trouble finding room for them in the last three months. Another ESL teacher, who was teaching supermarket vocabulary, had hung pictures of items with the words attached. Students often quizzed themselves going from the Spanish words to the English.

Luperón ESL teachers also used song and video enthusiastically. Building on the success of crossover pop stars who sing both in Spanish and English, the teachers incorporated translanguaging into singing, dancing, and watching film. One teacher taught new vocabulary words using the song "Stand by Me": as she read the printed lyrics in English, she asked for volunteers to translate each line into Spanish for those who could not understand. She explained idiomatic expressions. Then they played the song several times, and the students sang along. A biology teacher had her students compose and perform songs about cell diversity, using key vocabulary, specific pages from their textbook, a diagram displayed on the overhead, and a mini-lecture she provided. One group used the tune and refrain of a traditional Puerto Rican salsa song originally performed by Héctor Lavoe and later revived by Marc Anthony, "Que cante mi gente." The music teacher showed a video-biography about Beethoven during his unit on classical music; the video was in English with Spanish subtitles. By teaching language in these contextualized ways, and by capitalizing on translanguaging techniques, teachers supported students' burgeoning language practices in English.

Research in the anthropology of education has long suggested that teachers who understand the everyday lived contexts of students' lives, and who view their students primarily in terms of what they bring (their assets) instead of what they lack (their deficits), are better able to promote school success for minority and immigrant youth (González, Moll, and Amanti 2005; Valenzuela 1999a). This orientation fully informs the teaching approach at Luperón, and especially in ESL classrooms. In the intermediate levels of English, the teachers made sure to include works by Dominican and Dominican American authors such as Julia Alvarez and Junot Díaz, which were read in English but whose cultural content helped to support and engage students as they read. Some students had also read these authors in Spanish translation. While no class was limited to Latin American or Latino work, this literature was often used as a gateway or starting point. Although the teacher always led the discussion in English, students often discussed the English-language reading among themselves in Spanish.

Further, literacy teachers drew extensively on student autobiography in having students begin to write. A first-year ESL teacher had students write postcards to send home with some students using words in Spanish; a second-year ESL teacher had students write short autobiographies called "My Life Back Home" where again, Spanish phrases figured prominently; another second-year ESL teacher had students write essays about family members, complete with photographs. Students responded well to this sense of being known and valued, and the approach benefited their academic development. As Walqui (2000b) wrote, students learn "new concepts and language only when they build on previous knowledge and understanding. . . . Some students have been socialized into lecture and recitation approaches to teaching, and they expect teachers to tell them what lessons are about. But by engaging in activities that involve predicting, inferring based on prior knowledge, and supporting conclusions with evidence, students will realize that they can learn actively and that working in this way is fun and stimulating" (1).

Finally, given the immense pressure exerted by the students' and school's performance on standardized tests, it is not surprising that the faculty at Luperón developed strategies explicitly to teach students how to take the English Regents. In 2004, during a professional development session, an ESL teacher complained that immigrant students are expected to learn too much in too short a time. In order to help them pass the Regents exams, he said, "We have to be like the fox—this is the back door, this is the way you can get in." In response to this, the two of us worked alongside the faculty during several staff development sessions to look at the specific literacy tasks that different tests require, and then develop what they themselves called "outfoxing" strategies. It is interesting to note that these outfoxing strategies rely, in great part, on some use of translanguaging. The strategies named by the faculty included:

1. Contextualizing: Work from the inside out. Start with something students are familiar with, such as personal experience, proverbs, fables. Use cognates smartly. Read passages in Spanish, but give students practice in talking and writing about the books in English. Increase talk by having students put down their pencils or by having peers engage in dialogue.

2. Providing models: Give them prepared essays, skeleton paragraphs, samples of concluding sentences, transitions, vocabulary (e.g., clearly state, interpretation, analysis) and terms. Make sure they know that they should practice these structures and vocabulary in Spanish also.

3. Building up predictability and redundancy: Practice with old tests. Have students know the tests well, what they are being asked to do, how questions are to be answered, what each question requires. Take the test directions and have students develop topic sentences from those. Have them rephrase instructions. Practice across the curriculum, in English and Spanish classes. Know the tests well, what students are being asked to do, e.g., how document based questions (DBQs) are to be answered, what critical lens questions require.

4. Keeping it simple: Show students how to take the easier way out. For example, disagree in an essay rather than agree, so that you can make better arguments.

5. Looking elsewhere for meaning: If reading a passage to then answer multiple-choice questions, have students first look at the questions before they read, so that they know what they are looking for. Translate the question.

6. Looking closely: Teach students to follow directions closely, doing

what the task requests of them. Teach them to proofread carefully. Have students ask themselves, "Have I answered it?"

Throughout the lessons offered at the school, the language of the test looms large. In Spanish classes, and especially in English classes, attention is paid to developing decontextualized language. The way to do so, as Cummins said so long ago, is to build on contextualized language. For an emergent bilingual, the most contextualized language at his or her disposal is his or her home language. As Cummins (2009) says, "Bilingual instructional strategies can be incorporated into English-medium classrooms, thereby opening up the pedagogical space in ways that legitimate the intelligence, imagination, and linguistic talents of ELL students" (xi).

Conclusion

This chapter described Gregorio Luperón High School's struggles with how to rigorously educate adolescents with different levels of literacy in Spanish and little proficiency in English. As do all other high schools in the nation, the school focuses on developing these students' English. But to do so, it uses a model of bilingual acquisition that we are calling *dynamic bilingual macroacquisition*, after the dynamic bilingualism concept developed by García (2009a) and the macroacquisition model developed by Brutt-Griffler (2004).

We argue that this emphasis on dynamic bilingual macroacquisition has contributed to Luperón's success in cultivating emergent bilinguals and supporting them through high school (Michael, Andrade, and Bartlett 2007; García and Bartlett 2007). The leadership and the teaching staff understand that English development is important not only for individual students, but for the entire Latino Spanish-speaking immigrant community. In focusing on the community, and especially the school community, the school also understands that its students' languaging in English will have different features from that of monolingual English speakers. The teachers recognize that cultivating students' Spanish skills will also help their acquisition of English language abilities, support their academic attainment, and demonstrate respect and value for their home language. But beyond this, the educators understand that the bilingualism of the community is essential, not only for the students' lives in a Spanish-speaking community, but also as twenty-first-century citizens of a global world. And yet, the teachers also recognize that their students' Spanish will have different features from that of monolingual Spanish speakers. Luperón educators understand that these youth will have adult lives in a bilingual English/Spanish world. It is thus dynamic bilingualism that is at the center of the school community's macroacquisition.

To reach that point, the leadership of the school and the educators are continually experimenting, questioning, and dialoguing as they adjust their teaching practices to the different demands. To do so, they have developed, quite organically, a variety of translanguaging pedagogies. These approaches include a commitment to Spanish language and literacy development; an asset-based or "funds of knowledge" approach to students' cultural and linguistic experiential knowledge; a fluid use of Spanish and English for sense-making; Spanish oral proficiency to develop English oral proficiency; English oral proficiency to develop English literacy; Spanish academic literacy to develop English academic literacy; the use of contextualized language for new ideas and tasks; a commitment to teaching academic strategies, sociocultural expectations, and academic norms; and the explicit instruction of test-taking strategies.

However, it is important to understand that the success of these pedagogical innovations lies in the fact that they haven't been imposed from the top. That is, they haven't been handed down as instructional packages from the state, but rather they have been developed and negotiated in interaction between teachers and students. As such, they remain flexible and emerging, as different educators rely more or less on them to provide the education that these newcomer adolescents deserve and that allows them to graduate and go on to college.

6

Challenges Facing
Immigrant Youth at Luperón

THE PREVIOUS CHAPTER DETAILED the language education approach employed at Luperón, and how it helped develop emergent bilingualism. In this chapter, we broaden our focus on language to consider the social and cultural elements of youth development. This chapter describes the long and sometimes painful processes of adaptation experienced by Luperón youth; Chapter 7 then explains the efforts of the staff, faculty, administrators, and peers of the youth at Luperón to support social and cultural development among the students.

Immigration and Education: Relevant Debates

Scholars of immigration and education have long debated a process generally but controversially dubbed *assimilation*, through which immigrants adapt to their new surroundings. Ogbu's *cultural ecological theory* contrasted the assimilationist-oriented, generally positive schooling orientations among voluntary minorities such as newcomer immigrants against the oppositional attitudes toward assimilation exhibited by nonvoluntary minorities such as African American and Native American youth, which were framed in terms of maintaining a strong ethnic identity. Ogbu usefully revealed how the academic engagement of students is affected by cultural and social or institutional forces; as Foster (2008) argues, Ogbu pointed out that "cultural discontinuities between home and school were politically charged for involuntary minorities in a way they were not for voluntary minorities" (578). However, various scholars critiqued Ogbu's oversimplification of generational, locational, and social diversity. For example, in her landmark study, Gibson (1988) discovered among voluntary minorities such as Sikhs a strategy she titled "additive acculturation," in which the students maintained their ethnic distinctiveness but also developed a strategic orientation toward academic success. Perhaps the most durable legacy of Ogbu's work has been the way the broader public adopted as common sense his claim that involuntary minorities painted a positive academic orientation as "acting white"; scholars such as Carter (2007) have worked to document the unique and diverse cultural practices that nonwhite students bring to school, as well as to show how students' occasional portrayal of schooling as "white" provides an important criticism of ineffective, institutionally racist schools (see Schultz 1996). As we hope to show in this chapter and the next, an ethnically identified school such as Luperón avoids this false choice between ethnic identity and academic orientation. Instead, in the "local institutional opportunity structure" at Luperón, academic achievements are framed not simply as individual accomplishments but as communal victories (Kasinitz et al. 2008, 143).

The second major theoretical corpus in immigration and education, dubbed *segmented assimilation theory*, built on this foundation from Ogbu. Focusing on second-generation youth, segmented assimilation theory posited three possibilities for the incorporation of immigrants: acculturation to the white middle class; assimilation to the underclass, adopting academic disengagement; or selective acculturation, in which youth maintain their parents' culture and language and use their strong ethnic networks to sustain a positive attitude toward education and access opportunities (Portes and Zhou 1993, 82). As Smith, Cordero-Guzmán, and Grosfoguel (2001) indicated, the first two choices recall Ogbu's work on voluntary and involuntary immigrants, wherein "immigrant parents try to help children succeed and get them on the ethnic upward path before they Americanize to dangerous oppositional inner-city minority model in a sort of contagion effect" (15; see also Fordham 1996; Portes and Rumbaut 1990). Some have argued that selective acculturation explains the success of Asian immigrants in comparison to Latino and Caribbean immigrants, given that the former tend to maintain ethnic distinctiveness and distance themselves from their U.S.-born peers.

Recent work has documented that the context of reception—specifically spatial isolation, discrimination, and cultural inversion—unequally affect the educational trajectories of new immigrant groups (Portes and Rumbaut 2001). Immigrant youth received by communities with active political support and opportunities in the labor market are considered more likely to invest in schooling as a route to upward mobility (Reitz 2003). The ethnic fidelity posited as a factor in early studies of selective acculturation provides significantly more resources and opportunities to some groups than to others (see, for example, Louie 2006a, 2006b). In their study of immigrant youth in New York City, Kasinitz et al. (2008) detected "cumulative patterns of advantage and disadvantage" among different ethnic groups (169). For example, the Chinese immigrant students in their study generally benefited from selective acculturation: they tended to have both parents, who tended to settle in formerly white or mixed neighborhoods with good elementary schools, and the families tended to invest their meager savings in the education of their (comparatively fewer) children, rather than remitting back home. Chinese students enjoyed ethnic networks that included middle-class parents with knowledge about public schools, and they profited from Chinese media, which also provided key information about educational opportunities. These students clearly benefited from maintaining ethnic cultural, linguistic, and social ties. Their situation contrasted sharply with that of the Dominicans in the study by Kasinitz et al. (2008). For Dominicans, housing discrimination, segregation, and the high levels of remittances sent back home "channeled them into neighborhoods with low-performing elementary schools. Poorly educated parents [lacked] information about how to get their children into better schools, partly because they were a relatively homogeneously poor group" (170). Thus, "while the presence of 'ethnic capital' . . . clearly benefited many second-generation youth," Kasinitz et al. (2008) "found little evidence that maintaining ethnicity per se—or 'consonant assimilation' in Portes and Rumbaut's (2001) terms—helped them get more education" (170). As they concluded, ethnic solidarity could open opportunities or, alternately, constrain mobility, depending on community norms, resources, and information. In this chapter and the next, we examine the social and cultural challenges identified by immigrant youth and the extent to which a culturally additive school premised on ethnic solidarity helps students in the process of adaptation.

Further, scholars influenced by Ogbu have proposed the "optimism hypothesis," which states that first- and second-generation immigrants invest in education as a route to economic and social mobility (Kao and Tienda 1995). Work by Suárez-Orozco and Suárez-Orozco (2001) supported the optimism hypothesis among Mexican and other Hispanic youth. An expanding body of work has compared the academic performance of foreign-born immigrant youth and native-born children of immigrants, finding that immigrant students often hold more positive pro-school attitudes (Rosenbaum and Rochford 2008) and sometimes outperform children of immigrants on standardized tests in math and reading (Schwartz and Stiefel 2006) and on nonacademic indicators of school performance such as attendance and stability at school (Conger et al. 2007). However, optimism does not trump material realities: the potential benefits of immigrant optimism are moderated by high rates of poverty, residential segregation, and limited stocks of social capital (Rosenbaum and Rochford 2008) and other forms of capital (Alba and Nee 2005; Perreira et al. 2006), as well as concentration in poor-quality schools (Conger et al. 2007). These chapters consider a school constructed to channel immigrant optimism while also working directly to address limited social, cultural, and economic capital. As a first step in that process, this chapter examines the considerable obstacles faced by the youth at Luperón high school as they adapted to life in New York City.

Immigration

Families, as units or piecemeal, immigrate in search of opportunities for themselves and their children. And yet immigration entails significant costs. In this section, we consider the processes of crossing over experienced by the youth in our study, their optimistic orientation toward life in New York and the possibilities of education, and the role played by the school in maintaining that optimism.

The stories of migration among our participants were very similar. The students reported that one or both parents, often the father, decided that the adolescents would come to the United States. One of the boys who participated in the study reported that after visiting his father in New York, he asked to come. For most, however, a parent decided to initiate this important change. The following excerpt from an interview with Eduardo in 2005 is typical in this regard:

Interviewer: ¿Cómo viniste a los Estados Unidos? [How did you come to the United States?]

Eduardo: Yo vine solo en un avión en julio 2004. [I came by myself on a plane in July 2004.]

Interviewer: ¿Quién fue el que decidió venir para acá? [Who decided to come?]

Eduardo: Mi papá y mi mamá. [My father and my mother.]

Interviewer: ¿Y cómo lo hicieron para que tú vengas? [And what did they do so that you would come?]

Eduardo: Se pusieron de acuerdo a ver si mi mamá aceptaba que yo viniera con él. Bueno y pasó el tiempo y cuando llegaron los papeles, la cita y ahí decidieron que sí, que podía viajar. [They talked to see if my mom would allow me to come with my dad. And time went by, and when my documents arrived, and the appointment [for the visa], they decided I could go.]

Interviewer: ¿Y cuándo fue esa decisión? [When was that decision made?]

Eduardo: No sé muy bien . . . eh en 2004 pero como tres meses después que, desde cuando yo tenía los papeles, fueron tres meses después que yo vine. [I don't really know . . . uh, in 2004, because three months later, as soon as I had the papers, three months later I came here.]

Interviewer: ¿Y cómo fue así que tu vengas? [And why did you come?]

Eduardo: Para estudiar y superarme aquí. [To study and better myself here.]

Interviewer: Y ¿querías venir? [Did you want to come?]

Eduardo: No mucho, no, porque mi mama se quedaba, y entonces yo no había estado sin ella y eso me pone un poco triste. [Not really, no, because my mom was staying behind, and I had never been without her and that made me a little sad.]

Interviewer: ¿Cómo viajaste cuando viniste, en el avión, cómo fue eso? ¿Te acuerdas de eso? [How did you travel? Did you come in a plane? Do you remember that?]

Eduardo: No, vine directo, estaba un poco nervioso porque era yo solo, pero después me acotejé ahí y me dormí y ahí ya estaban por aterrizar y ahí mi papá me estaba esperando afuera y salí más rápido porque había que hacer unos papeleo, y ah, y salí más rápido porque él me estaba esperando; él habló con los de seguridad para

ayudarme. [No, I came straight here. I was a little nervous because
I was traveling alone, but after I got on the plane, I slept until we
landed, and my dad was waiting for me outside. I got out as quickly
as I could, because there was a lot of paperwork, and I got out
because he was waiting for me, he talked to some security guards to
ask them to help me.]

Ten of the twenty students came to live with their fathers, leaving
mothers behind. Some of them traveled alone, as did Eduardo; others
came with an adult and often with another sibling. The students often
spoke of the decision and the preparations to move to New York as something that happened to them and around them, rather than something in
which they were actively involved.

Like many transnational Dominicans, the youth in our study had
complicated familial migration histories and, once they arrived, often
participated in what Guarnizo (1994) called multinuclear households,
in which the parents live for long periods in different countries and the
family nuclei are located in different settings. Indeed, of the twenty youth
we followed in this study, only four were living with both parents when
they arrived in 2005. While it is true that only three of the study's participants had traveled to the United States before coming as teens, members
of their nuclear families had often been in New York for a long period. For
example, Jamie's father had been in New York for fourteen years; Juan's father for eleven years; Fausto's father for fifteen years; Francisco's mother
for nine years; Magda's father for eighteen years; and Gruna's mother for
three years.

The proximity of the Dominican Republic to New York facilitated
considerable mobility for family members. Several of the study's participants had parents who came and went from New York: the most extreme
example was a student whose mother visited in two-month stints using a
tourist visa; several others had fathers who lived in New York but regularly
returned to the Dominican Republic *para resolver* [to resolve things], often related to business ventures. Of the students themselves, at least fourteen of the twenty who participated in our project returned to the Dominican Republic for stays of one week to three months while studying at
Luperón.

Family Separation, Loss, and Change

Stepwise patterns of immigration have been shown to be multiply agonizing both for those who depart first and for those who are first left (Artico 2000; Escamilla-Toquica 2009). In particular, when immigrant children are separated from their biological parents for long periods of time, they are confronted with multiple challenges to their sense of identity, familial roles, and community belonging, even when they are later reunited with their parents in the United States (Artico 2000; Escamilla-Toquica 2009; Hine-St. Hilaire 2008; Marte 2008). These newcomer youth face questions about who they are, what they want, and what accommodations they might merit (Wortham, Murillo, and Hamann 2002).

The findings from Hine-St. Hilaire's (2008) study on West Indian immigrant youth suggest that multiple factors—including the adolescents' length of separation, their age at separation, age at reunion, experience during separation, and quality of child care during separation—affect their ability to adapt to life in the United States. In her study on Salvadoran immigrant youth who have been reunited with their biological parents and are living on Long Island, Escamilla-Toquica (2009) argues that the leaving of their communities and extended families in El Salvador created a loss of identity and sense of belonging. Suárez-Orozco and Suárez-Orozco (2001) emphasize that the

> cultural frame for the separation will influence how the child internalizes and responds to the experience. For example, in Caribbean countries there is a long-standing cultural practice of "child fostering." Children are sent to live with relatives either purposefully (as in when a mother has a live-in work position or when educational opportunities are better near a relative) as well as in response to a family crisis. In that social context, the separation is often *not* experienced as abandonment. When international separations occur, however, expectations in the host culture are likely to have important repercussions—especially when children enter a new social context where such separations are viewed as a symptom of a pathological family situation. (68; see also Waters 1999)

The youth in our study were accustomed to long separations from family; at Luperón, the separations were not considered abandonment. Nevertheless, the youth struggled with the disunifications necessitated by migration.

The pain of separation from key family members figured prominently in the youth's narratives of their experiences. In many cases, the youth talked specifically about the loss of their mothers. Several made significant efforts to keep in touch with their mothers: Eduardo reported calling his mother every weekend; Fausto said there were weeks when he called his mother every day; Fernanda reported calling her mother three times per week; Juan reported calling his mother every day except Sundays; Madali said she called as often as she could. When asked if she planned to stay in the United States her whole life, Fernanda replied, "No. I would want to be here if my mom and brother and sisters were here, but I want to leave after university."

In at least two cases, the students seemed to have developed depression in the absence of their mothers. For example, César, who lived with his father and stepmother, seemed devastated by the absence of his mother. He cried during a 2005 interview while talking about immigrating and leaving his mother behind. In 2006, his mother traveled twice to New York for two months at a time, staying on a tourist visa while providing child care. While she was in town, César lived with her in the Bronx. At the same time, he reported that he was very unhappy, and that his relationships with his father and stepmother had changed and that they rarely talked. He said he was only happy when his mother was in town, at which time he freely chatted with everyone. But, he said, when his mother leaves and he moves back in with his father and the rest of his family, he's quieter and bored and less happy again. He said in English, "I don't know what happened to me." Two years later, his mother was still making these trips, and César was still bouncing between living primarily with his father and staying with his mother during her visits.

Several of the young men were committed to supporting their mothers financially. For example, David was working in a music shop. When we asked if he keeps the money or shares it with his family, he reported that he generally keeps his paychecks or he'll send some money to his mom. When we asked Adrián, who was living with his single mother and his two younger brothers, what he saw himself doing in five years' time, he reported that he saw himself helping his mother "by working and being self-reliant" so his mother can concentrate on his younger brothers. He didn't see himself married or with children. He mostly wanted to help his mother *recompensarle* [to give back to her]. Likewise, when asked what he saw himself doing in five years, Luis responded, "I see myself studying at the university, with a future, with a good job, and to help my mother. To see her proud of my achievements. And I see myself in a good economic situation." Their sense of obligation to their mothers was palpable.

Further, between 2006 and 2008, several of the participants (David, Eduardo, Fausto, and Madali) discussed with us their desire to bring their absent mothers to New York to live with them. The following excerpt from our notes on an interview with Eduardo in 2008 exemplifies the students' sense of their responsibility and their own position in the migration chain:

> Eduardo says he is working on getting his mother here to New York. I ask him how he learns about the procedure to bring his mother to the States. He says he is waiting to have enough time in U.S. territory and become a citizen so he can start the procedure to bring his mother to the U.S. He says his father can help him with this procedure, since he has experience and is knowledgeable in this issue, since he has brought his whole family to the U.S. throughout the years. . . . He then adds that when he was really young his father "asked for him" [*lo pidió*] so he could come live with him in the U.S., but his visa was denied. He says they denied his visa because his father didn't have anyone that could take care of him in the Sates if he came. I ask him how this issue was solved, how he was able to come to the U.S. He says that the second time his father asked for him his age was appropriate. He also adds that this time around his grandmother was coming as well. I say that then it has been over twenty years of bringing people little by little to the States. Eduardo says yes, and adds, "Me toca a mí ahora" [Now it's my turn to bring people over].

The sense of loss was not limited to mothers, but extended to other relatives who had been central to their childhood. Studies of Dominican migration have demonstrated that when the mother migrates, the care of children left behind generally falls to another woman: her mother, her sisters, or the father's female relatives (Vargas 2010). Three of the youth in our study had been living with grandmothers before migrating; these women became symbolic mothers. For example, Francisco was raised by his grandmother until, at the age of fifteen, he came to live with his mother in New York. He reportedly spoke to his grandmother every few days on the phone during his first year. By his third year, he talked much less frequently to her but still missed her.

Whether the mother immigrated before the child or was left behind when the youth immigrated, the stories shared during the interviews for this study revealed the emotional hardship suffered by children in the absence of mothers and mother-figures. Previous studies have emphasized the high rates of migration among Dominican women, prompting debates about the impact of the "care drain" on children (see, for example, Ehrenreich and Hochschild 2003). As Sørensen (1994) explains, the migration of Dominican women disrupts traditional notions tying femininity to morality, domesticity, and motherhood; subsequent to their migration, Dominican women are often blamed by the media, the government, their partners and extended families, and some social scientists for any hardship faced by their children. Yet Sørensen critiques such a position, emphasizing that it

> is not only female-initiated migration that affects the ways in which men assert their masculinity, children face emotional deprivation, and relations of care and love become unfairly distributed between North and South, as the care drain approach would have it. Family disintegration also happens in the Dominican Republic, as well as in the diaspora, even when the traditional pattern of male migration and later family reunification with wives and children is being followed. (229)

Indeed, the idea that women's migration leads to family disintegration seems sexist, given that many Dominican men (and many of the fathers of the youth in our study) maintain multiple families, simultaneously or sequentially (see Petree and Vargas 2005; Vargas 2010). Further, as Petree and Vargas (2005) found in their study of women's migration to Switzerland, the migration of mothers and corresponding remittances sometimes had a markedly positive impact on children's educational opportunities. In our case study, the migration initiated by relatives eventually led to educational opportunities for the youth in the families—though it is important to note that the "opportunities" primarily came as a result of the arbitrary luck the youth had in landing at Luperón instead of comprehensive high schools in their neighborhoods.

In sum, experiences of familial loss marked the immigrant experience for these youth. As Liberato and Feagin (2007) wrote, based on their interviews in the United States, "The experience of being a Dominican immigrant was linked to ideas of personal pain. The painful circumstances narrated by respondents . . . include . . . personal suffering after leaving loved ones behind" (193). The fact is that anywhere transnational families are, they always leave someone behind (Guarnizo 1994). Tony eloquently explained the predicament during an interview in 2008, as we recorded in field notes:

> I ask him what the most difficult thing for a Dominican in New York is. He says not only for a Dominican but for all Latinos, one of the hardest things is to learn the language, and to keep an open mind to learning about another culture and assimilating. He says you have to learn how to assimilate to another culture without losing yours. He says you have to learn how to interact with different types of people. He says you also have to deal with the longing, with solitude and loneliness, with the desire of wanting to go back home, but still be able to function in your new society.

The changes in living circumstances also entailed important familial shifts, as youth adjusted to living with people with whom they did not have the closest relationships. As Suárez-Orozco and Suárez-Orozco (2001) note,

> migration tends to have a destabilizing effect on the family. It creates particular stresses on the family system that may translate into conflict between family members, particularly if there were tensions prior to migration. (75)

> In many cases, too, parental authority needs to be renegotiated— before, grandma and grandpa were the disciplinarians, and now the child may have to deal with a new set of rules. Indeed, many immigrant children reported to us that with the move they experienced a significant loss of freedom because immigrant parents are often very concerned about crime in their new neighborhoods. (69)

These observations held true for the youth in our study. Two of the girls who moved to New York to join their mothers complained about the tension generated by high levels of supervision. Adjusting to life with a father was equally if not more difficult. Fathers imposed new rules that were hard for youth to accept. For example, Madali, who lived with her father and brothers, complained that she had to do all the cooking and cleaning. Eduardo, who lived alone with his father and was responsible for the house, said he argued frequently over chores: "Hay problema en el hogar porque no le gustaba ver alguna cosa desordenada, pero las cosas van mejorando porque ya me acostumbré a él" [There are problems at home because he didn't like to see disorder, but things are improving because I'm getting used to him]. The fathers of the youth in our study, with two exceptions, strictly controlled the whereabouts of their children. Our discussion with Paulo in 2006 was illustrative in this regard:

Interviewer: ¿Cómo te sentiste sobre la decisión? [How did you feel about coming to New York?]

Paulo: Bien . . . por un lado bien, y por otro triste porque iba a dejar a mi mamá y a mis otros hermanos. [Good . . . on one side good, on another sad because I was leaving behind my mother and my other brothers and sisters.]

Interviewer: ¿Te gusta la ciudad? [Do you like the city?]

Paulo: A mí no me gusta. Yo a cada rato digo que me quiero ir, que no quiero estar aquí. [I don't like it. I often say that I want to go back home, that I don't want to be here.]

Interviewer: ¿Por qué? [Why?]

Paulo: Porque quiero estar con mi mamá. A mí no me gusta estar con mi papá. [Because I want to be with my mother. I don't like being with my father.]

Interviewer: Ah y ¿por qué? [Really? why?]

Paulo: Porque él jode mucho. [Because he annoys me a lot.]

Interviewer: Y ¿por qué tú dices que él jode mucho? [And why do you say he annoys you a lot?]

Paulo: Oh . . . no quiere que uno salga para ningún lado. . . . A mí no. . . . Quiere tener a uno tranca'o to' los días allá. . . . Es porque él no quiere que nosotros cojamos mal camino. . . . Pero nosotros no vamos a coger mal camino, ya nosotros sabemos qué es bueno y qué es malo. [Oh . . . he doesn't want me to go out anywhere. . . . I don't. . . . He wants to have us "locked up" at home every day. . . . It's because he doesn't want us to deviate into a bad path. . . . But we are not going to deviate or select a bad path; we know what is good and what is bad.]

Interviewer: ¿Ha cambiado su relación con su papa? [Has your relationship with your father changed?]

Paulo: Cambió un poco, porque allá yo andaba pa' donde quiera y aquí él se ha puesto medio raro. No me deja salir casimente pero . . . después yo me le revoltié y ahora me está dejando salir. [A little, because back home I went anywhere I wanted, and here he acts sort of strange. He barely lets me go out. But then I rebelled and now he is letting me go out.]

Interviewer: ¿Qué tú le dijiste? [What did you tell him?]

Paulo: No, porque él no me dejaba salir a ningún lao' y yo le dije que me mandara para Santo Domingo otra vez. [Well, because he didn't let me go out anywhere, and I told him to send me back to Santo Domingo again.]

According to the youth, the fathers were very concerned about where their children spent time and with whom. They worried considerably about gang and drug activities in the neighborhoods of upper Manhattan and the Bronx, and they were determined to steer the youth away from such activities.

Conflict with parents was exacerbated by the cultural differences the youth faced in this new land. The youth felt that their parents were authoritarian when compared to the new standards of parenting they saw in American media. In fact, two parents told us that their children had threatened to report them for abuse. In her study of the impact of migration to the United States on Dominican gender relations, Vargas (2010) noted a similar trend resulting from cultural differences in her accounts of parents attempting to maintain authoritarian attitudes and teens threatening to report them for abuse. Vargas reported that such reactions by the teens reduced their mothers' abilities to require the youth to help at home, thus leaving housework to the mothers in such a manner as to reinforce gender inequalities.

New rules from biological parents were not the only familial adjustments facing the youth. Often, when they moved to live with a father or mother, they had to adjust as well to that parent's partner and, sometimes, other children. Dominican families are commonly complex. Three of the students had to adjust to living with stepmothers, and one to living with a stepfather: of those four, three complained of significant levels of conflict with the stepparent. Many of the youth we interviewed had siblings who did not share both biological mother and father. These relationships seemed easier for the students. In fact, it was not unusual for participants in our study to have siblings who had been born in the United States or had spent significant periods of time here. Although the potential for jealousy was high, we saw little evidence of it. Especially if they were older, these siblings often helped the participants learn to navigate the city and were important connections to social networks. For example, in 2006, David explained that one of the most significant things to happen to him since moving to the United States was getting to know the eight siblings with whom he shared a father. In our field notes, we recorded that "he didn't know any of them before coming to the US, and he's so happy to get to know them. He says he spends the most time with [two older ones, one for whom he works after school]. . . . He spends much of his leisure time with them."

In sum, stepwise migration exposed the youth to several key stressors, including intense longing for loved ones left behind, tense renegotiations of parental authority, a loss of freedom, and a strong sense of responsibility to the extended family for the sacrifices made on their behalf.

Feeling *Tranca'o*: Space, Time, Trust, Mobility, and Safety in New York

One of the major differences experienced by the students in their transition from life in the Dominican Republic to life in New York was their changing sense of liberty. They often expressed their sense of the newfound limitations in terms of feeling *tranca'o*. Though *trancado* literally means "locked up," the students often used it more metaphorically to signify their perceived limitations in terms of public space, time, interpersonal trust, personal mobility, and safety.

Space

Spatially, their lives in New York were quite distinct from their lives back home. The colder climate meant that people spent more time inside. Apartment life seemed impenetrable and impersonal to many, especially to those more accustomed to seeing and hearing neighbors outside their houses much of the time. Given the high cost of living, many of the participants lived in small apartments with their extended families. Students often missed the *calor humano* [human warmth] that they felt was culturally more prevalent in the Dominican Republic. Though these elements were mentioned by many, they were most eloquently explained by Tony:

> Interviewer: ¿Qué te hace falta de Santo Domingo? [What do you miss about Santo Domingo?]
>
> Tony: Bueno, a mí me hace falta, el espacio. Como que uno tiene más libertad en un sentido, como que puede salir. Aquí muchas veces uno se siente como apretado en un apartamento, y no tiene mucho contacto con el exterior. El calor humano me hace falta. El clima me hace falta también. Me hace falta como los vecinos eran bien chéveres, que tú podías sentarte en la casa de alguien a hablar. Aquí tú lo puedes hacer también pero es más formal. Tienes que llamar como si fuera si tú vas a hacer una cita médica. [Well, I miss the space. One has more liberty there, one can go out. Here often you feel squeezed in an apartment, and you don't have much contact with the outside. I miss the affection. I miss the climate too. I miss my neighbors, who were cool, and you could sit down in people's houses to chat. Here you can do that, but it's more formal. Here you have to call ahead, as if you were making a medical appointment.]

Tony went on to explain that when he is in the Dominican Republic he misses New York, and when he is in New York he misses the Dominican Republic. He said he misses the "liberty" of home even more now that he is away at college and there aren't many Dominicans or Latinos where he is. He said he even misses speaking his own language—his particular way of speaking Spanish—because even though there are people from other Spanish-speaking countries at his college, it doesn't feel the same to talk to them. When asked what he means when he says he misses the "liberty" of the Dominican Republic, Tony explained that he misses having the opportunity to relax and "take things easy." He said that in New York everyone is always in a rush, whereas people in the Dominican Republic sit in rocking chairs in their front yards during the afternoons to take some fresh air. He says people in New York don't have time for that—they are never *tranquilos* [calm]. He said New Yorkers are always in a rush due to the capitalist essence of the United States. People don't take breaks, and if they do take breaks, they don't even speak to one another. They simply watch television, he said.

Similarly, when asked what he missed from home, Eduardo said he missed "espacio, y aire. Aquí uno está siempre rodeado por edificios; allá hay más espacio, más parques." [open spaces and fresh air. Here you are always surrounded by buildings, while there you have more open space and parks.] When asked about the rhythm of her life in New York, Fernanda answered, "Todos los días lo mismo. Muy rutinario." [Every day it's the same. It's very routine.] She explained that life in New York is about having so much to do, with no time to be quiet and no time for fun. People don't go out much, not like in Santo Domingo where everyone's out on the street or on the patio. She said here it's "muy aburrido" [very boring]. These feelings of spatial and cultural alienation persisted despite the fact that the majority of the students in the study were living in Washington Heights or the south Bronx, where large concentrations of Dominicans live.

Time

As Tony indicated, one of the major differences experienced by the students related to time. Whereas those who had attended public school in the Dominican Republic (all but one participant) were accustomed to being in school only four hours per day, in New York they suddenly had at least seven consecutive hours of schooling per day. Further, with the pressure of standardized testing, the school often required those who were having trouble in specific areas to attend after-school and Saturday morning tutoring sessions. In addition, several participated in one of the many after-school activities offered at the school, which over time included stalwarts such as journalism, school government, and anti-drug clubs, as well as more exotic offerings such as Japanese, chess club, opera, and filmmaking. About half of the participants had taken advantage of courses offered by community-based organizations at the local *Alianza Dominicana* [Dominican Alliance], the Dominican Women's Development Center, the Community Association of Progressive Dominicans, and the City College of New York. Finally, the students regularly had one to two hours of homework per night.

> Interviewer: ¿Qué es lo que no te gusta de Luperón? [What do you not like about Luperón?]
>
> Gruna: Okay, que cuando tú entras en el aula que tienes que sacar todo y escribir, escribir, no te dejan ni siquiera cinco minutos de descanso, como cuando te mandan a hacerle ahora, como que tú piensas no lo hice bien. Son como cinco minutos o tres, lo que te salga es lo que tú tienes que poner, y ellos te dan estos minutos, y a veces tú no tienes tiempo para hacer las cosas bien. [Well, when you go in the class and you have to take out your notebook and write, they don't give you even a five-minute break, they make you do the "do now" immediately, and you think you didn't do it well, it's like five minutes, or three, and you put down whatever comes out because they only give you a few minutes, and sometimes you don't have time to do things well.]

> Interviewer: Tus amigos, ¿qué dicen ellos de que estés aquí en Nueva York? [What do your friends think of you being here in New York?]
>
> Gruna: Para ellos todo y que, oh, que es el mejor país que tiene muchas oportunidades y muchas cosas. Pero en realidad ellos no saben que en muchas cosas ellos viven mejor que uno. Porque aquí tú pasas todo el día estudiando. Allá te da tiempo para todo. [For them, it's like this is the best country, and you have so many opportunities and stuff like that. But in reality they don't know much, and in many ways they live better than we do here. Because here you spend your entire day studying. There you have time for everything.]

Eduardo concurred regarding the lack of time in New York. As we recorded in field notes:

> Eduardo then added that here in New York you see your neighbors one day out of the year [*de cada año un día*]. He says people are always busy here in NY, or locked up in their apartments [*tranca'o*]. He says that in DR you see your neighbors more frequently. I ask him if he thinks

people on DR are not as busy as people here in NY. He says people
in DR are not as busy as people in NY because here there are many
responsibilities [*aquí hay muchas responsabilidades*]. . . . He then said that
in what concerns responsibilities, in Santo Domingo *no hay tanta presión*
[there isn't as much stress about it] as in New York.

It is interesting that Eduardo, who came from a very poor neighborhood
in Santo Domingo, felt a significant increase in financial and temporal
pressure in New York.

When asked about the pace of life in New York, most of the students answered with words such as *rápido* [fast], *apretado* [tight], *ocupado*
[busy], and *acelerado* [fast].When asked about the rhythm of life in New
York, Fausto explained:

> Bueno, el ritmo de vida aquí es un ritmo rápido, porque aquí casi
> no hay tiempo, todo el tiempo que uno tiene aquí uno siempre está
> ocupado en algo. Uno siempre algo tiene que hacer; allá en Santo
> Domingo el día como que le dura mucho, pero aquí el día se te va así,
> porque tú tienes muchas cosas que hacer. Aquí el tiempo no le da a uno
> para hacer todo lo que tiene que hacer.

> [Well, the rhythm of life here is a fast rhythm, because here there
> is almost no time, almost all the time you have you are busy with
> something. One always has something to do; over there in Santo
> Domingo days last forever, but here they go by very quickly, because one
> has many things to do. Here there isn't enough time to do everything
> you have to do.]

In a similar vein, Eduardo complained that he always felt *encerrado* [closed
in] in New York, working or studying. When asked how that was different from back home, Eduardo said that he hadn't cared much about his
studies back home. He cares more here, and he attributed this change
to being more mature, knowing what he wants, and having a precise set
of goals. In part because students see schooling as the means to achieve
personal (and familial) progress, and because they are aware of the familial sacrifices made to give them such opportunities, they feel significant
amounts of pressure to succeed in school and take advantage of any and
all opportunities.

The students feel pinched for time not only because of their radically expanded educational obligations, but also because many assume new responsibilities at home or at work. Though only two reportedly had domestic workers in their homes back in the Dominican Republic, others had had extended families and many female relatives doing such labor. Once in New York, many of the girls *and* boys found they were suddenly responsible for housework. Madali and Magda did all the housework, cleaning, and daily cooking at their homes: Madali had no other female in the apartment, and Magda's mother worked full time. Here's how Magda described her sense of time:

> Ay no no me gusta la vida aquí. El sistema, tú corres mucho, que el tren se te va, que que si yo sé que; en Santo Domingo . . . los carros conchan así como los taxis y se paran. Si se te va un carro, viene otro de una vez atrás y tú no tienes que mandarte, pero si un tren se te va, hay uno que se para uno no. Tú tienes que estar corriendo, que la babysitter se va para la universidad, que están los muchachos corriendo, que tengo que buscar los muchachos, corriendo, huyendo, que tengo que recoger la casa huyendo, y tú ves que allá tú haces tus cosas calmada, tú me entiendes, aquí no.

> [I don't really like it here. The system, you run around too much. Because the train is leaving, because I don't know what; in Santo Domingo . . . the cars go by, like the taxis and they stop. If you miss the public taxi, there's another one right behind it, and you don't have to run, but if you miss one, there's another one that stops for you. Here, you're always running, because the babysitter needs to leave for the university, because the children are running, because I have to get the kids, running, fleeing, because I have to clean the house, rushing, And you know that there things are calmer, you understand me, here they're not.]

As the person most responsible for caring for her younger brother, Magda felt the pressure of time. The boys especially complained about the increase in their labor at home. Adrián, David, Eduardo, Francisco, Nilton, and Tony all mentioned at various times that they were now expected to clean house and, in a few cases, care for younger siblings. Such labor greatly reduced their free time. As Adrián explained,

Adrián: Ha cambiado mi forma de ser, de actuar, de vivir, de
    alimentarme. [I've changed my way of being, of acting, of living, of
    eating.]
Interviewer: ¿Qué significa forma de ser? [What do you mean when you
    say your way of being?]
Adrián: Porque allá te sientes más libre, más intensidad, más amor. Y
    aquí estás encerrado. [Because (back home) you feel more free, more
    intensity, more love. And here you are penned up.]

Adrián's sense that he had lost important freedoms was palpable. Likewise, Paulo reported that he rarely left the house except to go to school,
after-school activities, or work; César reported that "in New York you
have fewer options than in the Dominican Republic. In New York the options are work, school, or home."

The expansion of responsibilities and sudden lack of free time echoes
a finding from a study of Dominican migration to the United States, in
which adult informants complained that their life's purpose had shifted
from living to working. According to the report,

> The social integration of migrants has translated into important changes
> in their nutrition habits, personal relations, social interactions and
> everyday life. The most startling social transformation is that "working"
> becomes more important than "living," and there is a reduction of social
> interaction with neighbours, friends, and family. Migrants understand
> their migration as an income-generating activity; their salary, working
> shifts, promotion opportunities and social relationships at work become
> the centre of "life." (UN-INSTRAW and UNDP 2010, 11)

Indeed, the youth we interviewed not only lacked the time to socialize
but had also left behind their primary social networks, including friends
and family. They reconstructed those networks with peers at Luperón who
became their social cohort. However, it must be noted that in some ways,
Luperón's heavy homework demands and long school day (extended by
the mandatory tutoring required by NCLB) contributed to their sense
of hurried, hectic lives. In other words, in relation to time, Luperón's demands clearly exacerbated the students' sense of time pressure.

Trust

The students' sense of freedom was also influenced by the changes in personal relationships that they felt. Several students reported having less personal contact with people and feeling less *confianza* [trust] with others in New York. For example, in 2005, six months after arriving in New York, David explained that he spent the majority of his time at home because he didn't trust anyone. Even after living in New York for three years, Eduardo still complained of a lack of interpersonal trust, as recorded in our field notes in 2008:

> I ask him if he found anything different about the way people socialize back home in Santo Domingo. He says things were the same, that the neighbors are always *compartiendo* [spending time together]. He says this is something he has always *añorado* [missed with nostalgia], spending time with neighbors. Eduardo says that even though one lives among Dominicans here in New York as well, the intensity and frequency of this sharing time together is not the same. He also adds that the *confianza* between them is not like with his neighbors back home. He says that *como no se comparte tanto aquí, no puede haber esa confianza* [since you don't spend much time with your neighbors here, you can't develop that trust].

Others noted important differences in the ways they made friends back home and the processes required in New York:

> Interviewer: Dime un poco de tu escuela allá. [Tell me about your school there (in the Dominican Republic).]
> Gruna: Allá era muy heavy, porque allá yo me sentía en confianza, yo conocía a todos los muchachos, yo me sentía como que oh, importante, no como aquí porque aquí yo casi no conozco a nadie. . . . Allá como que yo me sentía libre, no sé. [It was cool there, because there I felt trust, I knew all the kids, and I felt important, not like here because here I hardly know anybody. There I felt free, I don't know.]

> Interviewer: ¿Tienes nuevos amigos? [Have you made new friends?]
> Juan: Algunos. [Some.]
> Interviewer: ¿De dónde son? [Where are they from?]

Juan: Algunos son dominicanos, otros de otras partes. [Some are Dominican, others are from other countries.]

Interviewer: ¿Es difícil hacer amistad aquí? [Is it hard to make friends here?]

Juan: Aquí es difícil porque aquí uno casi no conoce a nadie, entonces aquí uno tiene que comenzar de nuevo, conocerlos, y no hay tanta confianza . . . porque allá en Santo Domingo los amigos que uno tenía uno creció con ellos desde chiquito. [Here it is harder, because here you barely know anyone, so you have to start all over again, meet people, and there is not as much trust . . . because in Santo Domingo, the friends you had you'd known since you were a child.]

Finally, for some students, issues of trust were clearly related to issues of safety. Especially during their first years, students were wary, based in part on stories they had heard from their frightened parents or through the immigrant grapevine:

Interviewer: ¿Cuáles son las diferencias entre la vida aquí y allá? [How is life different here from back home?]

Luis: Allá, para mí es mejor, uno se siente más seguro porque estás entre los tuyos, y si tu tienes algún problema, ellos lo evitan. Pero aquí no, aquí tú te sientes inseguro porque aquí cualquier persona te puede hacer una maldad, lo que sea, nada más para burlarte, para hacerte pasar la vergüenza delante de los demás. Por eso yo pienso que allá es mejor—porque estás más seguro, tienes amistades, vienen a tu casa, aquí no, tú los lleva a tu casa, después saben adónde tú vives y se atreven a robarte, atracarte; aquí no hay confianza. [There for me it's better, I feel more secure because there you are among your own, and if you have a problem, people avoid trouble. But here, no, here you feel insecure because here anybody can do something mean to you, whatever it is, just to make fun of you, to embarrass you in front of other people. That's why I think it's better there—you are more secure, you have more friends, they can come to your house. Here, no—here if you take them home, who knows, later they could know where you live and come to rob you, attack you, here's there's no trust.]

Magda voiced similar concerns:

Yo no tengo problemas pero tú no puedes confiar en nadie. Entonces en Santo Domingo tú puedes confiar, nadie te va a poner una droga en el vaso. Tú puedes hasta beber del vaso de tu amiga y ir a la casa de tu amiga. Por aquí, cuando tú vas a la casa de tu amiga que tú conociste y viene y los papás de tu amiga van y venden droga, y viene la policía y te llevan. No hay esa confianza que hay en Santo Domingo. [I have had no problems here, but you can't trust anybody here. In Santo Domingo you can trust people, no one will put a drug in your drink, you can even drink from the same cup as your friend and go home with your friend. Here, if you go home with a friend you met, you might see that the parents are selling drugs, and the police could show up and take you away. There's not the trust that exists in Santo Domingo.]

Like the Mexican students in Valenzuela's (1999b) *Subtractive Schooling*, these Dominican youth complained about the lack of *confianza* in their lives in New York.

Mobility

The cultural differences in space, time, and trust all influenced the students' sense of freedom. Most significant, however, was their greatly reduced mobility. Students reported being afraid to vary from their usual routes because they were afraid of getting lost. The girls, especially, reported not leaving the house alone. As Gruna said in 2005, "Porque no me gusta, por ejemplo que allá yo salía, podía estar afuera pero aquí no, es muy peligroso, y que allá yo sabía andar, más aquí no. Podía ir a las siete, pero aquí no, porque no se sabe; aquí es muy diferente." [At home I went out, I could be out of the house, but here, no, it's very dangerous, and there I knew how to get around but not here. I could go out until 7, but not here because you never know. Here it's really different.] Two years later, Gruna still reported feeling restricted in her movements. When asked if she left her neighborhood often, she replied, "Es muy raro, yo no salgo. Mi familia vive en esta misma calle . . . paso todo el día adentro. No puedo compartir mucho." [It's very unusual, I don't go out. My family members live on the same street . . . and I spend the whole day inside. I can't spend much time with others.] Whereas the students reported moving freely through their hometowns in the Dominican Republic, often in the company of relatives, they discussed at length their sense of reduced mobility in New York.

Their limited English in the early years likewise reduced their mobility, as exemplified in these excerpts from an interview with César in 2006:

> Interviewer: ¿Pasas más tiempo en la casa o en la calle? [Do you spend more time inside or outside the house?]
>
> César: En la casa. No tengo donde ir. Voy al mercado, a ver las vitrinas. No salgo casi nunca del barrio. [Inside. I have nowhere to go, I go to the store, to go window shopping. I don't ever really leave the neighborhood.]

> Interviewer: ¿Cómo tú puedes describir el ritmo de la vida en Nueva York? [How would you describe the rhythm here in New York?]
>
> César: Tranca'o, como en una jaula. No puedes salir, sólo vas a la escuela, y después a la casa, luego a la escuela, y a la casa. [Locked up, like in a prison. You can't leave, you just go to school, then home, then school, then home.]

> Interviewer: ¿Cuál ha sido la experiencia más importante que te ha pasado aquí? [What is the most important experience that has happened to you here?]
>
> César: Cuando cogí el tren. [When I took the train.] [*laughs*]
>
> Interviewer: ¿Qué pasó? [What happened?]
>
> César: Yo estaba preocupado, yo tenía . . . miedo. Sí. Porque era mi primera vez. [I was worried, I was . . . afraid. Yeah. Because this was my first time.]
>
> Interviewer: ¿Qué pasó en el tren? [What happened on the train?]
>
> César: Subí en el tren pero no sabía dónde bajar y por eso me perdí. [I got on the train but I didn't know where to get off and so I got lost.]
>
> Interviewer: ¿Dónde, sabes dónde? [Do you know where?]
>
> César: No.
>
> Interviewer: ¿Y entonces qué hiciste? [So what did you do?]
>
> César: Llamé a mi papa y él fue a recogerme en el carro. [I called my father and he came to get me in the car.]

Others told similar stories of feeling imprisoned by their inability to communicate in English and their lack of familiarity with transportation routes. For example, in 2006, Eduardo said, "No me gusta salir mucho por ahí sin saber inglés . . . [entonces] me voy para mi casa." [I don't like to go out much without knowing English . . . [so] I usually just go home.] Paulo told a funny story about himself and two other participants in the study that we recorded in field notes:

> Last Saturday Paulo went downtown and got lost. He went down to 42nd Street with César and Eduardo. He tells me they were first in GLHS and then in City College.[2] Then they decided to go down to 42nd Street. They were going to Chinatown, but they walked from 42nd to 18th street and then returned when they saw Chinatown was too far. When he got back to 42nd Street, he took the wrong train and ended up in the Bronx. He asked a policeman and he told him he was in the Bronx and explained to him how to get to the place where he could catch the train to Manhattan. He went there and he then asked a girl if the train went to Manhattan and she told him it did, but the train left him in a place where he had to take the "Shuttle" (he says this in English) to "Time Square." He tells me he spent from 3:30 to 6:00 riding on trains, and all this time he wanted to go to the bathroom!

Those with extended families, especially with siblings or cousins who had been in the United States for some time, were not quite as restricted in their movements because they could go out with their peers. In 2005, Eduardo explained:

> En este país afuera no conozco mucho. Tengo los hermanos míos, ellos viven en el Bronx, yo voy a veces y converso con ellos. . . . Yo casi no salgo, de la casa para los hermanos míos o ando con mi papá.

> [In this country, outside, I don't know too much. I have my brothers, they live in the Bronx. Sometimes I go see them, and talk. . . . I hardly go out, from my house to my brothers' house or I go out with my dad.]

By 2006, Eduardo seemed to be getting out more, but he still expressed concern about linguistic and cultural differences. He said that "hay que saber como lidiar con una persona y también con el idioma" [you have to know how to deal with people and also with the language] because if you offend someone, you can get yourself into trouble. He said that in the Dominican Republic, if you offend someone you can apologize and move on. But it is very different here. He said that someone might pull a weapon on you, so one ought to be careful. Later in the interview, he said that here in New York, he is more cautious about meeting people, so he and his friends stay at home, *tranca'o*. He noticed that in public spaces, people don't relate with one another. People are quiet and keep to themselves. The only student in our study who traveled through the city and beyond it with ease by the second year of our study was Jamie, a young man who was heavily involved in an evangelical group that proselytized frequently and went on church trips often.

Securing a job was an important means of increasing one's mobility, because it gave the student a new place to go, introduced him or her to new potential friends, and provided spending money. The boys in the study were more likely to be employed outside the home, which increased their mobility. David reported spending much more time outside his house in 2006 than in 2005, partly because he was working at his brother's music store (but also because he was hanging out with his U.S.-born nephews, who were older than him); in 2007, Eduardo started working at a photography studio, and reported getting out of the house more; Fausto was working at the school in 2006, but by 2007 had shifted to working at a local McDonald's, and reported getting out of the house more; Francisco worked in the summer of 2007 in a camp, and got to visit museums, parks, and other places with the children.

However, getting an after-school job negatively influenced the students in other ways (see Barling, Rogers, and Kelloway 1995; DeSimone 2006; Lillydahl 1990; Oettinger 1999; Rich 1996; Sabia 2009), especially those who were struggling the most in school, by leaving them limited time during the week to complete their homework. For example, the two students in our study who were struggling the most in school both took jobs at fast-food restaurants, working four hours in the afternoons and often eight-hour shifts on Saturdays and Sundays. One reported that with so little time, he ended up doing his homework on the train on the way to school. Research regarding the impact of part-time employment on students' educational experiences generally suggests that while working modest weekly hours does not reliably influence academic performance (Barling et al. 1995; Lillydahl 1990; Oettinger 1999; Sabia 2009), working more than twenty hours per week during the school year often negatively affects students (Weller et al. 2003). Gándara and Contreras (2009) also confirm that for many Latino high school students, finding good jobs leads to lower grades and less interest in going to college. These findings held true for the students we met at Luperón.[1]

Tranca'o

The most common term the students used to describe their sense of limited mobility was *tranca'o*. Almost every student described feeling *tranca'o* in New York. As Francisco stated:

> Cuando uno compara lo de aquí y lo de allá, uno . . . se encuentra el bueno y malo de allá . . . porque allá tú tienes más libertad, tienes amigos, familia; aquí uno 'ta tranca'o.

> [When you compare things here and back home, you find good things and bad about home . . . because over there you have more freedom, you have friends, and family . . . here you are locked up.]

The youth missed the mobility and the personal interchanges they had enjoyed back home. In part, their reduced mobility was due to the increased vigilance of their parents, who were worried about the kind of trouble the youth could get into in the city:

> Interviewer: ¿Cómo ha cambiado su forma de ser aquí? [How have you changed while here?]
> Paulo: Ah, mi forma, que yo allá andaba mucho, pero aquí no, aquí mi papa no quiere que uno ande. [Ah, my way of being, because I used to hang out a lot over there, but not here, here my dad doesn't want me to.]
> Interviewer: ¿Te gustaría ir a andar por ahí? [So you would like to hang out?]
> Paulo: Sí, porque me gusta mucho conocer el panorama. [Yes, because I like to go out and get to know the scene.]
> Interviewer: El panorama. ¿Qué es el panorama para ti? [What is the "scene" for you?]
> Paulo: Bueno, el pueblo, la sociedad. [Well, the town, society.]

The girls were even more restricted than the boys. This was evident in our notes, including those from an interview with Madali in 2008, when she was already nineteen:

> I ask her what things she is used to here. She says she is used to not going out a lot. She says that when she lived in Santo Domingo she used to go out a lot, to parties and to the discotheque, but over here she doesn't go out that much. I ask her, surprised, if she used to go to clubs more frequently in Santo Domingo when she was 14 years old, instead of here when she is already 19 years old. She says yes, because she used to go out a lot with her brothers and sisters over there. I ask her if she has gotten used to not going out here. She says she has.
> I ask her if she likes it. She says she does. She adds that she doesn't like to go out by herself, that she doesn't have many people to go out with, and that her father doesn't let her go out anyway.

For the youth in our study, it was clear that parents were more vigilant with girls, but nevertheless boys were also fairly restricted in their movements.

Luperón did not address the challenge of mobility directly. To be sure, the school established partnerships with neighborhood nongovernmental organizations such as the Community Association of Progressive Dominicans (ACDP) and with City College to integrate students into available after-school or weekend programs. Having a school-authorized reason for being out of the house on the weekends was valued by students. When we held a Saturday research methods workshop for a select group of students at Teachers College one semester, we were really surprised by the regularity of attendance until one young man explained, "¡Es que yo haría cualquier cosa para salir de mi casa!" [I'd do anything to get out of the house!] After the sessions, the students asked us to show them around the neighborhood and explain bus routes so they could do a bit of nearby exploring. In general, however, the strictures of limited mobility were not directly tackled by the school.

Safety

In part, the reduced mobility of the students was due to a perception, shared by the youth and their parents, that the city was a dangerous place and that their safety was potentially at risk. Several youth expressed views similar to the one communicated by Juan.

> Juan: Yo primero no quería venir para acá, porque no me gustaba mucho dejar la mama mía allá sola. Entonces después vine para acá, entonces después . . . que el papá mío me visó. . . . Y decían dizque que esto era bueno para acá. . . pero esto pa' acá no es que es tan bueno, no. [At first I didn't want to come here, because I didn't like the idea of leaving my mother back there, by herself. Then I came here . . . (when) my father got my visa. . . . And they said it was good here . . . but it's not as good as they said.]

> Interviewer: Pero, ¿qué fue que encontraste que no llenó tus expectativas? [But what did you find that didn't fulfill your expectations?]
> Juan: No que . . . cuando vi que era como . . . como el ambiente de Santo Domingo, que allá uno, to' es gozar y así, y no era así aquí . . . y que allá también era todos los días uno gozando. [No, that . . . when I saw that it was like . . . like the environment in Santo Domingo, there you, everything is fun, and here it is not like that . . . and over there every day that you had fun.]
> Interviewer: ¿Qué tú quieres decir con gozar? [What do you mean by having fun?]
> Juan: Porque aquí uno casi siempre 'ta tranca'o—cuando viene, eh, de la escuela a la casa, y a veces tal vez los sábados es que uno puede salir. . . . Allá en Santo Domingo no; allá en Santo Domingo desde que tú salías de la escuela era a . . . a gozar. [Because here you are almost always locked up—when you come from school you go directly home, and sometimes you can only go out on Saturdays. . . . In Santo Domingo it was not like that; when you got out of school you went to . . . have fun.]

> Interviewer: Pero por qué tú dices eso? Por qué tienes que estar tranca'o? Porque una cosa es que uno quiera estar tranca'o y otra es que uno tenga que estar tranca'o? Porque tú dices entonces que tienes que estar tranca'o? [But why do you say that? Why do you have to be locked up? Because it's one thing if you want to be locked up and another if you have to be locked up. Why do you say you have to be locked up?]

Juan: Porque casi no me gusta estar afuera, como que hay tantos
problemas que uno se puede encontrar afuera. . . . Si uno se
encuentra con problema tal vez pueden matar a uno, sin tú hacer
na' . . . y también pueden a veces culpar a uno de una cosa que uno
no hizo, ya que aquí la justicia y esa vaina de la policía es tan . . .
tan problemática así. [Because (here) I don't like to be outdoors
much, because there are so many problems you can bump into
out there. . . . If you encounter problems you can even get killed,
without you even doing anything . . . and they can also blame you
for things you haven't really done, since here justice and things with
the police are so . . . so problematic here.]

Half of the boys we interviewed had been involved in negative encounters or fights of one kind or another; sadly, these encounters often
involved African American youth (in the few direct encounters the Dominican students reported with them). Salvador said he had been attacked
at his New York middle school by a black boy who was jealous of the
attention Salvador received from some girls. Paulo told of two experiences when, in his opinion, he had been threatened by a group of African
American youth in the street who had thrown a stick at him: he recounted
that he had said nothing but reached into his waistband as if he were going to pull out a gun. According to our field notes, Eduardo told us that
he had gone out "to a movie somewhere in the southern part of the Bronx
near Grand Concourse with his two brothers (aged thirteen and fifteen).
They were assaulted by a gang. They hit Eduardo on his neck and hit one
of his brothers on the chin, cutting his lip. Eduardo said they were saved
not by the police officer, who didn't do much, but by his father, who arrived when the officer did." Such stories reveal the heightened sense of fear
that the boys had when in public spaces.

The students' sense of safety was also compromised by the activities
they witnessed in their neighborhoods. Many of the students lived in poor
neighborhoods, as their families were struggling to make it on incomes
from their work as taxi drivers, in-home health aides, beauticians, and
similar positions. In these neighborhoods, the students saw drug dealing,
fistfights, and even robberies. César's house was broken into while he and
his mother were out; Adrián warned that teenagers should stay away from
people who stand on the corner; Gruna talked often of the "delinquency"
in her neighborhood, and recounted a drug bust of the *morenos* [Afri-

can Americans] living in the apartment above hers; Eduardo complained about his neighborhood, saying that there were lots of "tigueres fumando" [delinquent youth smoking] on the street corner, and that one had to avoid them because sometimes police conduct "redadas" [raids]; when asked what was worse in New York compared to her life back home, Laura said "the delinquency," which she defined as "los muchachos jóvenes vendiendo drogas" [the young men selling drugs]; when asked what she liked least about her neighborhood in the Bronx, Marta replied, "Toda la delincuencia" [all the delinquency]. Fausto reported that his father moved them to a new apartment to avoid the "mucha delincuencia" [high levels of delinquency] around their old apartment, and that he had seen the police arrest "casi cincuenta tigueres" [about fifty delinquents]. He explained that "tigueres" could be "morenos," or they could be Dominican:

> Muchos dominicanos vienen a estudiar aquí, muchos dominicanos progresan, pero muchos se pierden, porque aquí hay mucha delincuencia, principalmente aquí en Manhattan que por dondequiera que tú pasas tú ves que hay un grupo en la esquina y eso también lo que hace es que los muchachos se pierdan aquí.

> [Many Dominicans come to study, come to advance, but a lot of Dominicans get lost, because there's a lot of delinquency here in Manhattan. Anywhere you go, you see a group on the corner, and that is what makes kids lose their way here.]

Unfortunately, such experiences often reinforced stereotypes Dominican youth had about African Americans. They knew very few African Americans personally. Our 2005 survey of fifty students who had been at the high school less than one year revealed that only a few had friends who were black or white; most socialized with extended family or, at most, with a friend from school. They knew very few white Americans at all; during the focus groups in 2004, we were struck by the absence of references to white Americans. Among the cohort that we followed over four years, only three of the students reported having African American friends: one met those friends through a summer enrichment program at a local university; another met them through his U.S.-born siblings; and a third met his American friends through a cousin. Otherwise, though the youth in the study lived in neighborhoods with African Americans, they consistently reported that even by their fourth year, most of their friends were from school, and all their friends spoke Spanish as their home language.

This social isolation and their perceptions of delinquency (and fear of straying from the straight path) bolstered students' stereotypes about African Americans. For example, our field notes record that when we asked Fernanda to recount a dangerous moment, she reported that "one day she and her cousin were walking and they looked down the street and saw a group of *morenos*. She passed them and they started walking toward them, so she and her cousin started walking faster. She eventually reached her apartment and nothing happened." When asked if he had experienced racism in the United States, David responded,

> Sí, yo he caminado por la calle, y un prieto me ve así, y yo le bajo la mirada o miro para otro lado porque si tú te quedas mirándolos ellos te quieren como entrar. . . . Y aquí los prietos algunos le tienen también racismo a los latinos. [Yes, I have been walking down the street, and a black guy looked at me like this, and I lowered my eyes or looked away, because if you keep looking at them they want to start something. . . . Here some blacks are racist toward Latinos.]

Later in the interview, we asked David to answer a question about advice to give to a newcomer:

> David: Si va a un party y se arma un problema de una vez irse lo más pronto possible, como sacar pie, irse rápido. No andar solo en la calle de noche, también es peligroso. También algunos bloques son peligrosos, algunas partes no. [If you go to a party and there's a problem, you should leave. Just get out of there fast. Also, don't walk alone at night, it's dangerous. Some blocks are dangerous, others aren't.]
>
> Interviewer: ¿Cuáles bloques? [Which blocks?]
>
> David: Específicamente en la 174 en el Bronx. Yo una vez pasé un día por un *bloque caliente*, como dicen, son morenos, aquí en Manhattan, en la 110, por ahí. Es un bloque de prietos y, a veces los prietos siempre le tienen como odio a los latinos. Y desde que te ven que andas en grupo. . . . Eso mismo también, no andar en grupo en la calle, andar solo, si tú andas solo ellos tal vez no te hacen nada, pero si tú andas con cinco haciendo coro y eso, a ellos como que

les da algo, yo no sé, y te quieren como preguntar de dónde tú eres, y como a darte golpe, a usar la violencia. [Specifically 174th in the Bronx. One time, I went by a "hot block," as they say. They are African Americans, here in Manhattan, at 110th, around there. That is a black block, and sometimes blacks hate Latinos. And if they see you in a group. . . . Also, you shouldn't walk in groups in the street. Walk alone. If you walk alone, maybe they won't bother you. But if you are in a group with five or so people, it's like it bothers them, I don't know, and they want to ask you where you are from, and want to hit you, use violence.]

These sorts of perceptions and stories seemed to circulate among the students, heightening their fear of African Americans. While students saw African Americans in their neighborhoods, some expressed a generalized sense that African Americans were dangerous and to be avoided. In part, their fear was based on an inability to understand what might be said to them or how to respond. As one student said,

Una persona te dice algo, tú′ no entiendes. . . . . Uno dice yes, yes. Uno no sabe qué le están diciendo y a quién. En todo esto está la raza y el idioma. Porque tú eres nuevo, porque no lo entienden.

[Somebody says something to you, you don't understand. . . . You say "yes, yes." You don't know what they are saying and to whom. In all of this is race and language. Because you are new, and you don't understand them.]

It is especially sad to see the stereotyping of African Americans given the profiling of poor male youth in the Dominican Republic as *tigueres*, or delinquents. In her studies of urban youth, Tahira Vargas discusses the extensive profiling of poor young men in the city, especially by police (Vargas 2006; Vargas and Kelly 2007). Though such cultural knowledge might have increased the empathy on the part of Dominican youth for other students of color, it did not appear to do so. Students' fears regarding their safety, and the unfortunate racial stereotyping to which it contributed, were major challenges for these Latino newcomer youth. In the next chapter, we discuss this lack of positive intercultural contact as a challenge facing the Luperón model of schooling.

Striving for English

Another obvious major challenge the students faced in their transition to life in the United States was their quest to learn English. Only one of the students in our project had studied English in any depth before coming to New York: unsurprisingly, his family was the best resourced of the group when they lived back on the island, and his studies in a private school meant he was able to place into the second semester of English upon his arrival. Only two others reported having had some formal instruction before arriving. All but one spoke little English upon their arrival in 2005; however, as we noted in Chapter 2, the students were familiar with some English thanks to their consumption of popular culture.

By and large, the students held positive attitudes toward English. Like Gruna, they generally felt that "es bueno aprender otro idioma" [it's good to learn another language]. They admitted feeling embarrassed and challenged by the language. As Gruna said, when she speaks English, "Yo me siento como nerviosa. Me pongo rojita." [I get nervous. I turn red.] When asked how she felt speaking English, Marta admitted, "A veces no me siento cómoda. No sé, como rara." [Sometimes I don't feel comfortable. I don't know, like strange.] Perhaps Isabel summed it up best:

> Interviewer: Para ti, ¿qué ha sido más facil en aprender inglés? [What have you found to be the easiest thing about learning English?]
> Isabel: Nada. [Nothing.]
> Interviewer: Para ti, ¿qué ha sido más difícil en aprender inglés? [What have you found to be the hardest thing about learning English?]
> Isabel: Todo. [Everything.] (*bursts into laughter*). . . . Es muy complicado, pero hay que aprenderlo. [It is very complicated, but you have to learn it.]
> Interviewer: ¿Por qué tú consideras que hay que aprenderlo? [Why do you think it is necessary to learn it?]
> Isabel: Porque uno vive aquí, y si tú no aprendes el inglés tú no vas para ningún lado, ni para el baño . . . para todo tú necesitas el inglés. [Because we live here, and if you don't know English you are going nowhere, you won't even be able to get yourself to the bathroom . . . for everything you need English.]

In general, the students talked about English like schooling—as a key in-gredient for self-improvement, even if it is difficult to learn. Jamie said, "El inglés es bueno porque nos ayuda a crecer como los inmigrantes que somos." [English is good because it helps us grow more, as immigrants that we are.] English, the students said, helps people "grow," and have more opportunities. Others used the familiar argument that English, like schooling, would help them *superarse*:

> Isabel: A mí me gusta ver televisión en inglés, porque cuando tú ves más la televisión en inglés tú vas a aprender más el vocabulario, se te pegan algunas cuantas palabritas; si la ves nada más en español tú no vas a superarte. [I like to watch television in English, because when you watch television in English you learn more of the English vocabulary, some words stick in your mind; if you see it only in Spanish you won't be able to better yourself.]

> Interviewer: ¿En qué cosas tú crees que te va a ayudar el seguir aprendiendo inglés? [How do you think continuing to learn English will help you in the future?]
> Isabel: En el futuro, para ir a la universidad, y para encontrar un trabajo. Y no tanto el inglés sino también el español, porque cuando tú eres bilingüe te pagan doble, porque tú no puedes atender sólo a los clientes anglosajones sino también a los inmigrantes. [In the future, to go to a university, and to find a job. And not only English but also Spanish, because when you are bilingual they pay you double the money, because you are going to serve not only Anglo-Saxon clients but also immigrants.]

> Interviewer: ¿Cómo has cambiado en este año? [How have you changed over the past year?]
> Isabel: Yo he cambiado bastante, yo he, como se dice, improved, y me siento mejor que antes. [I have changed a lot. I have, how do you say it, improved, and I feel better than before.]
> Interviewer: ¿Por qué? [Why?]
> Isabel: Porque cuando tú hablas otro idioma tú te sientes importante; te sientes que vales por dos como dice el anuncio de Inglés sin Barreras. [Because when you speak another language you feel you are important; you feel like you are worth two, like the ad from

English without Barriers says.] (*The ad was popular on the subway at the time.*)

Finally, students were convinced that English was necessary for opportunities to study in college and secure good jobs:

> Interviewer: ¿Qué tu opinas del inglés? [What do you think about English?]
>
> Paulo: Que no es tan difícil, pero que es un idioma que tengo que aprenderlo para poder ser alguien importante aquí en Nueva York. [That it is not that hard, but it is a language that I need to learn if I want to be someone important here in New York.]
>
> Interviewer: ¿Por qué tú crees que es importante aquí en Nueva York? [Why do you think it is important here in New York?]
>
> Paulo: Ah, porque aquí lo que se habla es inglés, y tú no puedes ir a una universidad así sin saber inglés. [Well, because here what they speak is English, and you can't go to any university, just like that, without knowing English.]

> Interviewer: ¿Qué tú opinas del inglés? [What do you think about English?]
>
> Juan: El inglés es bueno para las personas que quieran aprender algo. Algunas personas dicen que van a coger inglés pero es nada más para ir a cherchar y vainas así. Pero para el que quiere aprender, el inglés es un buen idioma, porque te facilita algunas cosas que uno pueda hacer, como alcanzar algo. . . . Por ejemplo, si tú no sabes inglés y vas a una tienda a comprar algo, ¿cómo tú vas a comprar si tú no sabes, o pedir algo . . . porque nada más hablan inglés? [English is good for people who actually want to learn something. Some people say they are going to take English classes, but it is only to go and have fun and play around. But for those who really want to learn, English is a good language to learn, because it facilitates for you a lot of things, like achieving other things. . . . For example, if you don't know English and you go to a store to buy something, how are you going to buy it if you don't even know how to ask for it because people in the store only speak English?]
>
> Interviewer: ¿Qué más beneficios tú le ves a aprender inglés? [What other benefits do you see in learning English?]

Juan: Que tú puedes conseguir un buen trabajo. [That you can get a better job.]

In general, though the students acknowledged that learning English is difficult, their attitudes toward English were positive. They spoke of English's instrumental value in helping them secure jobs; they suggested that English could help them *superarse,* or to improve themselves "as immigrants," as a speech community. Notable here is the students' sense that learning English, though hard, is possible. Such attitudes are far from the sentiments often reported for Latino students (see, for example, Valdés 2001, Valenzuela 1999a). Further, Luperón students did not frame English as "the language of 'White' people, a group that they perceived felt superior to their own ethnic group," as did the Mexican immigrant youth studied by Brittain (2005, 1). Instead, they tended to conceptualize and valorize themselves as emergent bilinguals. Learning English was not cast as subtractive, or as threatening to their ethnic identity, perhaps because they were learning English in the presence of their compatriots—as a group involved in macroacquisition.

However, it is clear from reviewing the data that the students lacked sufficient opportunities to practice their burgeoning English within and beyond the school. Most of the students reported that they would prefer to have more opportunities to speak, hear, read, and write English at school. Further, even by their fourth year, when asked when they had spoken English during the previous day or previous week, their answers were generally restricted to school-based interactions or to speaking to their school friends (who were also Spanish dominant) in English in order to practice. Some of the youth reported speaking in English with siblings or cousins who had been in the United States for a long period, but these interactions appeared to be fairly limited. The following notes from an interview with César in 2008 are typical in this regard:

I ask him what language he speaks with his family. He says he speaks with them in Spanish. I ask him what he speaks with his friends. He says it depends on the level of knowledge and abilities of the specific friend he's talking to. If his friend has more ability than the rest to talk in English he often talks to his friends in English. Some of these friends are from school. I ask him if the majority of his friends talk more in English or Spanish at the moment. He says the majority of them talk in Spanish. I ask him with whom else he gets a chance to talk in English. He says he talks in English with the school's teachers. I ask him if there is any other place where he gets a chance to talk English besides in school and with his friends. He says he speaks English when he goes to the hospital or the dentist for any appointment.

Obviously, medical appointments are not terribly frequent, nor would the English required in such interactions necessarily be of long duration. The youth needed sustained opportunities for English interaction in order to develop their English further.

Conclusion

This chapter examined the challenges Luperón students have faced in relation to immigration and dislocation; family separation, loss, and change; issues of safety and mobility; cultural differences in the use of public space and the management of time; and learning a new language. In the following chapter we demonstrate the extent to which the students, teachers, and administrators at Luperón are together able to create a culture of additive schooling, giving students the resources, support, and resilience needed to overcome these challenges.

7

Social Capital and Additive Schooling at Luperón

> If academic success is contingent upon engagement
> with agents who control access to institutional resources
> vital to educational achievement (as indicated by grades,
> test scores, etc.) and attainment (graduation, college
> enrollment), then our paradigm for understanding success
> and failure in school has to be a relational one.
> —Ricardo Stanton-Salazar

SOCIAL CAPITAL CAN BE UNDERSTOOD AS "those 'connections' to individuals and to networks that can provide access to resources and forms of support that facilitate the accomplishment of goals" (Stanton-Salazar 2004, 18). In a school, social capital refers to the social ties that connect students to each other (peer social capital) and the relationships developed with adults at the school or other educational support organizations, which are also known as *institutional agents* (Stanton-Salazar 1997). While functionalist definitions of social capital stress the value of shared norms, more critical definitions of social capital (drawing from Bourdieu 1991) emphasize the ways in which social capital reproduces social relations and excludes those with less economic capital (Stanton-Salazar 2004). So, for example, Valenzuela (1999b) demonstrated how a high school socially decapitalized Mexican and Mexican American youth through a process of subtractive schooling that led to

> cultural and linguistic divestment, including their de-identification from
> Mexican culture and the Spanish language; psychic, social, emotional,
> and cultural distance between immigrant youth and their more
> culturally assimilated U.S.-born peers; and finally, a limited presence

of academically productive social capital in the peer group networks of U.S.-born youth. (61)

However, social capital and cultural capital (here defined as institutionalized or widely shared high-status cultural signals such as beliefs, attitudes, preferences, knowledge, and behaviors) can not only exclude but also, when intentionally constructed and employed well, include. The construction and accessing of networks rich in cultural and social capital have been documented by several scholars (Achor and Morales 1990; Gándara 1999; Gándara and Contreras 2009; Stanton-Salazar and Spina 2003). Stanton-Salazar and Spina draw on a large study that investigated the social networks and help-seeking practices of Mexican-descent youth. They show that students experience greater academic success when they access nonfamily mentors and role models.

School culture matters a great deal in the construction of such social capital. Studies of schools (Gibson et al. 2004; Goodenow and Grady 1993; Osterman 2000) have shown that students, and especially immigrant students, do best when they experience a "sense of belonging" or "sense of community" at school. Some students find safe, familiar, and stable places of belonging within their schools (Gibson et al. 2004; Koyama and Gibson 2007; Raley 2004). In Raley's (2004) study of a small multiethnic high school, "peer-relations-like-family" are central to the students' sense of school as a place of safety, stability, caring, and belonging. He argues that the safety and familiarity of the school positively influenced the experiences of the students, all of whom attended college. Nuñez (2009) argues that a sense of belonging can be considered a form of social capital in its ability to evoke feelings of support. Social capital can bolster students' academic achievement; connections to social networks can evoke "feelings of reciprocity to and trust in the community and the institutions with which one is involved" (25).

Further, peer relations are an important factor. The sociological literature has established the value of cross-class social capital for working-class minority youth with middle-class youth and adults (Mehan et al. 1996; Stanton-Salazar and Dornbusch 1995; Gándara 2002). Recently, Stanton-Salazar and others have demonstrated the importance of within-class peer social capital. Stanton-Salazar (2004) argues that "the potential for working-class youth to experience high levels of motivation, increased effort engagement, and academic achievement exists when working-class peer relations are situated within a supportive school context founded by interlocking ties between the school, the community, and the student community" (28; see also Stanton-Salazar 2001). A sense of fitting in with peers and classmates contributes to academic persistence and well-being, especially among economically marginalized youth (Gibson et al. 2004).

In this chapter, we argue that Luperón's additive approach to schooling helps foster its students' social and cultural capital by encouraging the students' relationships with institutional agents such as teachers and community-based organizations, as well as the building of peer social capital. Luperón's founders and supporters managed to accumulate political influence that they translated into the quite tangible institutional resource of a bilingual high school; this institutional resource has greatly influenced the students' cultural adaptation processes. While we highlight areas in which we believe Luperón has excelled, we also identify the challenges the school faces, such as in fostering intercultural experiences for youth.

Opportunities and School: *Con los estudios, superándome*

The youth in this study held very high expectations of the opportunities offered by immigration. As Sørensen (1994) commented, "Massive Dominican out-migration has led to a veritable migration culture and a collective belief that in order to move up you need to move elsewhere" (228). Indeed, Rumbaut (2006) reports that a poll of Dominican Republic residents in the mid-1990s found that half of the 7.5 million Dominicans had relatives in the United States, and that two-thirds would move to the United States if they could. Such optimism was shared by the youth at Luperón. In general, though they were aware of (and sad about) the sacrifices that migration required, the students were exceedingly positive about the opportunities that life in the United States could bring. Most specified that the chance to study at a U.S. high school was a primary motivation for their move; they felt that the best way to meet their goals would be, in Eduardo's words, "con los estudios, superándome" [improving myself, through my studies]. The following commentaries give a sense of the perceptions held by the youth.

> Interviewer: Imagínate que estás dando consejos a una alumna dominicana que ha llegado a los Estados Unidos. ¿Qué la dirías a ella sobre la vida aquí? [Imagine you are giving advice to a student

from the Dominican Republic who is new to the United States. What would you tell her about life in the United States?]

Delia: Que hay muchas experiencias y oportunidades aquí. Que tiene que reconocer las oportunidades a crecer y cambiar. Que no se esté llevando por las personas de la calle. Que tiene que reconocer el valor y el sacrificio de los padres. [I would tell her that there are so many experiences and opportunities here. She needs to recognize all the opportunities to grow and change. I'd say, don't be influenced by the people on the street. She needs to recognize the value and sacrifice her parents made to bring her here.]

Interviewer: ¿Tu querías venir a Nueva York? [Did you want to come to New York?]

Isabel: Sí, hay muchas personas que quisieran estar en mi lugar y mira, muchos quieren venir. . . . Realmente yo quisiera estar allá porque sea . . . well, aquí es mejor porque hay muchas oportunidades, pero [*starts crying*] quisiera estar allá, no? . . . Ay, mi madre. [Yes. There are many people who would want to be in my place, many people want to come here. . . . Really, I would like to be there because . . . Well, it's better here because there are a lot of opportunities, but (*starts crying*) I would like to be there, no? . . . Oh my gosh.]

Interviewer: ¿Por qué decidió tu padre traerte a Nueva York? [Why did your father decide to bring you to New York?]

Paulo: Oh para que nosotros tengamos un mejor futuro y . . . a estudiar mucho. [Oh, so we can have a better future and . . . to study a lot.]

Interviewer: ¿Qué es diferente de la escuela? [How is your school here different?]

Paulo: Oh, allá no dan clases casimente. . . . Allá, si se fue la luz, to' el mundo pa su casa. [Oh, there we barely have classes. . . . There, if the lights go out, everybody is sent home.] (*Paulo had been attending school at night.*)

Interviewer: ¿Cómo tú compararías esa escuela con Luperón? En qué se parecen? En qué son diferentes? [How would you compare that school to Luperón? How are they similar? How are they different?]

Paulo: Oh porque aquí tengo que estudiar obligado—no tan obligado, pero sí tengo que estudiar. [Here I'm required to study—well, not required, but I have to study here.]

Interviewer: Y ¿allá no? [And over there you didn't have to?]

Paulo: ¡No! Allá tú vas a la escuela si tú quieres. Ahora estoy más
    interesado en estudiar. [No! Over there you go to school (just) if
    you want to. Now I'm more interested in studying.]

Interviewer: ¿Y allá no te interesaba? [And you weren't interested there?]

Paulo: Sí me interesaba. . . . Pero es que la escuela . . . le desencantaba
    a uno la escuela allá, na más todo el mundo jodiendo ahí, ni asunto
    le ponen a los profesores. . . . Por ejemplo, aquí le ponen asunto a
    los profesores. . . . que atienden a to' lo que los profesores dicen…
    que no se ponen a hacer otras cosas mientras los profesores están
    explicando. [I had the interest. . . . But the school didn't help
    that much. . . . the school disappointed me. . . . everyone was
    just playing around and didn't even pay attention to the teachers.
    For example, here (in GLHS) the students pay attention to the
    teachers. . . . They pay attention to what the teacher is saying
    . . . they don't do other things while the teachers are talking and
    explaining the class.]

Interviewer: ¿Por qué? [Why is that?]

Paulo: Bueno por el interés de que tenemos que echar para alante todos.
    [Well, because of the interest we have, that we all need to get
    ahead.]

Interviewer: ¿Que dirías tú a un inmigrante sobre la vida en Nueva York?
    [What would you tell an immigrant about life in New York?]

Fausto: Que aquí al americano se preocupa mucho por avanzar. Por eso
    este es un país también que progresa mucho, porque los americanos
    se preocupan mucho por estudiar y tener una buena educación.
    [That Americans care a lot about getting ahead. That why it's a
    country where there's a lot of progress, because Americans care
    about studying and getting a good education.]

Interviewer: ¿Te gusta Nueva York? [Do you like New York?]

Fausto: Bueno, sí me gusta porque aquí tengo más facilidades de tener
    cualquier cosa que yo no podía tener allá en Santo Domingo. Aquí
    hay más facilidad para estudiar que allá. Aquí te dan, en la escuela
    uno aprende más. No es como allá en Santo Domingo que uno
    nada más está de 8 a 12, cuatro horas en la escuela. Aquí uno se
    pasa la mayoría del tiempo estudiando. Y aquí uno tiene mucho
    más facilidades para cualquier cosa. [Well, yes I like it because here

I have more chances to have anything I couldn't have back home in Santo Domingo. Here there are more opportunities to study than there are back home. Here in school you learn more. It is not like in Santo Domingo where it's only from 8 to 12, four hours in school. Here you spend most of your time studying. And here you have more chances for anything.]

Interviewer: ¿Que dirías tú a una persona que acaba de llegar? [What would you tell a newcomer?]

Juan: Que venga a estudiar porque para acá no es fácil. Porque si viene dique pa' acá esto es dique el paraíso, porque así es que dicen allá en Santo Domingo, que el que viene para acá, y cuando llegan aquí. . . . Que se preocupe por él mismo. Que no se ponga a cuando llegue a estar andando y a juntarse con gente mala de la calle. Que haga lo que a él le guste, y que venga a estudiar, que a eso es lo que aquí se viene casi, para que venga y coja una carrera buena, de los estudios. [To come here to study because this isn't easy over here. Because if he comes here thinking this is a paradise, because that is what they say over there in Santo Domingo, that the ones that come here, and when they get here. . . . That he should take care of himself. That when he gets here not to be going around, hanging out and getting together with bad people from the streets. To do what he likes to do and to come to study, because that is what one comes here for, more or less, so he can come and choose a good career, focused on his studies.]

The youth concentrated specifically on the advantages that schooling in the United States offered. In many ways, these newcomer students are the classic voluntary minorities Ogbu and Simons (1998) discussed in their work: the students' dual frame of reference compared their potential in New York to the (lack of) possibilities back home (see Suárez-Orozco and Suárez-Orozco 2001; Suárez-Orozco, Suárez-Orozco, and Todorova 2008). They shared a folk theory of getting ahead through education and a sense of collective identity in making the journey with other co-ethnics they had met at the school. Finally, the students held a solid cultural frame of reference for judging appropriate behavior and affirming group membership and solidarity (Ogbu and Simons 1998).

The optimism of newcomer immigrants is legendary (Gibson 1988; Portes and Rumbaut 2001; Suárez-Orozco and Suárez-Orozco 2001;

Suárez-Orozco, Suárez-Orozco, and Todorova 2008; Waters 1999). Many scholars (Kao and Tienda 1995; Kao 2004) have argued that "immigrant optimism" and a keen sense of familial sacrifice fuels the academic perfor- mance of immigrant youth. Yet the students at Luperón were unusually committed to the idea of social and economic mobility through educa- tion. The youth seemed cheered by their dual frame of reference, believing that they are doing better than their peers back home (see Louie 2006a, 2006b).

We argue that the additive schooling at Luperón, including a com- mitment to social capital, channeled the immigrant optimism of these students. Similar to the accommodation without assimilation strategy documented by Gibson (1988) and later discussed by Portes and Zhou (1993), the youth attending Luperón were able to develop strong ethnic attachments and take advantage of the school provided by Latino activ- ists to develop very positive orientations toward schooling. This culture of additive schooling relied on the social capital constructed in and through schooling—the relationships between students and institutional agents, and the relationships among students (a.k.a. peer social capital).

Relationships with Other Students

While their relationships with teachers were clearly significant, the stu- dents also described the importance of peer relationships. By and large, the students' primary social relationships were with peers they met at school. During the first two years, in response to questions about how they spent their free time, the students almost always responded by de- scribing outings with family members or time spent socializing, often on the phone, with friends from Luperón. During this time, this socializing happened almost exclusively in Spanish. For some students, this pattern continued well into their final year of school, although by then their peers were more willing to experiment with English. The following excerpt from notes after our interview with Madali in 2008 is typical in this regard:

> I ask Madali where she gets a chance to practice English besides school. She says she gets a chance to practice English over the phone and on the computer. I ask her with whom. She says she practices it with her friends. She says some people only talk to her in English all the time. I ask her where these friends are from. She says some are from here from Luperón and some from outside the school. I ask her surprised if

people from Luperón speak to her in English all the time. She says that many times when they are speaking they add phrases here and there in English, and she answers back as well. I ask her if, at this moment, the majority of her friends prefer to speak English or Spanish. She says they prefer to speak Spanish because this is what they really know how to speak. I ask her if the majority of her friends are Dominican. She says all her friends are Dominican except for one that is Mexican whom she met in Luperón. She doesn't have any friends that are not Latinos.

The students in the study talked a great deal about *haciendo coro* [hanging out] with other Dominicans or Latinos, with whom they felt comfortable. They shared interests in music, school gossip, and most important they could speak to each other in Spanish.

However, lurking behind their comments about feeling comfortable with other Latinos were also concerns about safety. Our interview with Fausto in 2006 illustrated this point:

Interviewer: ¿Qué dirías a un muchacho nuevo de la vida en Nueva York? [What would you tell a new kid about life in New York?]

Fausto: Aquí dicen que las escuelas son malas, pero las escuelas no son malas, lo que pasa es que la mayoría de las escuelas de aquí, todas las escuelas tienen su parte mala, la mayoría de las escuelas aquí los muchachos lo que quieren es ir hacer coro en los pasillos, meterse al baño. No quieren coger clase, lo que vienen es a cherchar en la escuela, pero esos muchachos son la mayoría de personas que tú ves después en la calle, parados en la esquina, que tienen que estar pidiendo en los trenes, pidiendo dinero. Que no se junte con ellos . . . que no se junte no, porque él se va a juntar con ellos en la escuela, pero que no se lleve de los muchachos esos que andan en mal camino. [Here they say that the schools are bad, but the schools are not bad, what happens is that the great majority of schools here, I mean all schools have their bad part, but in the majority of schools here, what the kids want is to go to school to have fun, to skip classes, get into the bathrooms. They don't want to take classes, what they go to school for is to hang out, but those kids, in their majority, are the ones that you later see on the streets, standing on the corners, and are the ones that later have to beg for money on the subways. I would tell him not to hang out with them . . . not

to not hang out with them, because he is going to be with them at
school, but not to let himself be influenced by those who are on the
wrong path.]

Interviewer: ¿Qué tu le dirías de esta escuela? [What would you tell him
about this school?]

Fausto: Bueno yo le diría que la Luperón sería una buena escuela para él,
ya que si no sabe bien inglés aquí lo ayudan, pero hay que ponerse
a estudiar inglés, y que también aquí que no se puede juntar con
todo el mundo, porque como te digo en todas las escuelas hay
personas malas, personas de mala compañía. . . . Y si viniera a esta
escuela estuviera mejor porque estuviera aquí mismo entre nosotros
mismos, que aquí somos todos hispanos. [Well, I would tell him
that Luperón would be a good school for him, because if he doesn't
know English, well, here they help him out, but he has to study
English well, and that also, he can't get together with everyone here,
because as I told you before, in all schools there are good people
and bad people. . . . And if he did come to this school, he would
be better than in other places because here he would be among us,
because here we are all Hispanics.]

Juan had a similar answer:

Interviewer: ¿Qué tú le dirías de este colegio? [What would you tell him
about this school?]

Juan: Esto es una maravilla aquí. . . . Que es bueno, y que aquí uno está
en familia porque casi todos los que están aquí son dominicanos.
[This is a wonderland here. . . . That it is good, and that here one
feels like family because almost everyone here is Dominican.]

Indeed, fights were not common at Luperón. The school had a
student-run mediation service to arbitrate disagreements: several of the
students in our study participated as peer counselors. In fact, the students
reported feeling very safe at their school, which they contrasted to what
they had heard about the schools that their siblings, cousins, and neighbors attended. Eduardo, for example, was warned about another school;
as we recorded in field notes in 2006, "When asked about the other students at Luperón, Eduardo said that in general they are good people. He
continued by saying that the school is very safe, not because there is secu-

rity but because the students are good. He mentioned George Washington High School is known for having problems with students. He learned about stories from his friends and the news."

In contrast to the insecurity they felt outside the school, the students felt quite safe at Luperón. This is significant because studies have suggested that the school environment is linked to boys' declining engagement with school (Qin-Hilliard 2003). Feelings of safety and security are significant factors in such school environments. Boys, in particular, appear to be vulnerable to recruitment into the sort of oppositional cultures that too often pit one ethnic group against another (Gibson 1997).

In general, the students expressed a strong sense of belonging and connection to their peers and faculty at the school. They found the cultural familiarity to be comforting. As Suárez-Orozco and Suárez-Orozco (2001) note, for some immigrant youth "the general dissonance in cultural expectations and the loss of predictable context will be experienced as anxiety and an acute disorientation" (72). Instead, the students of Luperón appreciated the opportunity to share humor, cultural references, popular culture, and their burgeoning English; the students expressed a sense of connection to their peers in this school.

Relationships with Teachers

Over the course of our study, we found that students at Luperón expressed great satisfaction with the relationships they enjoyed with their teachers. Delia's comments in 2007 were typical in this regard:

> Interviewer: ¿Y qué le dirías a una nueva alumna sobre los maestros?
>   [And what would you say to a new student about the teachers?]
> Delia: Que son excelentes. Que los maestros siempre quieren lo mejor
>   para ti; cuando ellos ven que te va mal en un examen buscan la
>   manera de hablar contigo, de explicarte lo que tú no entiendes,
>   de que tú entiendas lo mejor de la clase, ellos siempre quieren
>   ayudarte. [I would say they are excellent. The teachers want what
>   is best for you; when they see that you are having trouble for
>   example on a test, they try to talk to you, explain what you didn't
>   understand, so that you understand the class better. They always
>   want to help you.]

Several commented that unlike their teachers back home, Luperón teachers were concerned about making sure students understood the content:

> Interviewer: ¿Qué opinas de tus profesores? [What do you think of your teachers?]
>
> Fausto: Hay gente que dicen que aquí los profesores son dique malos, pero lo que pasa es que allá en Santo Domingo lo que uno se acostumbra es a ir a la escuela, los profesores dicen "copia ese libro ahí," ¡y ya! Lo que tú aprendiste. Pero aquí no, aquí uno tiene que . . . ellos te explican, tú no sabes algo y tú le dices a ellos que te expliquen; y después de la escuela la mayoría de los profesores tienen un día que te dan tutoría, clases después de la escuela, entonces si tú estás atrasado en la materia de ellos tú vas y ellos te ayudan ahí, cualquier cosa que tú necesitas ellos te ayudan. [There are people who say that here in New York the teachers are bad, but what happens is that over there in Santo Domingo what one is used to is to going to school and having teachers tell you "copy what it says on this book" and that's it! What you learned was what you understood. But not here, here one has to . . . they (teachers) explain to you, if you don't know something you tell them to explain it to you; and after school most of the teachers have a particular day in which they give tutorships and classes after the regular school period, and if you need help with anything they help you.]

Juan offered a similar opinion:

> Interviewer: ¿Cuáles son las cosas buenas en los Estados Unidos, en comparación con la RD? [What things are better in the United States, compared to the DR?]
>
> Juan: El estudio que es mejor que allá . . . y que uno viene aquí a aprender otro idioma diferente, que allá no, es el español allá . . . y también que aquí los estudios son más . . . como que le dan más apoyo aquí que allá en Santo Domingo, porque allá en Santo Domingo casi na' ma' es para la política to' . . . casi . . . y aquí le dan como más apoyo al estudio, pa' que uno estudie, le dan tutorías para que uno coja, le dan clases que uno vaya también a coger a la universidad así, como para que uno se interese más en los estudios

y cosas así. [Studies are better than back home . . . and one comes here to learn another language, back there it is only Spanish . . . and also over here studies are . . . like they give you more support here than in Santo Domingo, because in Santo Domingo everything is for politics. . . . Here they give you more support so you can study, they give you tutorships, they give you classes that you can go take at universities, so you get more interested in studies and those things.]

Other students shared the opinion that the teachers at Luperón were more invested in whether they learned the content:

> Interviewer: ¿Cómo compararías los profesores de Luperón a tus profesores en Santo Domingo? [How would you compare your teachers at Luperón to your teachers in Santo Domingo?]
>
> Francisco: Los de aquí le ponen más interes a la clase y se preocupan por los estudiantes, y cualquier cosa llaman a sus papás . . . y dan las clases que tú las entiendes. Si tú no entiendes vuelven y te repiten. En Santo Domingo no—si tú no entendiste, te jodiste. [The teachers here show more interest in the class and they care more about the students, and if there is something wrong they call their parents . . . and they give classes that you can understand it. If you don't understand they repeat it again for you. Not in Santo Domingo—if you didn't understand, you were screwed.]

On a similar note, several stated that their teachers in the United States were better prepared.

Teachers helped to maintain a high value for Spanish and English at the school and modeled the utility of bilingualism. Many of the teachers were native Spanish speakers. At the beginning of our study, two of the ESL teachers spoke Spanish fluently, and two others who were not native Spanish speakers had studied it and were able to communicate in it. Given the structure of the curriculum, in which students spent approximately two years learning content in Spanish while acquiring sufficient academic English, Spanish was positioned as an asset, not a deficit. This equalization of status between the languages has led to very positive attitudes toward both English and Spanish. For example, a student told us:

El español es como la lengua con que tú te comunicas con tu cultura. El inglés es como la superación. Si no sabes inglés, uno no va a llegar a ningún lado. Es lo más importante después del español.

[Spanish is the language in which you communicate with your culture. English is like improving oneself. If you don't know English, you're not going to get anywhere. It is the most important thing after Spanish.]

Because English monolingualism has not become marked as the norm, there is no threat to the students' Spanish language identity. As a result, English and Spanish were both valued by students. For example, in one of the focus groups, a female student commented:

El español es mi lengua nativa. El inglés me encanta. En todos los países hablan ese idioma, es muy importante, para todo, más aquí, es el idioma oficial de aquí y tiene que serlo.

[Spanish is my native language. I love English. That language is spoken in all countries, it is very important, for everything, more than anything here. It is the official language here and it has to be.]

At Luperón, Spanish maintained a high status, and students continued to improve their academic Spanish while developing academic English. This focus, with their Spanish identity not threatened, helped them maintain a positive attitude toward English.

At Luperón, the teachers were also attentive to more than the students' academic selves; teachers offered important forms of emotional support as well. For example, when we asked Laura in 2005 what she considered to be most difficult about Luperón, she said, "Nada, porque siempre hay personas para ayudarte. Si hay algo no entiendes, te ayudan. Te dan tutoría. Te ayudan y es una forma de desahogarte." [Nothing, because there are always people to help at Luperón. If there is something you don't understand, they help you. And it's a way of unburdening oneself.]

Further, several students expressed a strong, mutual sense of identification between Dominican students and teachers. For instance, Tony said:

Desde que uno llega, le dan la mano. Le quieren ayudar, como que ellos no están solamente porque le están pagando sino porque realmente le importan los estudiantes, a ayudarlos, que progresen. Muchos de ellos vinieron aquí a la misma edad, jóvenes. Tuvieron que aprender inglés y no había educación bilingüe. Entonces entienden la situación que nosotros encontramos.

[From the time one arrives, the teachers here give a hand. They want to help you, as if they aren't here just for the salary but because students really matter to them—helping students advance matters. Many of them came at the same age, young. They had to learn English and there was no bilingual education. So they understand our situation.]

Though the students occasionally complained about the teachers, for the most part the students' comments about their teachers at Luperón were exceedingly positive—unlike anything we've heard before in a high school.

In fact, one of the few complaints we heard regularly about teachers was related to their high expectations for the students—and even those complaints were, in some ways, hidden praise. For example, when asked what she liked most about her teachers at Luperón, Isabel said that "ellos te molestan bastante para que tú hagas las cosas, pero ellos lo hacen porque saben que tú puedes hacerlo" [they bother you a lot, so you do the things you have to do, but they do it because they know you can do it].

> Interviewer: Cuándo tu dices que te molestan, ¿a qué tú te refieres?
> [When you say they bother you, what do you mean?]
> Isabel: Que practicamente te obligan a las cosas, porque ellos saben que tú tienes la capacidad suficiente para hacerlo. [That they practically force you to do things, because they know you have sufficient ability to do things.]
> Interviewer: Y ¿cómo tú te sientes con eso? [And how do you feel about that?]
> Isabel: Con mucha presión, pero tú sabes que tienen que hacerlo. . . . Aquí al menos tú tienes la opción de que tú tienes clases individuales y tú tienes tutorías. Allá en Santo Domingo eso no existe; allá tú tienes que pagar un tutor. [Under a lot of pressure, but you know they have to do it. . . . At least here you have the option of taking individual classes and tutorships. In Santo Domingo this doesn't exist; you would need to pay for a tutor.]

Francisco offered similar comments. When we asked Francisco what he would miss if he left New York, he first said his mom, the transportation system, and the friends he has made here. Then he added the school, explaining that he would miss "la jodedera de los profesores, todos los días encima de uno, que esto y que aquello" [the teachers nagging you, you know, every day they are on top of you, saying "do this" and "do that"].

Several students spoke quite specifically about their relationships with specific teachers—and not only with Dominican teachers. For example, several students mentioned their close relationships with their ESL teachers. One referred to a teacher as her "mamá," and that teacher called the student "her baby"; another said of his English teacher, "She's like my second mom. She taught me to speak all over again." At the end of our interview with Tony, which was conducted primarily in English, we asked if there were any other topics he'd like to talk about. Tony said, "Maybe that I speak a lot with [my English teacher]." He said that when school ends, in the ten-minute period before tutoring begins, he often goes up to speak to the teacher. "I feel an admiration for [him]," he said, "I like his ideas about things." They originally met through newspaper and chess club. They speak in English (the teacher did not speak Spanish) about college, life, and political points of view. Tony said he felt the teacher had become a mentor to him, in the absence of his brother who had left home. "He has shown me how to think about myself," said Tony.

The Luperón Family

The familial stresses created by immigration were somewhat assuaged by the intentional creation of a *familial* atmosphere at the school. The majority of the students, faculty, and parents we interviewed evoked the word to describe the unique environment at Luperón. One student was so inspired by the metaphor that she dubbed the adults at the school as fictive kin:

> Interviewer: ¿Qué le dirías a una alumna nueva de Luperón? [What would you tell a new student about Luperón?]
> Delia: Ay, Luperón. Que es la mejor escuela que yo he podido estar. A mí me encanta esta escuela. Yo me quedo aquí a veces hasta las siete de la noche, porque aquí tú te sientes como en familia, como que

tú estás en tu casa, que tú estás en República Dominicana. Más la gente con la que tú estás, tú te sientes como en familia, A Villar yo le digo "tío," a Santa yo le digo "grandmother," a toditos le tengo otro nombre, y yo me siento como en familia aquí. . . . Una escuela que tú aprendes el inglés rápido, que tú aprendes bien, que te ayudan cuando tú lo necesitas . . . si ven como que te va mal en las clases ellos buscan la mejor solución para acercarse a ti y explicarte las cosas como es, y los profesores sienten como que tú eres su hijo, y de hecho como para tu futuro, como que ellos se entran en tu vida, no para mal, sino para ayudarte. [That it's the best school that I could have hoped for. I love this school. I stay here sometimes until 7 p.m., because here you feel like a family, like you are at home, like you are in the Dominican Republic. The people here feel like family. I call Villar my uncle, I call Santa my grandmother, I give everyone a name, and I feel like I'm with my family. . . . It's a school where you learn English quickly, and learn well, and they help you when you need it. If they see that something is not going well in your class, they seek the best way to get close and explain things as they are; and the teachers act like you are their child, and think about your future; they get in your personal life, but not in a bad way, just to help you.]

The principal, in particular, took this role quite seriously. He often referred to students as "our kids." And it was more than mere rhetoric, as our observations bore out. For example, in the middle of an interview we conducted with him in 2006, three excited young women came in to tell him that they were departing for a tour of a college upstate. Villar quizzed them about their preparations before asking if they had sufficient pocket money and making sure they had his cell phone number with them. During a second interview, when we arrived, Villar was busy and worried because two students who had been to the Netherlands on a school trip couldn't return with the rest of the group because they had forgotten to bring their green cards, and they were stranded at the airport. They could fly to the Dominican Republic because they were Dominican and had their passports, but they were not allowed to fly back to the United States. Villar was taking responsibility for getting the youth home safely.

This sense of family was also present among several faculty and staff members. Several of the teachers had figuratively "adopted" students who worked for them in the afternoons and whom they called "my baby." During one observation, we saw the school janitor showing to several students pictures of his family, including his recently adopted child. We also noticed several of the young women seeking personal advice from Jessica, the secretary. These interactions between the faculty, staff, and students exemplify the ways in which a family environment was cultivated at Luperón. As feminists, we are keenly aware of the ways in which "family" quickly devolves into patriarchy; however, Luperón seemed to provide a kind of culturally congruent environment for these youth who had so recently experienced the trauma of migration.

These close relationships were enjoyed not only by the most high-achieving students: When Lesley once stopped by Villar's office to ask about a student she had not seen in a while, Villar reported that "he's doing okay, because he's not on my list." Upon asking about that list, Lesley learned that Villar keeps a list of the students who aren't doing well in classes, so he can coordinate more support for them and keep in touch with their parents. He said, "I enjoy working with these students; their progress makes me happier than to see students who always get 95 or more in all their classes. I would throw a party if Laura got a 65 in her English class, but it wouldn't be the same for someone who always gets As."

More generally, several students mentioned how Luperón faculty and staff were helping them in their overall adjustments to life in the United States. The comments of Tony, who had graduated from Luperón, were particularly eloquent, as recorded in our field notes in 2008:

> I ask him how he thinks teachers in Luperón helped him prepare
> for being in any type of situation in life, as he was describing, be it
> a minority or a majority. He engages in explaining how when one
> comes to the U.S. one experiences an identity crisis, in which you have
> to juggle values and ideas from your culture and the culture you are
> inserting yourself into. He says some people lose their culture when
> inserting themselves in a new one (or think this process needs to take
> place), and he says this happens because they don't have strong roots in
> their own culture and they eventually adopt the new culture with greater
> ease, but by "forgetting" their own. He says Luperón helps students
> learn about the culture they are coming from, feel pride about coming
> from where they come from, and about being who you are. He says
> that when the school took them to DR for the United Nations Model
> they took them to a lot of places and told them, "We want for you all
> to create a bond with your own country, your own culture; that's why

we think it is more important than you actually going and competing in this competition, which is not going to mean much to you when the years pass by . . . that you get to know your own country, your own neighborhoods." Tony said he enjoyed this part of the trip, and seeing his own people and how they are progressing.

I ask him how he thinks all this effort teachers put in emphasizing their history and culture helps him learn, as he was saying, how to navigate any given situation, whether it is as a majority or as a minority. He says that when you, as a Dominican, go to a college like the one he is going to (95 percent white), people relate to you as a Dominican, a Latino, a student of color, and after they know who you are and where you come from, then you automatically become like a small ambassador for your country. He says that it is important then to know what you represent or stand for (your history and culture). He then adds that one can't pretend to represent all Dominicans, but it is important to feel one does belong to a group of people, be it Dominican or Dominican-American, or Dominican-York. He also adds that knowing about the group you belong to, and feeling you belong to it, is the basis for learning about other cultures. He says one can't pretend to learn about white Americans, for example, without first knowing about one's own group.

Tony also says that as an immigrant (and even if one tries to adapt to the American mainstream), one is always going to have an internal conflict and feel one is not from either of the two societies one belongs to. He says that even if he tries to adapt to American white mainstream society, there are going to be factors like his skin color and accent that will point out right away that he is not white, and may make others think, "Why does he want to act white when he is not?" He says this all brings internal conflicts in which one might be trying to act white, but still have that "little bachata and merengue music inside."

The cultural familiarity that reigned at Luperón helped to address the youth's concerns about trust and *confianza,* expressed in the previous section. Unlike the first- and second-generation immigrant youth in Valenzuela's (1999a) study, the students at Luperón felt that the school provided precisely the *confianza* they needed. When asked what he liked most about the teachers at Luperón, Eduardo said, "Confianza, siempre ha habido confianza" [the trust, there has always been trust]. He elaborated by explaining that his brothers attended other schools where they were treated as numbers and people related to one another through laws and guidelines. In contrast, he said, "En Luperón hay confianza suficiente para poder compartir" [At Luperón there is enough trust to be able to share with each other] without the need for the laws that exist at other schools. Such comments were common among the cohort. Generally speaking, the students felt that their teachers were invested in their success and well-being; they enjoyed the *confianza* they shared at school. The school's evident community of commitment (Ancess 2003) served as a protective factor for these newcomer youth, for whom the process of migration had provoked feelings of vulnerability and a lack of trust.

The social relationships that students developed with teachers and administrators fostered their sense of belonging; the faculty carefully tracked low-performing students to try and build, with their parents, a safety net for them; and the high expectations teachers held for students pushed them toward achieving their potential more fully. Further, Luperón specifically worked with students to imbue them with a strong linguistic and cultural affiliation, in the hope that the identification would help them feel rooted during the alienating, lifelong process of adapting to life in the United States. Adults at Luperón helped ease students through the transition to new cultural rules and expectations of schooling in New York. As Suárez-Orozco and Suárez-Orozco (2001) argue, there are major stresses specific to what they call the acculturation process, in which "cultural practices are first learned in childhood as part of socially shared repertoires that make the flow of life predictable. The social flow changes in dramatic ways following immigration. . . . Without a sense of cultural competence, control, and belonging, immigrants are often left with a keen sense of loss and disorientation" (73).

Yet, at least within the school, the youth at Luperón avoided this sense of disorientation. The school felt familiar, and the shared sense of culture and language—and, more important, the academic and emotional investment on the part of teachers and administrators—buffered the immigrant youth from the shock of the transition.

Self-Determination—or Segregation?

Key elements of the Luperón model—bilingual schooling, the speech community model, translanguaging, high status for both languages, immigrant optimism, the familial culture based on *confianza,* the presence of immigrant teachers as role models, the formation of a culturally additive pedagogical model, the partnerships with Latino (and specifically Dominican) community groups, and the ethnic community politics that resulted first in the school itself and later in a new school building—depend on a certain ethnic and cultural homogeneity among the staff, faculty, administration, and students. Luperón was founded on what Moll and Ruiz (2002) call *educational sovereignty*, which "requires that communities create their own infrastructures for development, including mechanisms for the education of their children that capitalize on rather than devalue their cultural resources. . . . These forms of education must address Latino's self-interest or determination, while limiting the influence of the anglocentric whims of the white majority that have historically shaped their schooling" (2). While Luperón also deeply values the contributions of non-Latino teachers, administrators, and staff, a strong sense of Latino self-determination persists at the school.

This model has an obvious drawback, however, as it results in a sort of linguistic and social segregation. As discussed in Chapter 6, students wanted more opportunities to develop their English at school, especially since they often lacked such opportunities at home. Further, the absence of positive engagement with African Americans in particular did nothing to challenge the negative stereotypes held by Latino immigrants about black youth. It is important to acknowledge that self-determination and educational sovereignty was, in many ways, in tension with the social integrationist goal that many educators—and we include ourselves here—hold for schooling.

However, the fact is that Dominican students in New York are routinely segregated into underresourced and underperforming schools, where "96% of the students are poor. . . . [and] virtually all [are] black or Hispanic," while the schools' "test scores are significantly below average" and their "teachers are less experienced and less well educated," when compared to teachers for other immigrant groups (Ellen et al. 2002, 197). These findings are confirmed by Kasinitz et al. (2008), whose comparative study of second-generation West Indian, South American, Chinese, Russian Jewish, and Dominican immigrant youth highlighted the different "receptions" of ethnic groups. They showed that

Dominicans, who settled closest to Puerto Ricans and native blacks, lived in the worst school districts and had the most limited mobility. This reflects not only their comparatively low incomes but also the fact that many Dominican families chose to buy homes in the Dominican Republic rather than in New York City. Even higher-income Dominicans showed lower rates of home ownership. As these families paid larger shares of their income as remittances, the quality of public schools in the neighborhoods they could afford declined. (151)[1]

Because Dominicans tend to live in areas of concentrated poverty, they often attend overcrowded schools with limited resources. Since the students' families are struggling, and their parents have on average much lower educational levels than other immigrant groups, they do not always receive the support they need from home to succeed in school. Further, Kasinitz et al. (2008) found that Dominicans (and South Americans) had more limited information about how to navigate the public school system and secure the best schools for their children than did parents in other ethnic groups (Kasinitz et al. 2008, 153). As research by López (2003) and others has shown, the concentration in New York City of Dominicans and African Americans in low-performing schools has only exacerbated the stereotypes held by Dominican youth, especially among young men.

There is a critical difference between what is occurring at Luperón and the (quite common) social-class and ethnic resegregation of U.S. schools documented and decried by scholars (see, for example, Frankenburg and Lee 2002; Orfield and Yun 1999; Orfield and Lee 2005), or the "segregated oblivion" experienced by some immigrants at newcomer schools (Feinberg 2000). Rather than rejecting an ethnically homogeneous, educationally sovereign school on the grounds of the principle of desegregation, as some would, we suggest that the significant needs of the Latino immigrant population and the remarkable success of the Luperón model deserve serious consideration. As Villalpando (2003) argues, the "racial balkanization" argument—so rarely applied to white dominant institutions but easily leveled against informal and formal efforts at ethnic self-determination—rests in a type of institutional racism. Work by various scholars (Delgado Bernal 1999; Tatum 1997; Villalpando 2003) has demonstrated the social and educational benefits of intra-ethnic association.

Instead of promoting a simplistic approach to integration, we argue that schooling for immigrant youth needs to take into account their specific and often considerable social and linguistic needs. Luperón offers a model for how to do that. At Luperón, faculty members have used various approaches to educate immigrant youth about American urban teens. They have taught about the civil rights movement, drawing parallels with social movements for immigrants' rights; they have helped Dominican youth understand the racial and economic discrimination experienced by Haitians in the Dominican Republic before comparing that situation to racial politics in the United States. Now that they have moved into the new building, which has a gymnasium, they are using sports events as opportunities to meet and get to know teams from other schools, especially schools with large African American populations, and they are guiding students to participate in after-school and summer programs that have them working in ethnically diverse groups, such as STEM at City College, the English Program at Bronx Community College, and Double Discovery at Columbia University. It is clear that to compensate for the lack of intercultural exchange in an organization like Luperón, administrators and faculty should work to incorporate structured, regular, positive encounters between Latino immigrants and their American (particularly African American) peers. While we realize that this is much easier said than done, it is a feasible and worthwhile strategy.

Conclusion

This chapter demonstrated how Luperón's additive approach and its tight identification as a Latino institution foster students' social and cultural capital as well as their adaptation to the immense challenges of immigration. However, as we discuss in the next chapter, the gains of the school are severely constrained by the social and economic conditions facing the youth. As Stanton-Salazar (2004) argued, "Although . . . pockets of 'peer social capital' within a school may have little overall effect on the position of working-class students at the school or in their community, they do often enable a good number of students to successfully complete high school and to continue on to college" (30).

In Chapter 8, we consider the trajectories of the focal youth in this study as they passed through Luperón and then moved beyond it into the world of work, family, and (in some cases) postsecondary education.

8

The Political Economy of Education: Trajectories of Luperón Students through School and Beyond

IN HIS COMPELLING STUDY of first- and second-generation Dominican immigrants in Providence, Rhode Island, sociologist José Itzigsohn (2009) finds that U.S. economic and racial structures, as much as if not more than academic and professional preparation and hard work, shape Dominicans' social mobility. Itzigsohn posits, "The future of immigrant generations depends on the continuity or change of the current class and racial stratification system" (40–41); that is, it "depends more on the evolution of the American economic structure and on which forces become hegemonic in politics than on the characteristics of the group" (197).

The findings of our longitudinal study show something similar: while Dominican immigrant youth are generally encountering success at Luperón, their social mobility is conditioned by larger economic structures and the ethnoracial stratification of postsecondary education. In this chapter, we examine the experiences of the focal youth in our study as they transition out of Luperón into further schooling or work and family obligations. The chapter asks: To what extent is Luperón able to facilitate social and economic mobility for its students, given the political economic context? Our analysis demonstrates that although Luperón manages to get a higher proportion of its students through graduation and on to college than its peer institutions, many of the students end up taking low-wage jobs in the service and retail sectors with little opportunity for economic advancement, while those who go on to further schooling commonly end up studying part-time at community colleges with diminishing returns.

Thus, while the additive schooling experienced at Luperón is promising, the subtractive times severely constrain the social and economic trajectories of these youth. These sobering findings underscore the ways in which broader economic and social structures hamper schools' efforts to promote social change. In what follows, we look specifically at the factors shaping students' decisions to drop out, we consider the types of work secured by students after graduation, and we examine the educational trajectories of those students who continue on to postsecondary levels of education.

Persistence through High School

As mentioned in Chapter 1, Latino immigrant students have significant difficulties completing high school. Poverty, residential segregation, and low-quality schooling both before moving to the United States and (often) upon arrival are only a few of the factors that diminish their persistence. According to the National Center for Education Statistics, in 2000, Hispanics aged 16–24 born outside the United States had a status dropout rate of 44.2 percent (NCES 2001, 15; see also Fry and Lowell 2002).[1] This exorbitant figure includes many youth who came to the United States as teens and, though school-age, never sought a formal education. Foreign-born students who arrive as adolescents and enroll in school are highly vulnerable to dropping out. While only 8 percent of the nation's teens are foreign born, 25 percent of teen dropouts were born outside the United States (Fry 2005, 1). Many of these youth did not make adequate progress before arriving, and the transition further dampened their chances of graduation. Youth from Mexico predominate, but youth from Central America and the Caribbean are also overrepresented among dropouts (see Table 1). Dropout rates declined from 1990 to 2000 for all student populations, including foreign-born students; nevertheless, these high numbers are cause for concern.

Latino immigrant youth in New York City show abysmal persistence rates. In their analysis of the New York City Department of Education data for the cohort that entered high school in 1995, Rosenbaum and Cortina (2004) found that approximately 39 percent of Latino foreign-born students successfully graduated with a high school diploma. Different ethnic groups experienced markedly differentiated levels of success: only 34 percent of Mexican-born students and just under 40 percent of Dominican- and Salvadoran-born students graduated, while more than 50

Table 1. School dropout rates of foreign-born fifteen- to seventeen-year-olds, by place of birth (in percentage)

Place of birth	Early Childhood Immigrant		Recent Arrival	
	1990	2000	1990	2000
Mexico	11.1	8.1	36.4	32.6
El Salvador	7.5	5.3	20.6	23.9
Guatemala	5.5	6.5	23.5	26.9
Nicaragua	4.4	4.0	8.5	8.1
Cuba	9.1	11.0	11.0	4.9
Dominican Republic	11.1	4.7	9.8	5.5
Haiti	12.3	2.8	5.9	6.8

Source: Fry 2007, 586.

percent of students born in South America, Colombia, and Ecuador who started high school in New York City in 1995 were able to graduate. Consistent with national-level studies, Rosenbaum and Cortina found that the immigrants who arrived earliest were most likely to earn a high school diploma; those who arrived recently were more likely to be discharged before earning their diploma (see Fry 2005). Notably, while low, Dominican educational attainment rates seem to be improving in New York City. Drawing on data from the New York City Housing and Vacancy Survey, Cortina reports that from 1999 to 2005, "the percentage of Dominicans without a high school education decreased from 49.6 to 45.1. A more dramatic increase can be seen in those who enrolled in college: from 26 percent to 30 percent" (2009, 8).

Compared to national and citywide averages, Luperón has had remarkable success shepherding newcomer immigrant youth through graduation. Official rates show that in 2008, Luperón enjoyed an 83.8 percent rate of students graduating within four years. It far outperformed peer schools with similar populations, leading the New York City Department of Education to declare the school as performing at 119.8 percent of its "peer horizon" in graduation rates (NYC DOE 2008b). In 2007, the official four-year graduation rate was 67.2 percent, while the six-year rate was 76.1 percent (NYC DOE 2007). The question of graduation rates over extended periods of time matters, particularly for immigrant youth who need a longer period to develop the academic English necessary to pass the English Regents exam.

The dropout rate among students in our study was consistent with these numbers. Our complete longitudinal study included twenty students.[2] We purposely sampled participants in order to include students who were evenly distributed in terms of academic preparedness (according to their teachers). In other words, four of the students included were considered to have low levels of literacy in Spanish and were suspected or confirmed to have had interrupted formal education; four students were considered to have high levels of academic performance; and twelve students were considered to fall in the range of average performance. Four of those twenty students, or 20 percent, dropped out during the course of our study. The students who left Luperón included three boys and one girl, reflecting a national trend of higher dropout rates for male immigrant youth (Conchas 2006; Fry 2005; Gándara and Contreras 2009; López 2003, 2004; Portes and Rumbaut 2001). Further, two of the four students were among the most impoverished youth involved in our study.

The factors prompting students in our cohort to drop out are consistent with push factors found in other studies of immigrant youth. Class and locational advantages experienced in the Dominican Republic transferred to the United States; those who came from rural areas had attended lower-quality schools and, in two cases, experienced interrupted formal education, and so they struggled at Luperón (see also Fry 2007). Of the four who dropped out of Luperón, two had serious difficulties reading and writing in Spanish, while the others reported low grades. Standardized testing presents another obstacle. For example, Salvador passed only one Regent before dropping out. Juan had completed all the requirements for graduation, save one Regents examination; when he failed it a second time, he gave up and quit school. Scholars have documented how the high-stakes testing required under NCLB has exacerbated dropout rates for first- and second-generation Latino immigrant students across the country (Abedi 2004; Gándara and Contreras 2009) and specifically in New York State (De Jesús and Vásquez 2005). The pressures of poverty create a need and desire to earn money among newcomer youth. This concern figured heavily in the decisions of all four students who dropped out; each began working part time while still at Luperón, reducing the number of hours available for their studies. Finally, family insecurity made life difficult for the four, and family obligations such as pregnancy became a deciding issue for two of the four. In the case of Salvador, when his father found out that he had gotten his girlfriend pregnant, they had a huge argument and Salvador was kicked out of the house. Though he went to live with an aunt, the chaos of his personal life took a huge toll on his studies, and he failed his classes that semester. He soon decided to drop out and move to another city, where an uncle helped him get a job in construction.

Laura's story illustrates how the combination of these factors—low educational quality before migration, the pressure of testing, poverty, and familial instability and obligations—shapes life choices.

When we met her in 2005, Laura was sixteen years old and had been in the United States for just a few months. Her mother had left the Dominican Republic when Laura was very young, and she was raised by a neighbor and then an aunt in a rural area of the country. When Laura came to New York, she lived with her mother (who was unemployed but had previously worked at Macy's), her stepfather (who worked in a greenhouse in New Jersey), and two brothers, in a poor neighborhood. Laura reported living with the "apartment owner" in the one-room place at 178th and St. Nicholas; a year later, she, her stepfather, her mother, an aunt, and two brothers had moved to a one-bedroom place. According to one of her teachers, Laura had completed the second grade. Her difficulties reading and writing appeared to confirm interrupted formal schooling.

Laura had difficulty with all her classes during her first year, but especially with English. She was soon placed in a remedial English class along with three other participants in the study. Our observations during this semester documented that Laura was struggling, but her literacy skills were gradually improving. She attended an intensive after-school program with several female peers from Lupéron at a Dominican community organization that provided tutoring, computer skills, and other assistance. By June 2005, Laura was able to separate paragraphs and write down a short, dictated paragraph in English, spelling most of the words correctly. However, she got discouraged easily. She reported that her career goal was to become a secretary, but she did not know what kind of training was required.

In the summer of 2005, Laura started working at a Burger King in New Jersey, commuting long distances to her job. She continued to work throughout the fall, often working four hours after school and arriving home late. She seemed to increasingly disengage from school during that semester. In November 2005, we noted that Laura had "many compensation strategies for covering up the fact that she doesn't understand."

That fall, Laura's teachers noted that she had begun to arrive late to school and late to class almost daily, and that she often left the classroom during class for long periods. Further, adults at the school began making comments to us about Laura. The school secretary remarked offhandedly that Laura was "crazy," screaming at inappropriate times in the cafeteria, library, or classroom. Several teachers expressed frustration with Laura. Laura's Spanish teacher told us that Laura had "changed"—that she seemed really angry. The teacher reported that Laura's stepfather had moved out, Laura's mother had no control over her, and the family had very little money. "I am scared for her," said the teacher. Laura told another teacher that there were always people drinking and dancing in her house, at all hours, every day of the week, and she hinted that drug use and drug sales were occurring as well. At the same time, several teachers noted an escalation of what they considered inappropriately provocative actions on Laura's part.

In the spring of 2006, Laura failed all her academic classes. During one observation, Laura's English teacher complained aloud that Laura "does nothing" in class. The teacher later confided that Laura "needs counseling," and that she had been recommended for a "special evaluation" but "it hasn't happened." The teacher was clearly concerned but also clearly frustrated. While writing an essay in her Spanish class, Laura recorded that her mother had a lot of problems with her father and "took them out on" her. At the end of the class, Laura asked her teacher to read the essay, and then she remarked that she doesn't have much to say about her mother and that things are usually better when she's not with her. The teacher grimaced. During the same semester, the principal reported that he had asked a female assistant principal to speak with Laura about her provocative behavior because he thought it was not appropriate for him to approach her about the issue. He said he hoped she wouldn't end up pregnant like a friend of hers who was also at the school.

As the obstacles mounted, Laura increasingly withdrew from schooling until, in 2007, she got pregnant and finally dropped out. Laura's struggles were visible to all; faculty, staff, and community organizations had made unusual efforts to support her. And yet, ultimately, Laura could not be saved.

However, it is interesting to note that only two of the four students who were identified early on as facing significant challenges ended up dropping out. Though they began with low levels of literacy and faced significant difficulties during their first years at Lupéron, two of the four students identified at the beginning of the study as at academic risk managed to graduate from high school and enroll in community college. While it is difficult to pinpoint the dissimilarities that made the critical difference, it is worth noting that in their interviews, both of these students identified strong family and teacher support and the daily extracurricular tutoring they received at Lupéron to prepare for Regents exams as critical factors in their ability to complete high school.

Leaving School and Finding Work

In addition to the four students who dropped out of Lupéron, four more graduated and then sought work immediately. The work prospects for this group of eight were extremely limited. This is a small group, and so information on them is inconclusive. Further, we have incomplete data from three of the study participants because of geographical mobility or expressed disinterest in being interviewed. However, the data we do have is discouraging. Of the students who dropped out, one is at home taking care of a toddler, a second is working in construction, and a third is working at a supermarket. We have data for two of the four students who graduated and went immediately to work: one is working in retail and the other in a service position. Occupational levels are low for this group, reflecting the national- and city-level data for Dominicans that we discussed in Chapter 2. Their reported income levels are also low, reflecting the fact that nationally, Dominicans report a mean annual per capita household income that is almost half the average across the country (Hernández and Rivera-Batiz 2003). Further complicating their situation is the fact that these four are performing jobs with few opportunities for advancement. Like their counterparts across the nation, they have been incorporated into low-paying jobs, living one paycheck from poverty, and their incomes are not expected to improve significantly (see Guarnizo 1994; Itzigsohn 2009; Kasinitz et al. 2008). Itzigsohn (2009) finds that second-generation Dominican immigrants in Providence are experiencing "partial mobility" with "internal stratification" in comparison to the first generation, while disproportionately remaining in poverty and failing to finish high school (51). Our data suggests that this pattern, which Itzigsohn calls *stratified incorporation*, may pertain to newly arrived immigrants as well, though clearly a larger-scale study is required to determine it. Despite the wide-spread rhetoric regarding the importance of education to achieving the American Dream, those who graduated are not much better off than those who left Luperón before graduating. It would seem that, as Itzigsohn suggested, U.S. economic and racial structures shape Dominicans' social mobility as much as academic preparation.

The story of Gruna, who graduated from Luperón and had intended to go to college but ended up working full time, is instructive of how small obstacles can derail immigrant graduates.

WHEN WE MET HER IN 2005, Gruna was fourteen and had been at Luperón for six months. Three years earlier, her mother had left the Dominican Republic to join her siblings in New York. During that time, Gruna lived outside of La Vega with her sister in the home of a cousin. She had never lived with her father, who was from Santiago.

Gruna came to the United States in 2005 to reunite with her mother, who had gained residency status. Gruna had not wanted to come, and complained about leaving a boyfriend behind, but when we interviewed her, she said she had adjusted quickly and that she now liked the United States because "aquí hay mucha mejoría para yo hacer una carrera, y eso, y que las cosas son más comodas, como en las casas, y eso" [here there are better chances for me to have a career, and things are more comfortable, like in the homes].

Gruna moved to a Bronx neighborhood she described as somewhat problematic, with some dangerous *morenitos* on the corner and "mucha delinquencia. Aquí en mi building yo ni puedo salir para fuera. Hay mucha policía." [a lot of delinquency. I can't even go outside at my building. There are a lot of police around.] She described a drug bust in the building and reported that someone who got kicked out later returned and defecated in the halls. Her mother, who held an eighth-grade education, worked as a hair stylist from their home while Gruna and her younger sister attended Luperón.

In her first year, Gruna earned a B average in her classes. She reported feeling surprised that she had difficulties in her classes, because she had performed well in school in the Dominican Republic. At that time, Gruna hoped to graduate from Luperón and then study business administration or communications at a university. In 2006, she still had the same plans.

By 2007, Gruna's overall grade point average had fallen to 80. That year, she failed the Regents in Living Environment, Earth Science, and American History, but passed in math and Spanish. She was preparing to take the English Regents, which she eventually passed with a 75. She still hoped to study psychology or business at a university, though she was worried that the latter might require too much math. She was also interested in tourism.

In our final interview in 2009, we learned that Gruna had graduated from Lupéron in 2008. She tried to enroll at Bronx Community College but had problems with the paperwork for the Discovery Program that was supposed to help poor immigrant youth pay for college. She explained to us that she had filled out the paperwork and that she had been told all she needed to do was to return to pay a fee. When she went to pay the fee, the assistant told her she was no longer eligible because she had not completed the mandatory workshop. Gruna complained, stating that no one had told her about that requirement, but the assistant said she could do nothing since it was only three days until the start of classes. Gruna later learned that something similar had happened with an aunt of hers, leading her to state that, at the college, "quieren joder la vida a uno" [they just want to mess up your life].

Gruna got disenchanted with the idea of college and started working instead in the coat check at a casino, where she earned roughly $250 per week plus tips. She reported speaking English exclusively at work and was pleased with her speaking abilities. At work, most of her friends speak some Spanish, but they primarily speak to each other in English. She felt she had learned more English since leaving Lupéron, while working with people from all over the world.

In 2009, Gruna said she would like to study at a university, and would prefer some person-related service area like psychology or human resources. But she had no specific plans to begin college.

It is clear that Lupéron graduates who do not continue to college need more support in locating well-paying work. In 2007, Lupéron started a modest job-shadowing program with the Rotary Club, but the shadowing was limited to a few days. Also, participants were generally higher-performing students, not those who are most likely to start working after high school. Given the larger political economy of the city, immigrant youth need more intensive assistance to transition successfully from school to work.

Graduating and Going to College

The obvious goal for many educators of Latino youth is for their students to graduate from high school and continue on to postsecondary education. As a group, Latinos have increasing access to college. According to one source, two out of three Latino youth pursue postsecondary education by age twenty-six (Swail, Cabrera, and Lee 2004). Fry (2004) offers even higher estimates: according to him, of the Latino youth who finish high school, more than 80 percent go on to college by age twenty-six—the same rate as white high school completers (2). Foreign-born Latinos are even more likely to enroll in postsecondary education (Ganderton and Santos 1995; Hagy and Staniec 2002; Vernez and Abrahamse 1996). Completion rates, however, are another matter. Twice as many whites as Latinos complete a bachelor's degree by age twenty-six (Fry 2004, 2; Swail et al. 2004).

One important factor in the discrepancy in rates of completion is the selectivity of the institution. Latinos, and particularly foreign-born Latinos, are disproportionately enrolled in less-selective postsecondary institutions (Fry 2004; Gándara and Contreras 2009; Leinbach and Bailey 2006). According to data from the National Center for Education Statistics, 46 percent of all Hispanic undergraduates were enrolled in community colleges (Horn and Nevill 2006). Hispanics represented 14.4 percent of all students enrolled in community colleges, and only 8.9 percent of students enrolled in public four-year institutions were Hispanic (Provasnik and Planty 2008). As Fry (2004) argues, "Selectivity matters because college selectivity and college completion go hand in hand" (5). More selective institutions have higher completion rates; not only because students are better prepared but seemingly because of a culture of achievement (Alon and Tienda 2005; Kane 1998; Light and Strayer 2000). Numerous studies have cited higher dropout rates among students enrolled in two-year community colleges when compared to students enrolled in public four-year institutions. Controlling for race, socioeconomic status, and academic "aptitude," community college students are 10–18 percent more likely to drop out in the first two years than students enrolled in four-year colleges (Dougherty 1992). These numbers are particularly high for Latino students. A longitudinal study of Hispanic students who enrolled in a two-year institution in 1995–1996 found that six years later, 52 percent of the students had no degree and were no longer enrolled at any institute of higher education, compared to only 27.7 percent of Hispanic students enrolled in a four-year institution (Berkner, He, and Cataldi 2002). Un-fortunately, Latinos disproportionately enroll on campuses that have low bachelor's degree completion rates, so that their pathway through post-secondary education starts on a low trajectory. In addition, even when they are on the same college pathway as white youth, they are less likely than their white peers to graduate. The National Education Longitudinal Study (NELS) reveals that young Hispanic college students do not fare similarly to young whites of equal preparation. The best-prepared Latinos fare worse than whites of equal preparation. The least-prepared Hispanics fare worse than their least-prepared white peers (Fry 2004, 4; see also Ganderton and Santos 1995). In fact, fewer than 13 percent of Hispanic students who begin at community college complete a bachelor's degree, compared to 23 percent of their white peers (Fry 2004, 15).

In New York City, the 1990s witnessed a dramatic increase in the number of Latinos (including immigrant Latinos) who sought their education within the City University of New York (CUNY) system (Leinbach and Bailey 2006). Though Latinos as a group attend CUNY schools in general proportion to their representation in the city, immigrant Latinos do not: "While Hispanics represent 40.6 percent of the city's foreign-born population, they represent only 27.8 percent of the foreign-born first-time freshmen at CUNY" (15). However, foreign-born Latinos are over-represented at CUNY's community colleges, where they account for 35.5 percent of enrollment (14, 17). Though Dominicans and students from Central and South America (CSA) attend in greater proportions (relative to their share of the city's population) than do Puerto Ricans, Mexicans, and Cubans, "even the Dominican and CSA foreign-born populations do not attend CUNY at rates expected, given their representation among the citywide population. Specifically, 79.7 percent of Dominicans in the city are foreign born, yet only 58.9 percent of the Dominican students at CUNY are foreign born" (16).

Access is not the only problem facing Latinos. Native- and especially foreign-born Latinos have low rates of credit accumulation relative to other ethnic groups, placing their program completion in jeopardy. As Leinbach and Bailey (2006) found, "All Hispanics—but in particular Hispanic immigrants—have very low rates of bachelor's degree attainment relative to other native- and foreign-born populations at CUNY. Thus, by all measures, Hispanics have not been as successful as other populations at CUNY, with the contrast between Hispanic and other immigrants much greater than the contrast between native-born Hispanics and other native-born populations" (29). Interestingly, while national data demonstrates that selectivity influences college completion, Leinbach and Bailey found that beginning at a community college per se does not diminish a Latino student's chances of earning a bachelor's degree (26).

These statistics give a sense of the ethnoracial stratification of the postsecondary educational ecology facing Luperón graduates. Luperón prides itself on its success in placing immigrant graduates in college. For the past several years, between 80 percent and 90 percent of its graduates have continued to a two- or four-year college. According to Luperón's college counselor, every member of the 2006 graduating class enrolled in postsecondary education. Of the sixteen youth who participated in our longitudinal study and graduated in 2008, eight continued to community colleges, and four went to four-year colleges. These rates are certainly encouraging, and Luperón is to be applauded for the obvious boost it gives its students.

This success is attributable to the intensive work conducted by the college counselor and by various faculty and administrators, as well as the role modeling provided by Luperón graduates. Students at Luperón attended college fairs. The counselor took students to visit different colleges, and a few faculty members have visited their own alma maters with seniors from Luperón. According to the college counselor, the school reserves a small fund to finance college visits. She held information sessions for parents about the application process, and she helped them fill out federal forms such as the Free Application for Federal Student Aid (FAFSA). Further, the counselor cultivated strong relationships with the admissions and financial aid officers at many State University of New York (SUNY) campuses and other New York State schools, and she actively advocated for her students. She was often able to convince colleges to overlook students' verbal scores on the SAT if their math scores were high enough. In addition, Luperón offered free SAT preparation courses, several Luperón teachers assisted students in preparing their application essays, and the school invited graduates to visit, tell current students about their schools, and even conduct practice college interviews with the current juniors and seniors. The principal instills in graduates a sense of responsibility for those behind them. For example, at a Luperón reunion in 2006, Villar asked some current seniors to speak to the alumni about how the graduates have inspired them. He then reminded the graduates that they are role models for those who come after them, and that they can help "make a space" for the upcoming students at their colleges; he also spoke of the importance of receiving a college diploma and contributing to their community.

Getting Through College

While Luperón's rates of college admission are encouraging, the qualitative data allows us to see how contingent and tenuous are the educational trajectories of newcomer youth. In what follows, we consider the factors that influence the youth's progress through community colleges, focusing specifically on social class, academic English, and family obligations.

Higher social class provided obvious advantages to some students. Two of the four students who made it to four-year colleges were from the wealthiest families in our cohort. Both of them had enjoyed private schooling in the Dominican Republic; they had had better academic preparation and some explicit English instruction before arriving in the United States. These advantages accumulated during their time at Luperón, and they ended up in more highly ranked colleges than their peers. As Fry (2005) shows, newcomer immigrant students' previous educational experiences significantly shape their access, persistence, and attainment.

The story of Francisco reflects the accumulation of advantages, including social class, a stable family, educational quality, and the parents' educational background.

WHEN WE MET HIM IN 2005, Francisco was a fifteen-year-old living with his mom and his nineteen-year-old brother in upper Manhattan. Francisco had been in the country for less than six months. He had grown up in La Vega, living with his grandmother and a (U.S.-born) younger brother, while his mother, who had trained as a pediatrician in the Dominican Republic, worked as a doctor's assistant in New York City. In his last year in the Dominican Republic, Francisco had attended a private, bilingual school for eight hours per day that had helped him prepare for the transition to New York. He reported that he was doing well at Luperón, but "allá me gusta más porque allá yo tengo más libertad. Allá puedo hacer la tarea, es más fácil todo." [I liked it better there. Because I had more freedom. And I could do the homework there, everything was easier.] Francisco missed the relatively carefree days of his life on the island, and he missed his grandmother and brother.

By March 2006, the family had moved to the Bronx, to a neighborhood Francisco described as "calmer and more boring." He missed the Latinos in his old neighborhood; he said that most of the people living around him now were black, and he couldn't talk to them. In his second year at Luperón, Francisco was still studying all his content-area courses in Spanish, and he was in the fourth level of English classes, right on schedule. His academic average was 88, and he earned As in English. However, Francisco complained that he spoke English only in class, and that "eso es lo que me tiene a mí para'o" [that's what has me stuck]. Francisco was receiving tutoring two afternoons a week in earth sciences as well as tutoring to prepare for the English Regents, and participating in a computer class one afternoon a week. He was considering joining a Japanese class at the school on Fridays "para estar en algo los viernes . . . para no estar en mi casa sin hacer nada. A mí me gustaría aprender esos idiomas como chino, árabe o ruso. Algo es algo, nadie sabe." [to do something on Fridays . . . so I am not in my house doing nothing. I would like to learn those languages like Chinese, Arabic, or Russian. Something is something, you never know.] He was also considering joining a Saturday program at City College. He reported that he had spent his entire winter break studying, and that he had so much work he felt he was already in college. When asked to describe Luperón, Francisco said it is a good school, "not like other schools where everything is a problem." He compared it to JFK in the Bronx, which is "big" and "cuando se arma un lío eso es a matarse to' el mundo" [when there is trouble it is big trouble, people go at each other]. At the time of our interview, Francisco was eagerly awaiting the arrival of his younger brother, who was coming to study in New York. (That brother later attended Luperón.) Francisco reportedly wanted to study computer engineering. When asked what he needed to do to achieve that goal, he answered, "Estudiar duro . . . y llevar como una buena disciplina, porque también eso ayuda. Si uno no tiene buena disciplina no puede estudiar bien y no va a lograr lo que tú quieres." [Study hard . . . and be well disciplined, because that helps a lot too. If you are not disciplined you can't study well and won't achieve what you want to achieve.]

The summer before his junior year, Francisco worked in a summer camp for children. That job required him to speak English all day, and the counselors took the children to museums, parks, and on other field trips.

By 2007, Francisco was seventeen, and still living with his mother and his two brothers. By this time, all his classes were in English, except his history class. He had taken and passed (in Spanish) his Regents exams in Living Environment (67), Earth Science (65), Global History (84),

Math A (76), and Spanish (96), as well as (in English) the English Regents, which he passed with an 89. He still had to take the American History Regents. When asked what he liked most about his teachers at Luperón, Francisco said, "Que ayudan a uno, que cuando uno necesita ayuda" [that they help you, when you need help]. When asked if this was not the case in the Dominican Republic, he laughed and said the teachers there would tell you to "jódete" [bug off]. However, Francisco continued, "A veces los de aquí son muy estrictos y ponen demasiada tarea." [Sometimes teachers here are too strict and they assign too much homework.] When asked if he had learned enough English in three years at Luperón, Francisco answered, "Yo he aprendido, pero como allá uno siempre está hablando español, aunque las clases sean en inglés, con los compañeros uno siempre está hablando español." [I have learned (English), but since in the school one is always talking in Spanish, even though the classes may be in English, you always end up speaking Spanish with your classmates.] Finally, we asked Francisco how he had changed over the past three years, and he replied,

> En la forma de pensar, la forma de ver las cosas . . . como que antes a mí en realidad no me importaba nada . . . si pasaba algo en mi familia yo no me daba cuenta de nada, y ahora he asumido más responsabilidades, como para mi hermanito.

> [In my way of thinking, my way of looking at things . . . before, I really didn't care about things . . . if something happened in my family I wouldn't even notice, but now I have more responsibilities, like for my little brother.]

He reported that he has more responsibilities and is more dependable in school here than he had been in the Dominican Republic. At this point, Francisco still intended to study computer science, though he was not sure where he might study.

In his final year at Luperón, Francisco started working at McDonald's, first as a chef, then on the register. He served as vice president of the student council, and he graduated in June 2008 with an academic average of 89. Over the summer, McDonald's asked him to become a manager of a store, but he left to start college instead.

In 2009, Francisco started college in upstate New York thanks to financial support from an Educational Opportunity Program (EOP).

Though he lived with an American roommate, most of his friends spoke Spanish, and he returned home frequently to visit his family. In his first semester, he took five classes, including two college preparatory courses in self-management, study skills, and critical thinking for EOP students in which he received As. His grades in other subjects were lower—English composition (C), mathematics (B–), and engineering (C). He worked in the computer lab five hours per week. In his second semester, he started taking courses in computer science in addition to completing his other prerequisites, including English Composition Part 2. He reported feeling comfortable with lectures in English and with compositions in English, but still felt a bit timid speaking out in class in English.

When asked how Luperón had prepared him, Francisco answered that for the resources it had, Luperón had prepared him well for life and the university: "Yo llegué a la universidad ya habiendo cogido clases AP en la escuela. . . . Luperón me preparó muy muy muy bien." [I arrived at college already having taken AP classes. . . . Luperón prepared me very, very, very well.] In this final interview, we told Francisco that some people criticize Luperón for segregating Latinos, and we asked to what extent he agreed or disagreed with this criticism. Francisco responded,

> Yo no creo que esto es así. . . .Yo hablo con todo el mundo y hablo con gente de diferentes sitios por igual. . . . Es verdad que uno estaba acostumbrado a un ambiente así (donde habían muchas personas que hablaban español), pero uno sale (de Luperón) y le va bien. . . .Yo me hago amigo de cualquier persona aunque sea de cualquier otro país sin ningún problema.

> [I don't think it's like that. . . . I talk to everyone and to people from different places, equally. It's true that you get used to an environment where everyone speaks Spanish, but when you leave Luperón you do fine. I make friends with anyone from any country.]

When asked about his future plans, Francisco said that in five years he wanted to be working with computers and possibly studying for his master's degree. He felt his life was going well, and while one never knows what might happen tomorrow, or whether things will be easy, he said he believes he will meet his goals: "Si yo me fajo yo digo que se puede. . . . Por lo menos es lo que estoy planeando." [If I work hard, I know I can. . . . At least that's what I plan to do.]

The relatively comfortable status of his family's finances meant Francisco did not need to work during his first years in New York, and instead he could dedicate himself to extra tutorials that prepared him for standardized tests and attend Saturday classes that provided him a sense of college campuses. The bilingual, private education he enjoyed at home had prepared him linguistically and academically for the transition to an American high school, although he had nevertheless felt deeply the sudden loss of leisure and the increase in responsibilities.

Despite his relative economic comfort, even Francisco had concerns about how to pay for school. For the students, this issue influenced not only college selection but also the amount of time they could dedicate to postsecondary schooling, and their decisions to drop out. Only three students left New York City for schooling; two of those were from the wealthiest families in our study. Two of those (who had secured residence status) benefited from Higher Education Opportunity Programs. The other participants stayed in the city and continued living at home in order to reduce costs. In two cases, financial pressures forced the students to suspend their studies. Their decisions reflected data from a national survey conducted in 2003 by the Pew Hispanic Center and the Kaiser Family Foundation, in which over three-quarters of the Latino respondents agreed that "the cost of tuition" and "a need to work and earn money" are major reasons why people do not go to college or fail to finish college (Fry 2004, 12).

The need to work influenced the amount of time available to invest in schooling. Of the twelve students who continued to college, only three were studying full time. Two of the three studying full time were from the wealthiest families in our study, reinforcing yet again the ways in which economic factors shape educational trajectories. Nevertheless, two of the three studying full time worked part-time, on-campus jobs. The other students, who all went to school part time, were working service and retail jobs in locations such as fast-food restaurants, supermarkets, shoe stores, day cares, and on-campus computer centers. Sadly, none of the students held jobs that were linked to their career goals. Several were working as many as thirty-five hours per week. Several of the students interviewed indicated that as they found school to be difficult, they increasingly invested more energy in work than in school; this trend did not bode well for their academic futures.

Madali's story illustrates this trade-off. Despite arriving from Santo Domingo with a low-quality, public school education, Madali managed to maintain a B– average throughout her time at Luperón, and she even won a modest grant to help offset the costs of her first year at a CUNY community college. However, Madali found the courses challenging and expensive. As she gradually increased her hours working in a supermarket, she decreased the time available for study and decreased her emotional investment in schooling. Discouraged by her slow progress, Madali reportedly felt overwhelmed by the obstacles she faced in completing her program. As Fry (2005) noted, "One of the difficulties facing young Latinos at two-year colleges is their relatively low rates of full-time enrollment. Full-time students complete their degree programs quicker, and part-time enrollment is associated with failure to finish degrees. Less than half of young Hispanics in two-year colleges pursue their education on a full-time basis over the entire academic year, significantly below the rate for white students" (15).

In addition, academic English (as measured by institutionalized examinations) constituted a significant barrier for Luperón graduates. Most of the community colleges had instituted academic English course and exam requirements as screening mechanisms, and these hurdles proved difficult for several students. Fernanda reportedly spent much of her first year taking coursework in English composition, and when we last spoke in 2009, she still had not passed the Basic Skills Test in English required to progress toward program completion. Eduardo faced the same situation. He entered a New York community college to study computer systems. However, he spent his first two semesters taking courses in English, in preparation for the Basic Skills Test in English that the CUNY system administers. He failed the writing and reading exams the first time he took them, and he passed only the writing exam the second time. In addition to struggling to get past these hurdles, Eduardo was concerned about how to pay for school. He was working off the books and so could not report himself as independent, while his father's salary was too high to qualify him for sufficient amounts of financial aid. When we interviewed him in 2009, Eduardo had suspended his coursework and was seriously considering joining the military, which would provide funding for his college studies.

Even those who made it to good four-year schools could be derailed by the obstacles we have identified thus far: financial pressures, academic English demands, and familial obligations. Familial obligations weigh heavily on Latino undergraduates in comparison to their white peers: "They are nearly twice as likely as whites to have children or elderly dependents, and are more likely than white undergraduates to be single parents" (Fry 2004, 16). These responsibilities negatively affect students' chances of completing college.

Marta's story is illustrative of this point.

WHEN WE MET HER IN 2005, Marta was already seventeen years old. She complained that though she had been close to completing high school at home in Santiago, her lack of English necessitated that she start school all over at Luperón. Marta came to New York with her mother, an older brother, and a younger brother to join their father, who had lived in New York for years and worked as a taxi driver. The family lived in the Bronx. Luperón did not have space for her brother, so he ended up studying at Marble Hill, a small school within the JFK building in the Bronx. At the time, Marta said she hoped to join him at that school within a year, because she thought she would master English more quickly there. Marta proved to be a diligent student, with an A-minus average. She attended tutorials four times a week (including Saturdays), which was possible in part because she did not need to work. After finishing high school, she said she planned to attend a university, though she was unsure what she would study, perhaps fashion design.

In 2006, Marta remained at Luperón and continued to do very well, maintaining a 90 average. She passed three Regents exams (Earth Science, Math A, and English). In her interviews, Marta frequently mentioned her need to *progresar* [make progress]. When asked what kind of people she would advise a new student to avoid, she said, "People who don't care. Stay with people who think about the future." When asked to describe Luperón, she said it was a good school and that new students "should take advantage of it, enrolling in extra programs and community service; do your homework, and get good grades." Marta hoped to graduate in 2007. People were discouraging her from pursuing fashion design because such a career might not be lucrative, so she was considering international business. She was initially interested in general business, but a teacher encouraged her to pursue international business because of her language skills.

By 2007, Marta had taken and passed all her Regents exams. Even though she had passed the English Regents with a 73, she was planning on taking it again because she wanted to score above 75 to avoid taking the Basic Skills Test when she got to college.[3] In her final year at school, Marta took English, Math 4, AP Literature, AP Biology, AP Music, and Gym. She also enrolled in Saturday courses at City College. Marta hoped to transfer significant credits into college. She applied to three CUNY colleges—Baruch, Lehman, and City College; she did not apply anywhere outside the city because she wanted to stay with her family. When asked what she would do to achieve her goals, Marta responded, "No llevarme de las malas influencias" [Not to get swayed by bad influences].

Marta graduated from Luperón and enrolled in City College. However, she soon got pregnant. She married her Dominican boyfriend, left school, and had a baby. They moved to Pennsylvania, where she again enrolled part-time at a small college while working in a day care.

Conclusion

Drawing on a speech community approach to bilingual education that employs a pedagogy of translanguaging, and using a culturally additive approach that builds social capital among its students, Luperón has managed to achieve much higher graduation rates for Latino foreign-born youth than citywide averages. In addition, the school manages to place a high percentage of graduates in postsecondary schooling. This spectacular achievement is to be lauded, for it demonstrates precisely what a group of dedicated, trained educators can do for vulnerable newcomer Latino youth. As we discuss in the next chapter, there are many important lessons to be drawn from this case about how best to educate immigrant Latino youth.

However, after students complete their studies at Luperón, their social and economic mobility are constrained by larger economic structures and the ethnoracial stratification of postsecondary education, especially in New York City. Dropouts and graduates alike end up taking low-wage jobs in the service and retail sectors with little opportunity for economic advancement. Those who enroll in postsecondary schooling disproportionately end up studying part time at oversubscribed, underfunded community colleges, facing (once again) serious obstacles in the form of academic English testing and significant economic pressures. The grim reality faced by Luperón's graduates indicates how broader economic and social structures impede the social change sought by educators.

We turn now to the final chapter, where we seek to draw out the lessons of Luperón's experiences for the education of Latino immigrant youth.

9

Educating Immigrant Youth: Lessons Learned

IMMIGRANT CHILDREN AND YOUTH are enrolling in schools at an accelerated pace: "The school-age foreign-born population increased by one million over the 1990s, and by 2000, 6 percent of the nation's school-age children were born in another country" (Fry 2007, 579). The education of foreign-born students is a significant concern for major urban centers across the United States, but it is increasingly a preoccupation in geographically dispersed settings: in 2000, 67 percent of foreign-born students were being educated in the six largest traditional receiving states, down from 77 percent in 1990 (Capps, Fix, and Passel 2002; Fry 2007).

Immigrant Latino students, who constitute the majority of immigrant students, face significant obstacles. Thirty-five percent of immigrant Latino students live in poverty (Fry and González 2008, ii–iv), and they tend to live in highly segregated areas where the schools lack resources and well-trained teachers (Gándara and Contreras 2009; Orfield and Eaton 1996; Orfield and Lee 2005). Their previous educational experiences, if of low quality, hinder their success in U.S. schools (Fry 2005; Van Hook and Fix 2000; Vernez and Abrahamse 1996). While immigrant students bring to their schooling important resources, such as optimism toward schooling and a resolve to succeed (Kao and Tienda 1995; Portes and Rumbaut 2001; Suárez-Orozco and Suárez-Orozco 1995; Suárez-Orozco, Suárez-Orozco, and Todorova 2008), they "perform poorly on a variety of academic indicators, including achievement tests, grades, dropout rates, and college enrollment" (Suárez-Orozco, Pimentel, and Martin 2009, 713; see also Gándara 1994; Gándara and Contreras 2009; Ruiz-de-Velasco and Fix 2000). Immigrant students are also dropping out of school at alarming rates (Fry and Lowell 2002; Fry 2005, 2007; Rosenbaum and Cortina 2004). And yet, from a policy perspective, "the needs and problems of immigrant students are rarely considered independent of their status as non-English speakers" (McDonnell and Hill 1993, xi–xii). Because the language of immigrant students is considered a problem, educational policy focuses on how to make them transition toward English (Ruiz 1984); this deficit approach, in turn, generates all sorts of educational challenges (Gándara and Contreras 2009).

The case study of Gregorio Luperón High School developed in this book offers key insights into the successful education of Latino immigrant students. In this chapter, we consider the lessons learned that will help educators optimize academic experiences for newcomer children and youth.

The youth benefited from a school planned by and for Latino immigrants.

The story of Luperón demonstrates the value of a community school planned by and for Latino immigrants. The political battle to open and maintain the school united the educators of Luperón, and the sense of ownership and shared struggle among the founders fueled their commitment to the school and its students. Further, there was a palpable sense at the school of collective effort oriented toward the edification of an entire community. Luperón's founders translated the growing political influence of the Dominican community in Washington Heights into the concrete institutional resource of a bilingual high school.

It is hard to overstate the value of having a space in which immigrant Latinos assumed major leadership roles and formed the overwhelming majority of the faculty, staff, and student population. The educators of Luperón established what Moll and Ruiz (2002) call *educational sovereignty*, based on self-determination and self-reliance. Notably, Luperón constructed its sovereignty in an inclusive way that also valued the contributions of Anglo teachers and staff. The generous Luperón version of sovereignty was rooted in social justice. While many scholars and citizens are justifiably concerned about the class and ethnic resegregation of U.S. schools (e.g., Frankenburg and Lee 2002; Orfield and Yun 1999), there is evidence of the value of "majority minority" schools when such schools have sufficient funding, employ highly trained faculty and staff, and pay specific attention to the educational and linguistic needs of emergent bilinguals (Gándara and Contreras 2009; National High School Center 2009).

An engaged staff was essential to establishing a beneficial school culture.

An important feature of Luperón was the role played by the entire staff in establishing a healthy and positive school culture. The bilingual secretary was essentially the gateway to U.S. schooling; she greeted new parents and students warmly, and she graciously explained procedures. She not only used her bilingualism to help parents make appointments and understand rules and regulations but also drew on a bicultural vision to explain new cultural norms in relation to schooling in the United States. Likewise, several members of the custodial staff had been at Luperón for many years; they knew students by name, and they often talked with students about family events or personal struggles. The adults at Luperón established a climate of strong collaboration within the building. Padilla (2005) argues that schools that work for Latino students have coordinated systems with minimal hierarchy, making them flexible and adaptable. Luperón's *conjunto* [team] of staff, teachers, leadership, and parents work together to benefit the students.

The leadership of the school is essential in building a community of educators and students.

Principals play critical roles, especially in schools for Latino immigrant students. A transformational leader articulates a vision of the school mission; reaches out to parents; fosters a warm, safe, and inclusive school climate; and maintains high expectations for all the students in the school (Suárez-Orozco, Pimentel, and Martin 2009). But this type of principal is too often absent from schools for newcomers. Luperón's principal is an exception—a principal "of the hallways, of the street" who is committed to the success of the school and the students. Although mindful of accountability measures, Luperón's principal embraces a broader definition of success than other principals of schools for newcomers. He views success in his students' graduation, in seeing the young adults they become, and in the impact they have in the community as graduates of Luperón. For the principal, an immigrant himself, the school and the community are one and the same.

In a model of additive schooling, teachers become important agents in the generation of social capital.

The additive schooling model at Luperón was premised on the generation of social capital, understood as "'connections' to individuals and to networks that can provide access to resources and forms of support that facilitate the accomplishment of goals" (Stanton-Salazar 2004, 18). At Lu-perón, teachers became key institutional agents in the lives of students. Such relations may be particularly important given the cultural disorienta-tion felt by immigrant students regarding space, time, safety, and trust. As Gándara and Contreras (2009) point out, "Teachers and administrators who know and are engaged with their students and communities are more effective than those who are detached from them" (109).

The students spoke extensively about the ways in which teachers sup-ported and simultaneously challenged them. During our fieldwork, we witnessed close, warm relationships between teachers and students, and we documented the ways in which teacher support mattered to these youth. Further, students identified strongly with the immigrant teachers who had achieved professional success and who, students felt, "understand our situation."

The available literature has documented how students' attendance, academic competence and achievement, engagement, and high school completion rates increase when they have access to nonfamily mentors and role models (Achor and Morales 1990; Gándara 1999; Gándara and Contreras 2009; Hamilton and Darling 1996; Hamre and Pianta 2001; Pianta 1999; Ryan, Stiller, and Lynch 1994; Stanton-Salazar and Spina 2003). Work by Marcelo and Carola Suárez-Orozco and affiliated schol-ars suggest that social capital is particularly important for immigrant youth as it provides cultural attachment, a sense of safety, key informa-tion, and knowledge of cultural norms (Rhodes 2002; Roffman, Suárez-Orozco, and Rhodes 2003; Suárez-Orozco, Pimentel, and Martin 2009). As Suárez-Orozco, Pimentel, and Martin (2009) demonstrate, adults pro-vide "emotional school-based support . . . characterized by the emotional connections or feelings of support and closeness" that "provide a sense of safety and protection, help students build specific skills, confidence, and a sense of self-efficacy" while keeping "students engaged as they encounter inevitable obstacles in their academic paths" (733–34). Adults also offer "tangible support" in the form of help with homework and advice (733), and bicultural mentors help students by clarifying assignments and ex-plaining how to get to college. Mentors are critical to the success of new-comer immigrant students. Our study found that a successful school for Latino immigrants requires teachers who define their teaching duties be-yond the academic realm. Certainly Luperón teachers saw *educación* as much more than teaching a subject or teaching English; in the Latino sense of *educación,* the teachers drew upon "reciprocal and relational social capital" (De Jesús 2005, 358) to inculcate a sense of "moral, social, and personal responsibility" (Valenzuela 1999b, 23).

Immigrant parents can be effectively engaged as partners in the education of their children.

At Luperón, several key characteristics fostered the partnership that exists between educators and immigrant parents. First, the school's bilingual staff and especially the energetic, bilingual parent coordinator (herself an immigrant) promoted communication between teachers, administrators, and parents. Second, teachers used Spanish in phone calls and notes sent home. Third, PTA meetings, attended by key administrators and faculty members, were held in the home language of the parents. Lastly, the principal's door was always open to parents and the community, and parents felt free to call on him to discuss their children's progress.

Notably, then, Luperón parents did not manifest the "general belief among many immigrant parents that teachers are responsible for what goes on in school" noted by other scholars of immigrant students (Suárez-Orozco and Suárez-Orozco 2001, 149). The linguistic barriers, status differences, and fears of deportation faced by parents at other schools were not concerns at Luperón. Instead, the school built on the optimistic outlook that immigrant parents had for their children—a fact that has been corroborated, for example, in research by Portes and Rumbaut (2001) and Lucas, Henze, and Donato (1990)—and built on the strong social ties that connected students, parents, and educators.

A sense of political engagement, shared by educators, parents, and students, contributed to a productive environment for immigrant students.

In many ways, the political struggle necessary to establish the school and, later, to attain a new school building intensified commitment to the school. Parents collected signatures on petitions; they attended public hearings; parents, educators, and students organized press events and demonstrations at the school; and rallies included members of the community board and residents of Washington Heights. The *lucha* [struggle] solidified a sense of community ownership. The political struggle in getting a new school building engaged educators, students, and parents in a concrete project of social justice.

Immigrant youth were served well by an additive schooling approach based on *confianza*.

Luperón has established a model of additive schooling—a school culture based on *confianza, calor humano*, and caring relationships. In this school, family is the reigning metaphor. As many students told us, at Luperón "you feel like a family." The *confianza* carefully and regularly built among students, parents, staff, and faculty at Luperón produces a specifically Latino school culture.

Luperón epitomizes what De Jesús (2005, 368) and others have called "additive schooling," which seeks to disrupt the social and cultural reproductive processes associated with subtractive schooling through authentic caring relationships (Noddings 1984; Valenzuela 1999b) that are based in *confianza* (Moll and Greenberg 1990) and rich in social cultural capital (Bourdieu 1984, 1985, 1986, 1987, 1990, 1992; Coleman 1988, 1990; Putnam 1993, 1995, 2000).

It also reflects what Ancess (2003) calls a "community of commitment," characterized by "human scale school size," "caring relationships," "close working proximity of teachers who collaborate," and "strong, nurturing, and shared leadership," among other factors (1–56). Valenzuela (1999b) talks about "authentic caring" in reciprocal relationships between teachers and students. Antrop-González and De Jesús (2005) reconceptualize authentic caring as being rooted in values familiar to Latinos: *personalismo* [individual relationships] and *confianza*. Relationship-building in schools is a most important factor in improving the academic performance of Latino students. The culture of additive schooling matters a great deal, because studies show that students, and especially immigrant students, do best when they experience a "sense of belonging" or "sense of community" at school (Gibson et al. 2004; Goodenow and Grady 1993; Koyama and Gibson 2007; Nuñez 2009; Osterman 2000; Raley 2004). These effective schools constitute what Suárez-Orozco and Suárez-Orozco (2001) call "fields of opportunities."

Immigrant youth benefit from additive schooling that fosters peer social capital.

At Luperón, peers provided significant sources of social capital. Students reported feeling a strong emotional sense of belonging and mutual support. Their peers explained the cultural rules of schooling to newcomers, and they translated not only words and texts but also concepts and ideas that were specific to U.S. schooling. With the encouragement of the majority of their peers, students maintained positive feelings toward schooling, high levels of engagement, and a strong sense of agency within the school. The students in our study also discussed feeling safe and protected at the school, where they felt that people looked out for one another.

The existing literature suggests that peer social capital is a key factor in the education of minority and immigrant youth. Adaptation to schooling is influenced by school-based relationships (Zhou and Bankston 1998). A sense of fitting in with peers contributes to academic persistence and well-being, especially among economically marginalized youth (Conchas 2001; Gibson et al. 2004; Stanton-Salazar 2001). Classmates establish expectations for one another by modeling academic engagement (Berndt 1999; Ogbu and Simons 1998; Stanton-Salazar 2004). In these ways, positive peer relationships can foster academic engagement and achievement (Fredricks, Blumenfeld, and Paris 2004; National Research Council 2004; Suárez-Orozco, Suárez-Orozco, and Todorova 2008).

Learning from peers can only occur in a safe environment (Scheckner et al. 2002). And yet, in 2005, 10 percent of Latino students in the country reported that they were worried about their physical safety at school (Gándara and Contreras 2009). One of the most important factors in Luperón's success is that its students feel safe with each other and in school, permitting connections among each other that are essential for learning.

Additive schooling builds on immigrant students' optimism.

The additive culture at Luperón—specifically the social capital constructed between teachers and students and among students—built on the resilient optimism of the immigrant student body. Fueled by a keen sense of familial sacrifice, the youth at Luperón shared a conviction of the importance of school success. Students developed strong ethnic attachments to the school and each other, and many (though obviously not all) relished the opportunity to "prove themselves" in schooling, even when they had not assumed such goals back home. For example, one of the students in the study insisted that we take her picture in front of the honor roll bulletin board when she made the list. The youth explicitly discussed the advantages that schooling in the United States offered and the necessity of schooling to achieve economic and social mobility. Such immigrant optimism has been documented by various scholars (Gándara and Contreras 2009; Gibson 1988; Kao and Tienda 1995; Kao 2004; Portes and Rumbaut 2001; Suárez-Orozco and Suárez-Orozco 2001; Waters 1999), and it constitutes a potent cultural resource among immigrant youth in the right cultural setting.

Strong content-area instruction provided by a highly educated faculty provides advantages for immigrant students.

A key feature of Luperón is the provision of strong content-area instruction in both Spanish and English by a highly educated faculty. Taking advantage of ethnic social networks, Luperón administrators recruited faculty members who not only brought applied math and science knowledge from their previous careers in fields such as medicine and engineering but also developed strong pedagogical skills by participating in teacher education programs in the United States. Luperón faculty teach rigorous content in Spanish, presenting complex ideas and engaging students to synthesize, generalize, explain, hypothesize, and arrive at conclusions and interpretations (Walqui, García, and Hamburger 2004). They provide direct instruction in Spanish language structures and discourse for specific subject-topics. Obviously, this strategy has been possible only because of New York's provision of high-stakes content-area testing in several languages—a political conquest of Latino activists. Nonetheless, it is clear that schools should offer challenging content-area courses to immigrants, just as they would to English-speaking students (National High School Center 2009).

Luperón's decision to provide content instruction in Spanish in its students' first years and in English in the later years promoted the students' social and academic advancement. This contrasts sharply to the more common provision of low-level content too often offered to students in ESL or transitional bilingual educational programs (Suárez-Orozco and Suárez-Orozco 2001; Walqui 2006). This rigorous content instruction in Spanish corresponds to a rigorous curriculum in English, where teachers also amplify the language used and the concepts included (Walqui 2006).

Bilingual faculty members draw on experiential and emotional knowledge of language development in relating to immigrant students.

Of course, not all faculty members can be co-ethnics, especially in a more diversified school, but Luperón benefits from the presence of teachers who are co-ethnics. There is much evidence that Latino students benefit from exposure to Latino teachers (Hidalgo and Huling-Austin 1993) since these teachers are more likely to bring to their work at least some understanding of the language and culture of Latino learners (García-Nevarez, Stafford, and Arias 2005; Rueda, Monzó, and Higareda 2004). Gándara and Contreras (2009) state that teachers and administrators from the students' own communities "are more likely to understand the issues that students and their families face, and to be familiar with both problems and resources in those communities" (109).

Another lesson learned from Luperón is the value of faculty members who are themselves bilingual, something that has been demonstrated by research on bilingual education (García 2009a; Genesee et al. 2006). This has proved particularly important among the ESL faculty of Luperón. When faculty members spoke and wrote Spanish, they drew on that knowledge to identify cognates, signal important spelling differences, and denote key differences in linguistic structures. However, even when bilingual faculty members did not speak Spanish, they often drew on their own experiential and emotional knowledge of language development in relating with students.

Immigrant students benefit enormously when their home language maintains a high status at the school.

One notable characteristic of Luperón is the high status of the students' home language, Spanish. Unlike most bilingual programs, where the students' home language rarely achieves the same prestige as English, in this school the status of Spanish and English are more equalized. Many of the authority figures in the school (including the principal, most of the teaching staff, and the office staff) are speakers of Spanish born in the Dominican Republic. Bilingualism seems to be a goal held by all for all. This equalization of status between the languages has led to very positive attitudes toward both English and Spanish. At Luperón, English monolingualism has not become marked as the norm, and therefore there is no threat to the students' Spanish-language identity. As a result, both English and Spanish are valued by students. The high status of Spanish, alongside the importance given to English, is an important feature of this unusual high school, contributing positively to the students' development of a bilingual identity. The higher status of a minority language in school has been shown to be an important predictor of the academic success of language-minority children (see, for example, García and Otheguy 1988).

Successful schools for immigrants educate in the students' home language.

As a bilingual school, Luperón insists on developing students' academic Spanish through Spanish language and literacy instruction as well as rigorous content-area instruction. This decision builds the literacy skills of students with low literacy in Spanish, who constitute a significant proportion of the immigrant student population, while extending the academic Spanish of all students through course content that counts toward graduation from high school.

Many studies have confirmed the wisdom of this strategy. Academic development in students' home languages is "positively related to higher long-term academic attainment" (Ferguson 2006, 48; see also Genesee et al. 2006; Ramírez 1992; Thomas and Collier 1997, 2002; Lindholm-Leary 2001). Thomas and Collier (1997) state, "The first predictor of long-term school success is cognitively complex on-grade level academic instruction through students' first language for as long as possible (at least through grade 5 or 6) and cognitively complex on-grade level academic instruction through the second language (English) for part of the day" (15).

The research evidence is clear. Students who are in educational programs that provide extended instruction in their home language outperform students who only receive instruction in English or short-term instruction in the home language.

Bilingual education promotes immigrant students' English language development.

As a result of Luperón's extended investment in bilingual education, its students achieved higher levels of English development (as measured by pass rates on the English Regents exam) than many immigrant students at many schools that focused on drilling and remediation in English only. Further, contrary to citywide pressure to graduate students within four years, our study demonstrates the value of giving immigrant students more time to develop the specialized academic English skills necessary to pass high-stakes examinations (Collier 1992; Cummins 1981a, 1981b).

Studies confirm that bilingual proficiency and biliteracy are positively related to academic achievement in both languages (Genesee et al. 2006). As the National Literacy Panel on Language Minority Children and Youth concluded, "Language-minority children who are instructed in their first language, as well as English, perform better on English reading measures than students instructed only in English. *This is the case at both sec-*

ondary and elementary levels" (August and Shanahan 2006, 639; emphasis added).

Successful schools for immigrant students recognize that bilinguals have specific needs. Immigrant students are well served by a dynamic bilingual and social approach to language education.

Luperón rejects the usual, linear, subtractive or additive models of language education and instead adopts a vision of dynamic bilingualism that emphasizes the ways in which students adapt their linguistic resources to make meaning in context-specific communicative situations. Educators at Luperón recognize that bilinguals have two dynamically interdependent language systems whose interactions create new structures that are not found in monolingual systems (Herdina and Jessner 2002; see also Cook 2002; Dworin 2003; García 2009a; Grosjean 1985, 1989; Moll and Dworin 1996; Valdés 2004). From this perspective, bilingualism is not something students ultimately possess, but rather something they use with increasing levels of communicative competence.

Further, educators at Luperón emphasized the value of a *social* approach to teaching emergent bilinguals, one that situates language learning as a community (rather than individual) phenomenon that evolves within a sociocultural and sociopolitical context. Luperón affords opportunities for the acquisition of a second language by a broader speech community, in a process similar to that described by Brutt-Griffler (2004) as *macroacquisition*.

In so doing, Luperón teachers do not aim to make students use English in the same ways as monolingual students. Instead, their goal is to have students use English academically in ways that make them competent bilingual speakers and writers, using bilingualism and not monolingualism as the norm. Teachers understand that for Luperón's bilingual students, English is dynamically interrelated to Spanish, and Spanish is necessary for them to make sense of English lessons and life in the United States.

Translanguaging pedagogies benefit immigrant students.

Building on this dynamic bilingualism, teachers at Luperón drew on both Spanish and English, translanguaging to develop students' academic languages. Translanguaging pedagogies (García 2009a; Williams, as cited in Baker 2001) are particularly important for newcomer adolescent youth.

Both teachers and students at Luperón used multiple bilingual discursive practices to make sense of teaching and learning in content-area classes as well as in ESL lessons. Teachers at Luperón showed that it is possible to alternate and blend language practices to promote effective learning and to normalize bilingualism without strict functional separation. Luperón's teachers experimented with language and pedagogical practices that built on cross-linguistic relationships in order to enhance transfer. Beyond providing a context to deepen dialogue and thus conceptual information, translanguaging can spur English language acquisition.

Translanguaging reduces the risk of alienation at school by incorporating languaging and cultural references familiar to newcomer youth. Further, bilingual education programs that treat the home and second languages not as two autonomous and separable systems but rather as functionally and dynamically interrelated can support the mutual development of both languages (García 2009a). The evidence has shown that translanguaging, if properly understood and suitably applied, can in fact enhance cognitive, language, and literacy skills (Creese and Blackledge 2009; Cummins 2007; Ferguson 2003; Gajo 2007; García 2009a; Heller and Martin-Jones 2001; Lewis 2008; Wei 2009; Lucas and Katz 1994; Martin-Jones and Saxena 1996; Serra 2007).

Accountability measures significantly constrain the education of immigrant students and have to be negotiated.

As Luperón transitioned from a newcomer school to a four-year high school, and New York City intensified accountability measures, test scores increasingly constrained the education of immigrant students. Rarely are state-mandated high-stakes tests or locally mandated periodic assessments developed with emergent bilinguals in mind. The English Regents exams require students to display high levels of academic-register English. The four essays prove difficult for emergent bilinguals, who generally "develop receptive skills more rapidly than the productive skills needed to write an essay in academic English" (Menken 2008, 69; see also Cummins 1992; García and Menken 2006). Further, many items on the English Regents are not context-embedded and offer no visual support; they too frequently make historical or cultural references likely to be unfamiliar to immigrant Latinos, and they employ sophisticated vocabulary more appropriate to the students with eleven years of U.S. schooling for whom the test was originally designed than for the immigrant students taking it (Menken

2008). The intensification of testing particularly affects English and math instruction, the two content areas most frequently highlighted by accountability measures. The pressure to improve test scores inevitably results in more time being spent on test preparation, with consequences for content instruction (see Menken 2008). Schools for immigrant students need to anticipate these demands and plan strategically how to maintain bilingual programs in the face of such pressure.

High-stakes exams—and especially high-stakes, English-medium exams—negatively influence the persistence of immigrant youth. In our study, two of the focal students dropped out when exams became a seemingly impossible obstacle.

Teachers have had to negotiate the testing policies, and over the years, they have dropped the Princeton periodic assessments and designed their own. They also have become very familiar with the tests, developing strategies—including "outfoxing"—to enable students to do better on the exams. The educators at Luperón, understanding that four years is simply not enough to develop the English language skills needed to graduate, have also advocated for additional high school time for their students.

High-stakes tests should be offered in immigrant students' home languages.
Given their prominence, high-stakes tests become "de facto language policy" (Menken 2008; Shohamy 2006), pushing schools to reduce the hours devoted to bilingual education in order to focus on English instruction. However, in New York State, content-area Regents tests can be taken in the five languages spoken at home by the largest number of immigrant students. This testing practice allows schools to build on students' linguistic resources by offering content-area courses in the students' home language. New York State is an exception in offering high school graduation tests in Spanish. Advocates for the education of immigrant children should lobby state legislatures to make similar provisions in their states, since English-medium exams are first and foremost a test of the students' English rather than of their knowledge of the content.

Additive schooling may have a surprisingly limited impact on the social and economic trajectories of immigrant students.
As we demonstrate in Chapter 8, although Luperón managed to shepherd a significantly higher proportion of its students through graduation than its peer institutions, many of the students stalled in their educational

trajectories: some ended up taking low-wage jobs in the service and retail sectors with little opportunity for economic advancement, while others enrolled part-time in community colleges and faced uncertain futures. Thus, while the story of what happens with and for students within a school like Luperón is hopeful, the outcomes in relation to students' social and economic mobility outside of the school context are considerably less sanguine. These sobering findings underscore the ways in which broader economic and social structures constrain the efforts of schools to promote social change.

Latino immigrant youth need structured, regular, positive opportunities for intercultural exchange with American peers.

In urban areas, immigrant youth are routinely segregated with other poor youth of color in underresourced, underperforming schools (Ellen et al. 2002, 197); these conditions only exacerbate the stereotypes held by immigrant youth, especially among young men. Less common but equally problematic is the "segregated oblivion" experienced by some immigrants at newcomer schools (Feinberg 2000). While we support the idea of linguistically homogeneous, educationally sovereign schooling to meet the educational needs of newcomer Latino immigrant youth, we also recognize the critical importance of providing these youth with opportunities for intercultural exchange with their urban peers.

Schools for immigrants need to pay careful attention to the school-to-work transition.

As we show in our longitudinal study, and as other studies have documented (Suárez-Orozco, Suárez-Orozco, and Todorova 2008), the students who graduate from school and even many of those who initially attend a two-year college commonly end up in low-wage jobs. As sociologist José Itzigsohn suggested, U.S. economic and racial structures shape Dominicans' social mobility as much as academic preparation (2009). In such a context, schools for immigrants need to attend carefully to the school-to-work transition. Schools need to build relationships with area employers and expand opportunities for high-quality vocational educational experiences. In her study, Valenzuela (1999b) found that vocational courses helped some Latino students remain in school and acquire work skills while bolstering academic knowledge and preparing students for postsecondary education (102). Immigrant students may well benefit from more attention to the school-work relationship, especially because many immigrant students work throughout high school and college. It is important to perceive engagement in academic work and employment not in opposition, but in interaction. Schooling models that can simultaneously tend to both aspects of immigrant students' lives will be more successful.

Highly skilled college counselors with extensive networks are critically important to immigrant students.

One thing was clearly evident from our study of Luperón: the critical importance of a skilled college counselor. Thanks to the tireless efforts of Luperón's counselor, between 80 percent and 90 percent of its graduates regularly went on to some sort of post-secondary schooling. Aided by faculty members, admissions and financial aid officers, and alumni, the counselor's assiduous efforts helped immigrants navigate the mysteries of college. For Latino immigrant students, the counselor has been found to be crucial (Bohon, Macpherson, and Atiles 2005; Gándara and Contreras 2009; Lucas, Henze, and Donato 1990). In the case of Luperón, the counselor was assisted by teachers as they prepared students who were learning English to aim high and apply to college.

Educators of immigrant youth need to attend more to the critical juncture between high school and college.

As various studies have demonstrated, with which our study concurs, immigrant youth who enroll in two-year post-secondary programs are particularly vulnerable to dropping out (Alon and Tienda 2005; Fry 2004; Kane 1998; Light and Strayer 2000; Leinbach and Bailey 2006). Persistence has been a particular problem for Latino immigrants in the two-year colleges of the CUNY system, where the majority of college-bound Luperón students enrolled. Studies have demonstrated that the demands of academic English, financial distress, and familial commitments easily derail immigrant youth.

Some form of continued support for students as they transition into college programs may be necessary to increase persistence in and successful completion of college programs among immigrant youth. Summer bridge programs have been shown to confer considerable benefits (Gándara and Contreras 2009), but that support has to be continued as Latino students enter college so that they can excel (see Gándara and Maxwell-Jolly 1999 for examples).

Conclusion

The dilemmas and the pedagogical responses at Luperón, like at any contemporary school, continue to evolve. The pressures resulting from high-stakes testing and accountability movements continue to mount. The Department of Education's decision to remove the option of a local diploma (with its lower requirement for Regents scores) threatens to exacerbate dropout rates among African Americans and Latinos in the city. Though the acquisition of a sparkling new facility was a major community achievement, it also brought new challenges. The faculty and staff have struggled with the bureaucratization and hierarchy that have resulted from an expansion in size. An increase in the size of the student body makes it difficult to maintain the sense of family among faculty and students. The school now admits not only very recent newcomers, but also those who have been enrolled in school in the United States less than three years. This move diversifies the linguistic and social needs of the students. Further, a few students bring with them a disaffection for school that was previously rare among the student body. As the policy context and the students' linguistic, social, and cultural needs change, so too do the strategies employed by the faculty, staff, and administration.

The achievements and the challenges experienced by the faculty, staff, students, and parents at Gregorio Luperón High School have much to teach us about educating the growing, vulnerable population of immigrant Latino youth. The lessons drawn from this remarkable school should inspire and humble educators regarding the tasks that lie ahead. What we do with such knowledge will determine whether we will manage to use schools in the United States to construct a more just and equitable future for all.

Notes

CHAPTER 1

1. We prefer the term *home language* to *native language* or *first language* because we write from a perspective that privileges bilingualism. Seen from a bilingual perspective, the terms *native* and *first* sometimes fail to account for variability in bilingual usage.
2. Fry (2005) asserts that many of the status dropouts are foreign-born males with previous schooling difficulties who came as labor migrants and may never have sought schooling in the United States.
3. These patterns hold true for Latino immigrants. Specifically, among the Mexican-born population, "twenty-one percent of recent arrivals who do not appear to have had schooling difficulties before migration are dropouts. However, of recently arrived Mexican-born teens who did not keep up in school before coming to the United States, 83 percent are not enrolled in school. About 11 percent of recently arrived Puerto Rican-born youths who stayed on track in Puerto Rico are currently not enrolled in school. Among their counterparts who fell behind in Puerto Rico, 54 percent are out of school" (Fry 2005, 9).
4. Newcomers are defined as having been in U.S. schools for less than three years.
5. Other studies have shown that newly arrived, working-class immigrants tend to settle in poor urban areas with underresourced, struggling schools (Rong and Brown 2002).

CHAPTER 2

1. By the late 2000s, the poorest half of the Dominican population received less than one-fifth of the GNP, while the richest 10 percent enjoyed nearly 40 percent of national income (CIA *World Factbook*, at *www.cia.gov*).
2. The high percentage of GDP allocated to the financing of public education in 2002 was reflected in a greater proportion of expenditures on education within the total budget of the central government (nearly 16 percent), and in a real increase (11.7 percent) of public expenditures for education.
3. The survey was conducted by Encuesta Nacional de Hogares de Propósitos Múltiples (ENHOGAR).

4. Secondary school teachers earn on average 7,000 DOP (216 USD) per month, based on a thirty-hour week (OECD 2008).

5. The Consorcio de Evaluación e Investigación Educativa (CEIE) is a consortium of three universities: the Instituto Tecnológico de Santo Domingo (INTEC), the Pontificia Universidad Católica Madre y Maestra en Santiago (PUCMM), and the University at Albany, State University of New York.

6. According to the 2009 American Community Survey, there were 2,315,041 persons of Latino descent living in New York in 2009 (U.S Census Bureau 2009). Of these, 942,235 (41 percent) were foreign-born. Of this foreign-born population, 360,401 (or 38 percent) were naturalized U.S. citizens, and 581,834 (or 62 percent) were not U.S. citizens.

7. Approximately 30 percent of the Latinos in New York lived in households with incomes below the poverty line in 1989 as well as 1999; however, the population of Latinos increased significantly during this time. Therefore, while the percentage of Latinos in New York below the poverty line remained the same, the number of those living in poverty had in fact increased (Rivera-Batiz 2002). As such, Rivera-Batiz (2002) points out that while Latinos in New York have made some gains in certain areas, they have not become better off in recent years, particularly as compared to their non-Latino counterparts.

   Such levels of poverty have stimulated demand for public assistance. Approximately 16 percent of New York City Latinos were on public assistance during 1994–1995, and 10 percent were on public assistance during 1997–1998. This percentage is larger among Latino non-citizens living in New York City, of whom 25 percent were on public assistance during 1994–1995, and 18 percent during 1997–1998 (Chernick and Reimers 2001). During 1994–1995, 32 percent of Latino New Yorkers were on welfare, which dropped to nearly 20 percent in 1997–1998 (Chernick and Reimers 2001). Moreover, a greater portion of Latinos' median household income in New York City is from public assistance, as compared to the city's total population. Estimates from the 2007 American Community Survey show that for Latinos, 7 percent of their household income comes from cash public assistance, as compared to 3.7 percent for the total population, and 25.6 percent comes from food stamp benefits, as compared to 13.3 percent for the total population (U.S. Census Bureau 2007).

8. In 1989, the per capita income for Latino New Yorkers was $11,419, which indicates only a 4 percent rise in per capita income for Latino New Yorkers over ten years—the slowest rate of income growth among all the major racial and ethnic groups in New York (Rivera-Batiz 2002). Furthermore, Rivera-Batiz (2002) finds that in 2000, Latinos' average per capita income was only 1/3 that of whites, and estimates show this to be the case as well in 2005, when Latinos' per capita income rose to $15,000, while for whites this reached $45,000 (NYC DCP 2005). Estimates show that the median household income for Latinos in New York in 2007 is $34,390, and the median family incomes is $36,003— significantly lower than the $48,683 median household income for the total population and the $52,871 median family income for the total population (U.S. Census Bureau 2007).

9. In all, the 2000 U.S. census found that Latinos make up 142,391 out of the

345,834 families living below the poverty line in New York City—nearly 42 percent. Latinos furthermore make up 654,716 of the 1,668,938 individuals in New York City living below the poverty line, or nearly 40 percent (U.S. Census Bureau 2000).

10. This information is taken from a study conducted by INSTRAW on Dominican migration to the United States. The project summary was retrieved from *www.un-instraw.org.*

11. However, notably, students in the Bronx were exposed to more English than were students in Washington Heights. As one student told us, "La diferencia de vivir en Manhattan es que aquí te sientes bien, te sientes en familia. Es mejor viviendo aquí. Lo bueno de vivir en el Bronx es que es más rápido oficial, aprender inglés. Pero no te vas a sentir mejor." [The difference between living in Manhattan is that here you feel good, you feel as if in a family. It is better to live here. What's good about living in the Bronx is that it is faster, more official, to learn English. But you're not going to feel better.]

12. See "Secretaría de Educación dispone enseñanza de inglés en las escuelas públicas," retrieved from *www.perspectivaciudadana.com.*

13. For examples on popular culture and second language and literacy acquisition, see Black 2009a, 2009b; Cenoz and Gorter 2008; Jacquemet 2005; Lam 2006, 2007, 2009; Lam and Rosario-Ramos 2009; Thorne and Black 2007.

14. For example, one of the youth we interviewed who had just arrived a month before we first spoke to him explained this complex language use in families that have been reconstituted and that include those who have just arrived, some who have been here longer, and others who have been born in the United States: "El hermanastro mío es americano y está aprendiendo español. Hablamos mediante mi hermana que está aprendiendo inglés." [My stepbrother is American and he's learning Spanish. We speak through my sister who is learning English.]

CHAPTER 3

1. The founding fathers of the United States had largely relegated education to the states; the U.S. Bureau of Education (founded in 1867) lacked policy-setting authority. Historically, legally, and practically, public schools have been largely controlled by state laws and have been locally governed.

2. This figure comes from "Closing the Achievement Gap: Strategies to Improve the Performance of LEP/ELL Students," a memo written on November 21, 2006, by Jean Stevens of the State Education Department (see *www.regents.nysed.gov*).

3. At the elementary level, the intense focus on literacy and math had the unfortunate effect of gutting support and time for social studies, science, art, physical education, and recess. So, for example, in 2005, "the National Association of Educational Progress survey of science found that two-thirds of New York City's eighth-grade students were 'below basic,' the lowest possible ranking," and "a DOE survey of arts in the schools in 2008 revealed that only 4 percent of the city's elementary schools met the state's requirements for arts education" (Ravitch 2010, 76).

4. For a more in-depth explanation and analysis of Children First reforms, see Koyama 2010.

5. Data retrieved from *schools.nyc.gov/Accountability/DOEData/GraduationDropoutReports/default.htm*. This graduation rate reflects the state's calculations. The state and city calculate graduation rates differently: city rates include those who graduate in August after summer school and some who earn GEDs while excluding special education students who largely fail to graduate. This calculation puts them at odds with NCLB, which is intended to improve education for special needs children as well. By the city's measures, then, 59 percent graduated on time. There was a statewide and citywide increase in students who graduated after five and six years.

6. The staff members at international schools work to promote both English and home language learning through a content-based approach, as they believe that language is best acquired when it is integrated into understandable content (Feinberg 2000; González and Darling-Hammond 1997). Home language skills are encouraged, and staff members exhibit a commitment to maintaining and encouraging students' home languages, as they are all "firm believers in bilingualism as an individual gift and a societal resource" (Walqui 2000a, 159). Nurturing students' home languages boosts students' self-esteem and self-confidence, as well as assisting with the creation of community; as Fine et al. (2005) note, the "safe" linguistic environment leads to students feeling "encouraged to take risks without being laughed at" (11).

CHAPTER 4

1. In 1999, George Washington High School was divided into four academies.
2. Less than a third of the Class of 1996 graduated on time at George Washington High School in Washington Heights (Sengupta 1997).
3. In late 2009, after our study was finished, Ydanis Rodríguez was elected to the New York City Council.
4. Nadelstern was a well-known educator during the early 1990s; at the time of our study, he was CEO of the Empowerment Schools in New York City. In 2010, Nadelstern became Chief Schools Officer; he headed the Division of School Support and Instruction, which includes the former Division of Teaching and Learning, a unit that managed administrative assistance to principals in the various networks. He retired in 2011.
5. In September 2009, after our study was completed, the school moved to a new building on 165th Street.
6. All the original support staff were still at the school fourteen years later in 2008.
7. By the time the study ended, one faculty member had left the school.
8. At the time of this writing, the media had reported no outcome regarding the charges against these youth.
9. In early 2010, the New York Department of Education once more underwent restructuring. The new organization includes six clusters with ten networks in each for a total of sixty Children First networks. Each network supports twenty operationally self-sufficient schools.
10. For more on the challenges faced by immigrant youth when reunited with biological families, see Escamilla-Toquica's (2009) study of Salvadoran adolescent newcomers on Long Island.

11. The cibaeño accent, common in the northern part of the Dominican Republic, is often stigmatized. Cibaeños are said to "hablar con la i" as they engage in liquid gliding.

CHAPTER 5

1. Because the term *trancado* [locked up] was so important to the students, and the concept became so central to our study, we spell it in several ways (including *trancao* and *tranca'o)* that approximate the pronunciation of our informants. Generally, however, we follow traditional Spanish spelling in rendering the voices of our informants, regardless of pronunciation.

2. The students were reading *Drown*, a book by Pulitzer Prize–winning author Junot Díaz that consists of ten short stories describing the hope, fear, and disappointment that result from immigration to the United States, as well as memories of Santo Domingo. Díaz had visited the school and talked to the students.

3. For more on textual structures in content areas, see Alvermann, Phelps, and Ridgeway 2007.

4. By *contextualized language*, we mean language that is supported by paralinguistic cues and does not rely solely on linguistic cues. For example, the pieces of writing that young children interpret are usually accompanied by pictures.

5. These include Math (Sequential I), Global History and Geography, U.S. History, Living Environment, and Earth Science. The Physics and Chemistry Regents are not translated.

6. An additional Math and an additional Science Regents are also needed for an advanced Regents diploma.

7. In 2011 the format of the English Regents was changed.

CHAPTER 6

1. Notably, several of the young men reported very negative experiences with African Americans on the job site; their encounters in the street and at work merely reinforced their existing stereotypes.

2. GLHS in notes refers to Gregorio Luperón High School.

CHAPTER 7

1. The study found high levels of ethnic segmentation. The authors write, "Three-quarters of Puerto Rican and native blacks growing up in the region went to non-magnet public high schools in New York City, as did most Dominicans and West Indians. . . . More than a third of the Puerto Rican, native black, Dominican, and West Indian students attended high schools in the lowest quintile [on measures of educational quality], compared to less than one-tenth of the Chinese, Russian Jews, or native whites; but a quarter or more of the latter groups went to high schools in the top quintile, compared to roughly one-tenth or fewer of the Puerto Ricans, native blacks, Dominicans, or West Indians" (Kasinitz et al. 2008, 138–40).

CHAPTER 8

1. According to NCES, the status dropout rate reports "the percentage of individuals in a given age range who are not in school and have not earned a high

school diploma or equivalency credential, irrespective of when they dropped out" (see *nces.ed.gov/pubs2007/dropout/#f3*).

2. We originally included twenty-two students, anticipating that we would lose some participants. Two of the students moved during our study, and we lost touch with them; therefore, we only have graduation status and longitudinal data for twenty participants.

3. A 75 on a Regents is a CUNY requirement for exemption from the Basic Skills Test.

References

Abedi, J. (2004). The No Child Left Behind Act and English language learners: Assessment and accountability issues. *Educational Researcher, 33*(1), 4–14.

Abedi, J. (Ed.). (2007a). *English language proficiency assessment in the nation: Current status and future practice.* Davis: University of California, School of Education.

Abedi, J. (2007b). Utilizing accommodations in the assessment of English language learners. In N. H. Hornberger (Ed.), *Encyclopedia of language and education* (Vol. 7, Language testing and assessment, 331–48). Heidelberg, Germany: Springer.

Abu El-Haj, T. (2007). I was born here, but my home, it's not here: Educating for democratic citizenship in an era of transnational migration and global conflict. *Harvard Educational Review, 77*(3), 285–316.

Achor, S., and Morales, A. (1990). Chicanas holding doctoral degrees: Social reproduction and cultural ecological approaches. *Anthropology and Education Quarterly, 21*(5), 269–87.

Advocates for Children of New York and Asian American Legal Defense and Education Fund. (2009). *Empty promises: A case study of restructuring and the exclusion of English language learners in two Brooklyn schools.* Retrieved from *www.advocatesforchildren.org/reports/php.*

Ahmed, S. (2000). *Strange encounters: Embodied others in post-coloniality.* London: Routledge.

Alba, R., and Nee, V. (2005). Rethinking assimilation theory for a new era of immigration. In M. Suárez-Orozco, C. Suárez-Orozco, and D. B. Qin (Eds.), *The new immigration: An interdisciplinary reader* (35–66). New York: Routledge.

Alon, S., and Tienda, M. (2005). Assessing the "mismatch" hypothesis: Differentials in college graduation rates by institutional selectivity. *Sociology of Education, 78*(4), 294–315.

Alvarez, A. (1975). New York's Latins: The Dominicans. *New York Post*, February 24. Retrieved from *www.nypost.com.*

Alvermann, D. E., Phelps, S. F., and Ridgeway, V. G. (2007). *Content area reading and literacy: Succeeding in today's diverse classrooms* (5th ed.). Boston: Allyn and Bacon.

Amnesty International. (2004). *Dominican Republic: Human rights violations in the context of economic crisis.* London: Amnesty International.

Amrein, A., and Berliner, D. (2002). High-stakes testing and student learning. *Education Policy Analysis Archives, 10*(18). Retrieved from *epaa.asu.edu/ojs/article/view/297.*

Ancess, J. (2003). *Beating the odds: High schools as communities of commitment.* New York: Teachers College Press.

Ancess, J., and Allen, D. (2006). Implementing small theme high schools in New York City: Great intentions and great tensions. *Harvard Educational Review, 76*(3), 401–16.

Antrop-González, R., and De Jesús, A. (2005). Breathing life into small school reform: Advocating for critical care in small schools of color. In B. M. Franklin and G. McCulloch (Eds.), *The death of the comprehensive high school?* (73–109). New York: Macmillan.

Aparacio, A. (2007). Contesting race and power: Second-generation Dominican youth in the new Gotham. *City and Society, 19*(2), 179–201.

Appadurai, A. (1996). *Modernity at large: Cultural dimensions of globalization.* Minneapolis: University of Minnesota Press.

Artico, C. I. (2000). Perceptions and memories of Latino adolescents separated in childhood due to piecemeal patterns of immigration. PhD diss., George Mason University. ProQuest (AAT 9985096).

August, D., and Shanahan, T. (Eds.). (2006). *Developing literacy in second-language learners: Report of the national literacy panel on language-minority children and youth.* Mahwah, NJ: Lawrence Erlbaum.

Avitia, D. (2009). English language learners. In Ravitch et al. 2009 (141–45).

Baker, A. (2009). Uptown drug ring is disrupted, officials say. *New York Times,* March 10. Retrieved from *cityroom.blogs.nytimes.com.*

Baker, C. (2001). *Foundations of bilingual education and bilingualism* (3rd ed.). Clevedon, UK: Multilingual Matters.

Barling, J., Rogers, K. A., and Kelloway, E. K. (1995). Some effects of teenagers' part-time employment: The quantity and quality of work make the difference. *Journal of Organizational Behavior 16*(2), 143–54.

Bartlett, L. (2007). To seem and to feel: Situated identities and literary practices. *Teachers College Record, 109*(1), 51–69.

Bartlett, L. (2010). *The word and the world: The cultural politics of literacy in Brazil.* Creskill, NJ: Hampton Press.

Batalova, J., Fix, M., and Murray, J. (2007). *Measures of change: The demography and literacy of adolescent English learners—a report to Carnegie Corporation of New York.* Washington, DC: Migration Policy Institute.

Bean, F. D., and Stevens, G. (2003). *America's newcomers and the dynamics of diversity.* New York: Russell Sage.

Berkner, L., He, S., and Cataldi, E. (2002). *Descriptive summary of 1995–96 beginning postsecondary students: Six years later.* Washington, DC: U.S. Department of Education, National Center for Education Statistics.

Berndt, T. J. (1999). Friends' influence on students' adjustment to school. *Educational Psychologist, 34*(1), 15–28.

Bernhardt, E., and Kamil, M. (1995). Interpreting relationships between L1 and L2 reading: Consolidating the linguistic threshold and the linguistic interdependence hypotheses. *Applied Linguistics, 16*(1), 15–34.

Bialystok, E., and Cummins, J. (1991). Language, cognition, and education of bilingual children. In E. Bialystok (Ed.), *Language processing in bilingual children* (222–32). Cambridge: Cambridge University Press.

Bilingual Education Act. (1968). Title VII, Bilingual Education, Language Enhancement, and Language Acquisition Programs of Elementary and Secondary Education Act, P. L. 90-247.

Bilingual Education Act. (1974). Title VII of Elementary and Secondary Education Act, 1974 reauthorization, P. L. 93-380.

Bilingual Education Act. (1978). Title VII of Elementary and Secondary Education Act, 1978 reauthorization, P. L. 95-561.

Bilingual Education Act. (1984). Title VII of Elementary and Secondary Education Act, 1984 reauthorization, P. L. 98-511.

Bilingual Education Act. (1988). Title VII of Elementary and Secondary Education Act, 1988 reauthorization, P. L. 100-297.

Bilingual Education Act. (1994). Title VII of Improving America's Schools Act of 1994, P. L. 103-382.

Black, R. W. (2009a). Online fanfiction, global identities, and imagination. *Research in the Teaching of English, 43*(4), 397–425.

Black, R. W. (2009b). English language learners, fan communities, and twenty first century skills. *Journal of Adolescent and Adult Literacy, 52*(8).

Bloomfield, D. (2009). Small schools: Myth and reality. In Ravitch et al. 2009 (49–56).

Bohon, S. A., Macpherson, H., and Atiles, J. H. (2005). Educational barriers for new Latinos in Georgia. *Journal of Latinos and Education, 4*(1), 43–58.

Bourdieu, P. (1986). The forms of capital. In John G. Richardson (Ed.), *Handbook of Theory and Research for the Sociology of Education* (241–58). New York: Greenwood Press.

Bourdieu, P. (1991). *Language and symbolic power.* Cambridge, MA: Harvard University Press.

Boyson, B. A., and Short, D. J. (2003). *Secondary school newcomer programs in the United States* (Research Report 12). Washington, DC: Center for Research on Education Diversity and Excellence.

Brittain, C. (2005). *On learning English: The importance of school context, immigrant communities, and the racial symbolism of the English language in understanding the challenge for immigrant adolescents.* San Diego: Center for Comparative Immigration Studies, University of California at San Diego.

Brutt-Griffler, J. (2004). *World English: A study of its development.* Clevedon, UK: Multilingual Matters.

Callahan, R., Wilkinson, L., Muller, C., and Frisco, M. (2008). ESL placement and schools: Effects on immigrant achievement. *Educational Policy, (23)*2, 355–84.

Canagarajah, S. (1999). *Resisting linguistic imperialism in English teaching.* Oxford: Oxford University Press.

Capps, R., Fix, M., Murray, J., Ost, J., Passel, J., and Herwantoro, S. (2005). *The new demography of America's schools: Immigration and the No Child Left Behind Act.* Washington, DC: Urban Institute.

Capps, R., Fix, M., and Passel, J. S. (2002). *The dispersal of immigrants in the 1990s.* Washington, DC: Urban Institute.

Carson, J. E., Carrell, P. L., Silberstein, S., Kroll, B., and Kuehn, P. A. (1990). Reading-writing relationships in first and second language. *TESOL Quarterly 24*(2), 245–66.

Carter, P. (2007). *Keepin' it real: School success beyond black and white.* New York: Oxford University Press.

Cenoz, J., and Gorter, D. (Eds.). (2008). *Multilingualism and minority languages: Achievements and challenges in education* 21. Amsterdam, Netherlands: John Benjamins.

Chernick, H., and Reimers, C. (2001). Welfare reform and New York City's low-income population. *Economic Policy Review, 7*(2), 83–97.

Coleman, J. S. (1988). Social capital in the creation of human capital. *American Journal of Sociology, 94*, 95–120.

Collier, V. P. (1992). A synthesis of studies examining long-term language minority student data on academic achievement. *Bilingual Research Journal, 16*(1–2), 187–212.

Collier, V. P., and Thomas, W. P. (1989). How quickly can immigrants become proficient in school English? *Journal of Educational Issues of Language Minority Students, 5*, 26–38.

Commission on Independent Colleges and Universities. (2007). *Solutions for New York's future.* Retrieved from *www.cicu.org/publicationReports/solutionsny.php.*

Conchas, G. Q. (2001). Structuring failure and success: Understanding the variability in Latino school engagement. *Harvard Educational Review, 71*(3), 475–504.

Conchas, G. Q. (2006). *The color of success: Race and high-achieving urban youth.* New York: Teachers College Press.

Conger, D., Ellen, I. G., and O'Regan, K. (2009). Immigration and urban schools: The dynamics of demographic change in the nation's largest school district. *Education and Urban Society, 41*(3), 295–316.

Conger, D., Schwartz, A. E., and Stiefel, L. (2003). *Who are our students: A statistical portrait of immigrant students in New York City elementary and middle schools.* New York: New York University Taub Urban Research Center.

Conger, D., Schwartz, A. E., and Stiefel, L. (2007). Immigrant and native-born differences in school stability and special education: Evidence from New York City. *International Migration Review, 41*(2), 402–31.

Cook, V. J. (1991). The poverty-of-the-stimulus argument and multi-competence. *Second Language Research, 7*(2), 103–17.

Cook, V. J. (2001). Using the first language in the classroom. *Canadian Modern Language Review, 57*, 402–23.

Cook, V. J. (2002). Background to the L2 user. In V. J. Cook (Ed.), *Portraits of the L2 user* (1–28). Clevedon, UK: Multilingual Matters.

Cortina, R. (2009). *The education of Latinos in northern Manhattan schools.*

Policy paper. Albany, NY: New York Latino Research and Resources Network (NYLARNet).

Crawford, J. (2004). *Educating English learners: Language diversity in the classroom* (5th ed.). Los Angeles: Bilingual Educational Services.

Crawford, J. (2008). No Child Left Behind: Misguided approach to school accountability for English language learners. In *Advocating for English learners: Selected essays* (128–38). Clevedon, UK: Multilingual Matters.

Creese, A. and Blackledge, A. (2009). Meaning-making as dialogic process: Official and carnival lives in the language classroom. *Journal of Language, Identity, and Education, 8*(4), 236–53.

Creese, A., and Blackledge, A. (2010). Translanguaging in the bilingual classroom: A pedagogy for teaching and learning? *Modern Language Journal, 94*(1), 103–15.

Cummins, J. (1979). Linguistic interdependence and the educational development of bilingual children. *Review of Educational Research, 49*, 222–51.

Cummins, J. (1981a). *Bilingualism and minority language children.* Toronto: Ontario Institute for Studies in Education.

Cummins, J. (1981b). *The role of primary language development in promoting educational success for language minority students.* Sacramento: California Department of Education.

Cummins, J. (1991). Conversational and academic language proficiency in bilingual contexts. *AILA Review, 8*, 75–89.

Cummins, J. (1992). Bilingual education and English immersion: The Ramírez report in theoretical perspective. *Bilingual Research Journal, 16*, 91–104.

Cummins, J. (2000). *Language, power, and pedagogy: Bilingual children in the crossfire.* Clevedon, UK: Multilingual Matters.

Cummins, J. (2007). Rethinking monolingual instructional strategies in multilingual classrooms. *Canadian Journal of Applied Linguistics, 10*(2), 221–40.

Cummins, J. (2008). Teaching for transfer: Challenging the two solitudes assumption in bilingual education. In J. Cummins and N. Hornberger (Eds.), *Encyclopedia of language and education* (Vol. 5, Bilingual education, 1528–38*)*. Boston: Springer.

Cummins, J. (2009). Foreword to *Writing Between Languages,* by Dangling Fu (ix–xii). Portsmouth, NH: Heinemann.

Cummins, J., and Swain, M. (1986). *Bilingualism in education: Aspects of theory, research and practice.* London: Longman.

De Jesús, A. (2005). Theoretical perspectives on the underachievement of Latino/a students in US schools: Toward a framework for culturally additive schooling. In P. Pedraza and M. Rivera (Eds.), *Latino Education: An agenda for community action research* (343–74). Mahwah, NJ: Lawrence Erlbaum.

De Jesús, A., and Vásquez, D. W. (2005). Exploring the Latino education profile and pipeline for Latinos in New York State. *Centro de Estudios Puertorriqueños Policy Brief, 2*(2): 1–14. *www.centropr.org.*

Delgado Bernal, D. (1999). Chicana/o education from the civil rights era to the present. In J. F. Moreno (Ed.), *The elusive quest for equality: 150 years of Chicano/Chicana education* (77–108). Cambridge, MA: Harvard Educational Review.

DeSimone, J. (2006). Academic performance and part-time employment among high school seniors. *Topics in Economic Analysis and Policy, 6*(1), 1–34.

Donley, B., Henderson, A., and Strand, W. (1995). *Summary of state educational agency program survey of states' limited English proficient persons and available educational services, 1993–1994* (Special Issues Analysis Center annual report, year 3). Washington, DC: Office of Bilingual Education and Minority Languages Affairs. ERIC (ED389179).

Dougherty, K. J. (1992). Community colleges and baccalaureate attainment. *Journal of Higher Education, 63*(2), 188–214.

Duany, J. (1994). *Quisqueya on the Hudson: The transnational identity of Dominicans in Washington Heights.* New York: City University of New York, Dominican Studies Institute.

Duany, J. (1997). The creation of a transnational Caribbean identity: Dominican immigrants in San Juan and New York City. In J. M. Carrion (Ed.), *Ethnicity, race, and nationality in the Caribbean.* Rio Piedras: University of Puerto Rico, Institute of Caribbean Studies.

Duany, J. (2003). Los países: Transnational migration from the Dominican Republic to the United States. In Sagás and Molina 2003 (29–52).

Dworin, J. (2003). Insights into biliteracy development: Toward a bidirectional theory of bilingual pedagogy. *Journal of Hispanic Higher Education, 2*(2), 171–86.

Earle, C. (2003). *The American way: A geographical history of crisis and recovery.* Lanham, MD: Rowman and Littlefield.

Ehrenhalt, S. M. (1993). Economic and demographic change: The case of New York City. *Monthly Labor Review, 116*(2), 40–50.

Ehrenreich, B., and Hochschild, A. R. (2003). *Global woman: Nannies, maids, and sex workers in the new economy.* New York: Metropolitan Books.

Ellen, I. G., O'Regan, K., Schwartz, A. E., and Stiefel, L. (2002). *Immigrant children and urban schools: Evidence from New York City on segregation and its consequences for schooling.* Brookings-Wharton Papers on Urban Affairs, 183–214.

Emerson, R., Fretz, R., and Shaw, L. (1995). *Writing ethnographic fieldnotes.* Chicago: University of Chicago Press.

ERIC (Education Resource Information Center). (2001, February). *Latinos in school: Some facts and findings* (ERIC Digest Number 162). Retrieved from *www.ericdigests.org/2001-3/facts.htm.*

Escamilla-Toquica, C. (2009). Central American adolescents reuniting with their families after a long separation: What happens during reunification period? PhD diss., New York University. ProQuest (AAT 3353017).

Farr, M., and Barajas, E. (2005). Latinos and diversity in a global city: Language and identity at home, school, church, and work. In M. Farr (Ed.), *Latino language and literacy in ethnolinguistic Chicago* (3–22). New York: Routledge.

Feinberg, R. C. (2000). Newcomer schools: Salvation or segregated oblivion for immigrant students? *Theory into Practice, 39*(4), 220–27.

Ferguson, G. (2003). Classroom code-switching in post-colonial contexts: Functions, attitudes, and policies. *AILA Review, 16*(1), 38–51.

Ferguson, G. (2006). *Language planning and education.* Edinburgh: Edinburgh Press.

Fernández, J. A., and Underwood, J. (1993). *Tales out of school: Joseph Fernandez's crusade to rescue American education.* New York: Little, Brown.

Fernández, M. (2007, March 4). New winds at an island outpost. *New York Times.* Retrieved from *www.nytimes.com.*

Fetler, M. (2008). Unexpected testing practices affecting English language learners and students with disabilities under No Child Left Behind. *Practical Assessment Research and Evaluation, 13*(6). Retrieved from *pareonline.net/pdf/v13n6.pdf.*

Fine, M. (1991). *Framing dropouts: Notes on the politics of an urban high school.* Albany: State University of New York Press.

Fine, M., Jaffe-Walker, R., Pedraza, P., Futch, V., and Stoudt, B. (2007). Swimming: On oxygen, resistance, and possibility for immigrant youth under siege. *Anthropology and Education Quarterly, 38*(1), 76–96.

Fine, M., Stoudt, B., and Futch, V. (2005). *The internationals network for public schools: A quantitative and qualitative cohort analysis of graduation and dropout rates; Teaching and learning in a transcultural academic environment.* New York: Graduate Center, City University of New York.

Fischer, K., and Bidell, R. (1998). Dynamic development of psychological structures in action and thought. In R. M. Lerner and W. Damon (Eds.), *Handbook of child psychology* (5th ed., Vol. 1, Theoretical models of human development, 467–561). New York: Wiley.

Fishman, J. A. (2004). Language maintenance, shift, and RLS. In T. K. Bhatia and W. C. Ritchie (Eds.), *The handbook of bilingualism* (406–36). Oxford: Blackwell.

Foley, D. E. (1990). *Learning capitalist culture: Deep in the heart of Tejas.* Philadelphia: University of Pennsylvania Press.

Fordham, S. (1996). *Blacked out: Dilemmas of race, identity, and success at Capital High.* Chicago: University of Chicago Press.

Foster, K. M. (2008). Forward looking criticisms: Critiques and enhancements for the next generation of cultural ecological theory. In J. U. Ogbu (Ed.), *Minority status, identity, and schooling* (575–90). Mahwah, NJ: Lawrence Erlbaum.

Frankenburg, E., and Lee, C. (2002). *Race in American public schools: Rapidly resegregating school districts.* Cambridge, MA: The Civil Rights Project, Harvard University. Retrieved from *www.civilrightsproject.ucla.edu.*

Fredricks, J. A., Blumenfeld, P. C., and Paris, A. H. (2004). School engagement: Potential of the concept, state of the evidence. *Review of Educational Research, 74*(1), 54–109.

Friedlander, M. (1991). *The newcomer program: Helping immigrant students succeed in U.S. Schools* (Program information series guide, No. 8). Washington, DC: National Clearinghouse for Bilingual Education.

Fry, R. (2003). *Hispanic youth dropping out of U.S. schools: Measuring the challenge.* Washington, DC: Pew Hispanic Cener.

Fry, R. (2004). *Latino youth finishing college: The role of selective pathways.* Washington, DC: Pew Hispanic Center.

Fry, R. (2005). *The higher dropout rate of foreign-born teens: The role of schooling abroad.* Washington, DC: Pew Hispanic Center.

Fry, R. (2007). Are immigrant youth faring better in U.S. schools? *International Migration Review, 41*(3), 579–601.

Fry, R., and González, F. (2008). *One-in-five and growing fast: A profile of Hispanic public school students.* Washington, DC: Pew Hispanic Center.

Fry, R., and Lowell, B. L. (2002). *Work or study: Different fortunes of U.S. Latino generations*. Washington, DC: Pew Hispanic Center.

Gabriele, A., Troseth, E., Matohardjono, G., and Otheguy, R. (2009). Emergent literacy skills in bilingual children: Evidence for the role of L1 syntactic comprehension. *International Journal of Bilingual Education and Bilingualism, 12*(5), 1–15.

Gajardo, M. (2007). *Dominican Republic: Country case study* (profile prepared for the Education for All Global Monitoring Report 2008). New York: UNESCO.

Gajo, L. (2007). Linguistic knowledge and subject knowledge: How does bilingualism contribute to subject development? *International Journal of Bilingual Education and Bilingualism, 10*(5), 563–81.

Gándara, P. (1994). The impact of the education reform movement on limited English proficient students. In B. McLeod (Ed.), *Language and learning: Educating linguistically diverse students* (45–70). Albany: State University of New York.

Gándara, P. (1999). *Review of research on the instruction of limited English proficient students: A report to the California legislature*. Santa Barbara: University of California at Santa Barbara, Linguistic Minority Research Institute.

Gándara, P. (2002). *Peer group influence and academic aspirations across cultural/ethnic groups of high school students*. Santa Cruz: University of California at Santa Cruz, Center for Research on Education, Diversity, and Excellence.

Gándara, P., and Contreras, F. (2009). *The Latino education crisis: The consequences of failed social policies*. Cambridge, MA: Harvard University Press.

Gándara, P., and Maxwell-Jolly, J. (1999). *Priming the pump: Strategies for increasing the achievement of underrepresented minority undergraduates*. New York: College Board. Retrieved from *www.williams.edu*.

Ganderton, P., and Santos, R. (1995). Hispanic college attendance and completion: Evidence from the high school and beyond surveys. *Economics of Education Review, 14*(1), 35–46.

García, E. (2001). *Hispanic education in the United States: Raíces y alas*. Lanham, MD: Rowman and Littlefield.

García, O. (1993). From Goya portraits to Goya beans: Elite traditions and popular streams in U.S. Spanish language policy. *Southwest Journal of Linguistics 12*(1–2), 69–86.

García, O. (1999). Educating Latino high school students with little formal schooling. In C. Faltis and P. Wolfe (Eds.), *So much to say: Adolescents, bilingualism, and ESL in the secondary school* (61–82). New York: Teachers College Press.

García, O. (2001). Writing backwards across languages: The inexpert English/Spanish biliteracy of uncertified bilingual teachers. In M. Schleppegrell and C. Colombi (Eds.), *Developing advanced literacy in first and second languages*. Mahwah, NJ: Lawrence Erlbaum.

García, O. (2009a). *Bilingual education in the twenty-first century: A global perspective*. Malden, MA: Wiley/Blackwell.

García, O. (2009b). Education, multilingualism, and translanguaging in the twenty-first century. In T. Skutnabb-Kangas, R. Phillipson, A. K. Mohanty, and M.

Panda (Eds.), *Social justice through multilingual education* (140–58). Bristol, UK: Multilingual Matters.

García, O. (2009c). Emergent bilinguals and TESOL: What's in a name? *TESOL Quarterly, 43*(2), 322–26.

García, O., and Bartlett, L. (2007). A speech community model of bilingual education: Educating Latino newcomers in the USA. *International Journal of Bilingual Education and Bilingualism, 10*(1), 1–25.

García, O., Bartlett, L., and Kleifgen, J. (2007). From biliteracy to pluriliteracies. In P. Auer and Li Wei (Eds.), *Handbooks of applied linguistics* (5, 207–28). Berlin: Mouton de Gruyter.

García, O., Flores, N., and Chu, H. (2011). Extending bilingualism in U.S. secondary education: New variations. *International Multilingual Research Journal 5*(1), 1–18.

García, O., and Kleifgen, J. A. (2010). *Educating English language learners as emergent bilinguals.* New York: Teachers College Press.

García, O., Kleifgen, J. A., and Falchi, L. (2008). *Equity in the education of emergent bilinguals: The case of English language learners.* The Campaign for Educational Equity Research (Vol. 1). New York: Teachers College Press.

García, O., and Menken, K. (2006). The English of Latinos from a plurilingual transcultural angle: Implications for assessment and schools. In S. Nero (Ed.), *Dialects, other Englishes, and education* (167–84). Mahwah, NJ: Lawrence Erlbaum.

García, O., and Otheguy, R. (1988). The bilingual education of Cuban American children in Dade County's ethnic schools. *Language and Education, 1,* 83–95.

García-Nevarez, A. G., Stafford, M. E., and Arias, B. (2005). Arizona elementary teachers' attitudes toward English language learners and the use of Spanish in classroom instruction. *Bilingual Research Journal, 29*(2), 295–316.

Genesee, F., Lindholm-Leary, K., Saunders, W. M., and Christian, D. (Eds.). (2006). *Educating English language learners.* New York: Cambridge University Press.

Georges, E. (1990). *The making of a transnational community: Migration, development, and cultural change in the Dominican Republic.* New York: Columbia University Press.

Gibson, M. A. (1988*). Accommodation without assimilation: Sikh immigrants in an American high school.* Ithaca, NY: Cornell University Press.

Gibson, M. A. (1997). Complicating the immigrant/involuntary minority typology. *Anthropology and Education, 28*(3), 431–54.

Gibson, M. A., Bejínez, L. F., Hidalgo, N., and Rolón, C. (2004). Belonging and school participation: Lessons from a school migrant club. In Gibson, Gandara, and Koyama 2004 (129–49).

Gibson, M. A., Gándara, P., and Koyama, J. P. (Eds.). (2004). *School connections: U.S. Mexican youth, peers, and school achievement.* New York: Teachers College Press.

Glick, J., and White, M. (2003). The academic trajectories of immigrant youths: Analysis within and across cohorts. *Demography, 40*(4), 759–83.

González, D. (1992, July 8). Events don't surprise Dominican residents: Policy harassment said to be common. *New York Times.*

González, J. M., and Darling-Hammond, L. (1997). *New concepts for new challenges: Professional development for teachers of immigrant youth* (Topics in Immigrant Education, 2). Washington, DC: Center for Applied Linguistics.

Gonzalez, N., Moll, L., and Amanti, C. (2005). *Funds of knowledge: Theorizing practices in households, communities, and classrooms.* Mahwah, NJ: Lawrence Erlbaum.

Goodenow, C., and Grady, K. E. (1993). The relationship of school belonging and friends' values to academic motivation among urban adolescent students. *Journal of Experimental Education, 62*(1), 60–71.

Gotbaum, B. (2006). *Public Advocate Newsletter,* April 28. Retrieved from *pubadvocate.nyc.gov.*

Graddol, D. (2006). *English next.* UK: British Council. Retrieved from *www.britishcouncil.org.*

Grant, S. G. (2001). An uncertain lever: Exploring the influence of state-level testing in New York State on teaching social studies. *Teachers College Record, 103*(3), 398–426.

Grasmuck, S., and Pessar, P. (1991). *Between two islands: Dominican international migration.* Berkeley: University of California Press.

Gregory, S. (2007). *The devil behind the mirror: Globalization and politics in the Dominican Republic.* Berkeley: University of California Press.

Grosjean, F. (1982). *Life with two languages.* Cambridge, MA: Harvard University Press.

Grosjean, F. (1985). The bilingual as a competent but specific speaker-hearer. *Journal of Multilingual and Multicultural Development, 6*(6), 467–77.

Grosjean, F. (1989). Neurolinguists, beware! The bilingual is not two monolinguals in one person. *Brain and Language, 36*(1), 3–15.

Guarnizo, L. (1994). Los Dominicanyorks: The making of a binational society. *Annals of the American Academy of Political and Social Sciences, 533*(1), 70–86.

Guarnizo, L. (1998). The rise of transnational social formations: Mexican and Dominican state responses to transnational migration. *Political Power and Social Theory, 12*, 45–94.

Gutiérrez, K., Baquedano-López, P., and Tejada, C. (1999). Rethinking diversity: Hybridity and hybrid language practices in the third space. *Mind, Culture, and Activity, 6*(4), 286–303.

Gutiérrez, K., and Jaramillo, N. E. (2006). Looking for educational equity: The consequences of relying on Brown. In A. Ball (Ed.), *With more deliberate speed: Achieving equity and excellence in education—realizing the full potential of Brown v. Board of Education* (Yearbook of the National Society for the Study of Education, *105*, part 2, 173–89). Malden, MA: Blackwell.

Gutiérrez, K., and Orellana, M. F. (2006). At last: The "problem" of English learners: Construction genres of difference. *Research in the Teaching of English, 40*(4), 502–7.

Hagy, A. P., and Staniec, J. F. O., (2002). Immigrant status, race, and institutional choice in higher education. *Economics of Education Review, 21*(4), 381–92.

Haimson, L. (2009). "Children First": A short history. In Ravitch et al. 2009 (7–22).

Hakuta, K. (2001). Key policy milestones and directions in the education of English language learners. Paper presented at the Rockefeller Foundation Symposium, "Leveraging Change: An Emerging Framework for Educational Equity," April, Washington, DC. Retrieved from *faculty.ucmerced.edu*.

Hakuta, K., and Beatty, A. (Eds.). (2000). *Testing English language learners in U.S. schools: Report and workshop summary*. Washington, DC: National Academies Press.

Hakuta, K., Butler, Y. G., and Witt, D. (2000). *How long does it take English learners to attain proficiency?* Berkeley: University of California at Berkeley, Linguistic Minority Research Institute.

Hall, K. D. (2002). *Lives in translation: Sikh youth as British citizens*. Philadelphia: University of Pennsylvania Press.

Hamilton, S. E., and Darling, N. (1996). Mentors in adolescents' lives. In K. Hurrelmann and S. E. Hamilton (Eds.), *Social problems and social contexts in adolescence* (121–39). Hawthorne, NY: Aldine.

Hamre, B. K., and Pianta, R. C. (2001). Early teacher-child relationships and the trajectory of children's school outcomes through eighth grade. *Child Development, 72*, 625–38.

Haugen, E. (1972). *Ecology of language*. Palo Alto, CA: Stanford University Press.

Hawkins, J. (2007, July 24). Dominicans' numbers soar. *New York Daily News*. Retrieved from *www.nydailynews.com*.

Heller, M., and Martin-Jones, M. (Eds.). (2001). *Voices of authority: Education and linguistic differences*. Westport, CT: Ablex.

Hemphill, C. (2009). Parent power and mayoral control: Parent and community involvement in New York City Schools. In J. Viteritti (Ed.), *When mayors take charge: School governance in the city* (187–205). Washington, DC: Brookings Institution.

Hemphill, C., Nauer, K., Zelon, H., and Jacobs, T. (2009). *The new marketplace: How small school reforms and school choice have reshaped New York City's high schools*. New York: Center for New York City Affairs and the New School for Management and Urban Policy.

Herdina, P., and Jessner, U. (2002). *A dynamic model of multilingualism: Changing the psycholinguistic perspective*. Clevedon, UK: Multilingual Matters.

Hernández, R. (2002). *The mobility of workers under advanced capitalism: Dominican migration to the United States*. New York: Columbia University Press.

Hernández, R., and Rivera-Batiz, F. (1997). *Dominican New Yorkers: A socioeconomic profile*. New York: City University of New York, Dominican Studies Institute.

Hernández, R., and Rivera-Batiz, F. (2003). *Dominicans in the United States: A socioeconomic profile*. New York: City University of New York, Dominican Studies Institute.

Hidalgo, F., and Huling-Austin, L. (1993). Alternate teacher candidates: A rich source for Latino teachers in the future. In R. Castro and Y. R. Ingle (Eds.), *Reshaping teacher education in the Southwest—a forum: A response to the needs of Latino students and teachers* (13–34). Claremont, CA: Tomás Rivera Center.

Hine-St. Hilaire, D. (2008). When children are left behind: The perceptions of West Indian adolescents separated from their mothers during childhood due to migration, and the effects of this separation on their reunification. PhD diss., New York University. ProQuest (AAT 3287893).

Hirschman, C. (2001). The educational enrollment of immigrant youth: A test of the segmented-assimilation hypothesis. *Demography, 38,* 317–36.

Hoffnung-Garskof, J. (2008). *A tale of two cities: Santo Domingo and New York after 1950.* Princeton, NJ: Princeton University Press.

Holland, D., and Eisenhart, M. (1990). *Educated in romance: Women, achievement, and college culture.* Chicago: University of Chicago Press.

Honig, M. I. (Ed.). (2006). *New directions in education policy implementation: Confronting complexity.* Albany: State University of New York Press.

Horn, L., and Nevill, S. (2006). *Profile of undergraduates in U.S. postsecondary education institutions, 2003–2004: With a special analysis of community college students.* Washington, DC: U.S. Department of Education, National Center for Education Statistics.

Hornberger, N. (1990). Creating successful learning contexts for bilingual literacy. *Teachers College Record, 92*(2), 212–29.

Huebner, T., Corbett, G. C., and Phillippo, K. (2006). *Rethinking high school: Inaugural graduations at New York City's new high schools.* San Francisco: WestEd. Retrieved from *www.wested.org.*

IADB. (2009). *Dominican Republic and remittances.* Washington, DC: Inter-American Development Bank. Retrieved from *www.iadb.org.*

IFAD. (2007). *Sending money home: Worldwide remittance flows to developing countries.* Rome: International Fund for Agricultural Development. Retrieved from *www.ifad.org.*

Itzigsohn, J. (2009). *Encountering American faultlines: Race, class, and the Dominican experience in Providence.* New York: Russell Sage.

Itzigsohn, J., and Cabral, C. D. (2000). Competing identities? Race, ethnicity, and pan-ethnicity among Dominicans in the United States. *Sociological Forum, 15*(2), 225–48.

Jacobson, R., and Faltis, C. (Eds.). (1990). *Language distribution issues in bilingual schooling.* Clevedon, UK: Multilingual Matters.

Jacquemet, M. (2005). Transidiomatic practices: Language and power in the age of globalization. *Language and Communication, 25*(3), 257–77.

Jennings, J., and Dorn, S. (2008). The proficiency trap: New York City's achievement gap revisited. *Teachers College Record,* September 8. Retrieved from *www.tcrecord.org.*

Jennings, J., and Haimson, L. (2009). Discharge and graduation rates. In Ravitch et al. 2009 (77–85).

Jennings, J., and Pallas, A. (2009). The racial achievement gap. In Ravitch et al. 2009 (31–39).

Kane, T. J. (1998). Misconceptions in the debate over affirmative action in college admissions. In G. Orfield and E. Miller (Eds.), *Chilling admissions: The affirmative crisis and the search for alternatives* (17–32). Cambridge, MA: Harvard Education Publishing Group.

Kao, G. (2004). Social capital and its relevance to minority and immigrant populations. *Sociology of Education, 77*(2), 172–75.

Kao, G., and Tienda, M. (1995). Optimism and achievement: The educational performance of immigrant youth. *Social Science Quarterly, 76*(1), 1–19.

Kasinitz, P., Mollenkopf, J. H., Waters, M. C., and Holdaway, J. (2008). *Inheriting the city: The children of immigrants come of age.* New York: Russell Sage; Cambridge, MA: Harvard University Press.

Kelly, S., and Monczunski, L. (2007). Overcoming the volatility in school-level gain scores: a new approach to identifying value added with cross-sectional data. *Educational Researcher, 36*(5), 279–87.

Kenner, C. (2000). Biliteracy in a monolingual school system? English and Gujarati in south London. *Language, Culture, and Curriculum, 13*(1), 13–30.

Kenner, C. (2004). *Becoming biliterate: Young children learning different writing systems.* Stoke-on-Trent, UK: Trentham Books.

Kim, J. S., and Sunderman, G. (2005). Measuring academic proficiency under the No Child Left Behind Act: Implications for educational equity. *Educational Researcher, 34*(8), 3–12.

Kindler, A. (2002). *Survey of the states' limited English proficient students and available educational programs and services: 2000–2001 summary report.* Retrieved from *www.ncela.gwu.edu.*

Klein, E., and Martohardjono, G. (2009, May 22). *SIFE students in NYC schools.* Paper presented at the Research Institute for the Study of Language in Urban Society (RISLUS) Forum, City University of New York.

Koyama, J. (2010). *Making failure pay: For-profit tutoring, high-stakes testing, and public schools.* Chicago: University of Chicago Press.

Koyama, J., and Gibson, M. A. (2007). Marginalization and membership. In J. V. Galen and G. W. Noblit (Eds.), *Late to class: Social class and schooling in the new economy* (87–111). Albany: State University of New York Press.

Kramsch, C. (1997). The privilege of the nonnative speaker. *PMLA, 112,* 359–69.

Kramsch, C. (2009). *The multilingual subject.* Oxford: Oxford University Press.

Krashen, S. (1981). *Second language acquisition and second language learning.* Oxford: Pergamon.

Krashen, S., Rolstad, K., and MacSwan, J. (2007). Review of "research summary and bibliography for structured English immersion programs" of the Arizona English Language Learners Task Force. Takoma Park, MD: Institute for Language Education and Policy.

Lam, W. S. E. (2006). Re-envisioning language, literacy, and the immigrant subject in new mediascapes. *Pedagogies: An International Journal, 1*(3), 171–95.

Lam, W. S. E. (2007). Language socialization in online communities. In P. Duff and N. Hornberger (Eds.), *Encyclopedia of language and education* (Vol. 8, Language socialization, 2859–69). Boston: Springer.

Lam, W. S. E. (2009). Multiliteracies on instant messaging in negotiating local, translocal, and transnational affiliations: A case of an adolescent immigrant. *Reading Research Quarterly, 44*(4), 377–97.

Lam, W. S. E., and Rosario-Ramos, E. (2009). Multilingual literacies in transnational digitally-mediated contexts: An exploratory study of immigrant teens in the United States. *Language and Education, 23*(2), 171–90.

Lambert, W. E. (1974). Culture and language as factors in learning and education. In F. E. Aboud and R. D. Meade (Eds.), *Cultural factors in learning and education* (91–122). Bellingham: Western Washington State College.

Lambert, W. E. (1975). *Culture and language as factors in learning and education.* Toronto: OISE Press.

Lapkin, S., and Swain, M. (1996). Vocabulary teaching in a grade 8 French immersion classroom: A descriptive case study. *Canadian Modern Language Review, 53*(1), 242–56.

Larsen-Freeman, D., and Cameron, L. (2008). *Complex systems and applied linguistics.* Oxford: Oxford University Press.

LeCompte, M., and Preissle, J. (1993). *Ethnography and qualitative design in educational research.* Bingley, UK: Emerald Group.

Leinbach, D. T., and Bailey, T. R. (2006). *Access and achievement of Hispanics and Hispanic immigrants in the colleges of the City University of New York.* New York: Community College Research Center, Teachers College, Columbia University. Retrieved from *ccrc.tc.columbia.edu.*

Levinson, B., Foley, D., and Holland, D. C. (Eds.). (1996). *The cultural production of the educated person.* Albany: State University of New York Press.

Levinson, B., and Sutton, M. (Eds.). (2001). *Policy as practice: A sociocultural approach to the study of educational policy.* Westport, CT: Ablex.

Levitt, P. (2001). *The transnational villagers.* Berkeley: University of California Press.

Lewis, W. G. (2008). Current challenges in bilingual education in Wales. *AILA Review 21,* 69–86.

Liberato, A. S. Q., and Feagin, J. R. (2007). Becoming American and maintaining an ethnic identity: The case of Dominican Americans. In Y. Shaw-Taylor and S. A. Tuch (Eds.), *The other African Americans: Contemporary African American families in the United States* (177–215). Lanham, MD: Rowman and Littlefield.

Light, A., and Strayer, W. (2000). Determinants of college completion: School quality or student ability? *Journal of Human Resources, 35*(2), 299–332.

Lillydahl, J. H. (1990). Academic achievement and part-time employment of high school students. *Journal of Economic Education, 21*(3), 307–16.

Linares, G. (1989). Dominicans in New York: Superando los obstáculos y adquiriendo poder; The struggle for community control in District 6. *Centro Bulletin, 2*(5), 78–84.

Linares, G. (2005). Who wins? Who loses? A case study of a parent-teacher conflict in an urban immigrant school district. EdD diss., Columbia University Teachers College. ProQuest (AAT 3175706).

Lindholm-Leary, K. J. (2001). *Dual language education.* Clevedon, UK: Multilingual Matters.

Logan, J. (2001). *The new Latinos: Who they are, where they are.* Albany, NY: Lewis Mumford Center for Comparative Urban and Regional Research, University at Albany. Retrieved from *www.s4.brown.edu.*

López, M. H. (2009). *Latinos and education: Explaining the attainment gap.* Washington, DC: Pew Hispanic Center.

López, N. (2003). *Hopeful girls, troubled boys: Race and gender disparity in urban education.* New York: Routledge.

López, N. (2004). Urban high schools: The reality of unequal schooling. In López 2003 (39–65).

Loucky, J., Armstrong, J., and Estrada, L. J. (2006). *Immigration in America today: An encyclopedia.* Westport, CT: Greenwood Press.

Louie, V. (2005). Immigrant newcomer populations, ESEA, and the pipeline to college: Current considerations and future lines of inquiry. *Review of Research in Education, 29,* 69–98.

Louie, V. (2006a). Growing up ethnic in transnational worlds: Identities among second- generation Chinese and Dominicans. *Identities, 13*(3), 363–94.

Louie, V. (2006b). Second-generation pessimism and optimism: How Chinese and Dominicans understand education and mobility through ethnic and transnational orientations. *International Migration Review, 40*(3), 537–72.

Lucas, T., Henze, R., and Donato, R. (1990). Promoting the success of Latino language-minority students: An exploratory study of six high schools. *Harvard Educational Review, 60*(3), 315–40.

Lucas, T., and Katz, A. (1994). Reframing the debate: The roles of native languages in English-only programs for language minority students. *TESOL Quarterly, 28*(3), 537–62.

Lukose, R. (2005). Consuming globalization: Youth and gender in Kerala, India. *Journal of Social History, 38*(4), 915–35.

Mace-Matluck, B. J., Alexander-Kasparik, R., and Queen, R. M. (1999). *Through the golden door: Educational approaches for immigrant adolescents with limited schooling.* Washington, DC: Center for Applied Linguistics.

MacLeod, J. (1995). *Ain't no makin' it: Aspirations and attainment in a low-income neighborhood.* Boulder, CO: Westview Press.

Mahoney, K. S., and MacSwan, J. (2005). Reexamining identification and reclassification of English language learners: A critical discussion of select state practices. *Bilingual Research Journal 29*(1), 31–42.

Makoni, S., and Pennycook, A. (Eds.). (2007). *Disinventing and reconstituting languages.* Bristol, UK: Multilingual Matters.

Marte, L. (2008). Migrant seasonings: Food practices, cultural memory, and narratives of "home" among Dominican communities in New York City. PhD diss., University of Texas at Austin. ProQuest (AAT 3325319).

Martin-Jones, M., and Jones, K. (2000). *Multilingual literacies: Reading and writing different worlds.* Amsterdam: John Benjamins.

Martin-Jones, M., and Saxena, M. (1996). Turn-taking, power asymmetries and the position of bilingual participants in classroom discourse. *Linguistics and Education, 8*(1), 105–23.

Mazrui, A. (2004). *English in Africa after the Cold War.* Clevedon, UK: Multilingual Matters.

McDonnell, L. M., and Hill, P. T. (1993). *Newcomers in American schools: Meeting the needs of immigrant youth.* Santa Monica, CA: Rand.

Mehan, H., Villanueva, I., Hubbard, L., and Lintz, A. (1996). *Constructing* school success: The consequences of untracking low-achieving students. New York: Cambridge University Press.

Menken, K. (2008). *English language learners left behind: Standardized testing as language policy.* Clevedon, UK: Multilingual Matters.

Menken, K., and García, O. (Eds.). (2010). *Negotiating language policies in schools: Educators as policymakers.* New York: Routledge.

Mercado, C. (2005a). Reflections on the study of households in New York City and Long Island: A different route, a common destination. In N. González, L. C. Moll, and C. Amanti (Eds.), *Funds of knowledge: Theorizing practices in households, communities, and classrooms* (233–55). Mahwah, NJ: Lawrence Erlbaum.

Mercado, C. (2005b). Seeing what's there: Language and literacy funds of knowledge in New York Puerto Rican homes. In A. C. Zentella (Ed.), *Building on strength: Language and literacy in Latino families and communities* (134–47). New York: Teachers College Press.

Michael, A., Andrade, N., and Bartlett, L. (2007). Figuring "success" in a bilingual high school. *Urban Review, 39*(2), 167–89.

Migration Policy Institute. (2006). *U.S. in focus: The Central American foreign-born in the United States.* Retrieved from *www.migrationinformation.org.*

Moll, L. C., Amanti, C., Neff, D., and González, N. (1992). Funds of knowledge for teaching: Using a qualitative approach to connect homes and classrooms. *Theory into Practice, 31,* 132–41.

Moll, L. C., and Dworin, J. (1996). Biliteracy in classrooms: Social dynamics and cultural possibilities. In D. Hicks (Ed.), *Child discourse and social learning* (221–46). Cambridge: Cambridge University Press.

Moll, L. C., and Ruiz, R. (2002). The schooling of Latino students. In M. Suárez-Orozco and M. Paez (Eds.), *Latinos: Remaking America* (362–74). Berkeley: University of California Press.

Monzó, L. D., and Rueda, R. (2009). Passing for English fluent: Latino immigrant children masking language proficiency. *Anthropology and Education Quarterly, 40*(1), 20–40.

Mühlhäusler, P. (1996). *Linguistic ecology, language change, and linguistic imperialism in the Pacific region.* London: Routledge.

National High School Center. (2009). *Educating English language learners at the high school level: A coherent approach to district- and school-level support.* American Institutes for Research. Retrieved from *www.betterhighschools.org.*

National Research Council (2004). *Engaging schools: Fostering high school students' motivation to learn.* Washington, DC: National Academies Press.

NCELA (National Clearinghouse for English Language Acquisition and Language Instruction Educational Programs). (2006). *The growing number of limited English proficient students 1991–2002.* Washington, DC: U.S. Department of Education.

NCES (National Center for Education Statistics). (2000). *Dropout rates in the United States: 1999.* Washington, DC: U.S. Department of Education.

NCES. (2001). *Dropout rates in the United States: 2000.* Washington, DC: U.S. Department of Education.

Nespor, J. (1997). *Tangled up in school: Politics, space, bodies, and signs in the educational process.* Mahwah, NJ: Lawrence Erlbaum.

Newman, M. (1994). Graduation rate declines to lowest in eight years. *New York Times,* December 30. Retrieved from *www.nytimes.com.*

No Child Left Behind Act of 2001. (2001). 20 U.S.C. 6301 et seq. (2002).

Noddings, N. (1984). *Caring: A feminine approach to ethics and moral education.* Berkeley: University of California Press.

Noguera, P. A. (2003). *City schools and the American dream.* New York: Teachers College Press.

Noguera, P. A. (2004). Social capital and the education of immigrant students: Categories and generalizations. *Sociology of Education, 77*(2), 180–83.

Norton, B., and Toohey, K. (2001). Changing perspectives on good language learners. *TESOL Quarterly, 35*(2), 307–22.

Novak, J., and Fuller, B. (2003). *Penalizing diverse schools? Similar test scores but different students bring federal sanctions.* Berkeley: Policy Analysis for California Education.

Nuñez, A.-M. (2009). Latino students' transitions to college: A social and intercultural capital perspective. *Harvard Educational Review, 79*(1), 22–48.

NYC DCP (New York City Department of City Planning). (2000). *The newest New Yorkers 2000: Executive summary.* Retrieved from *www.nyc.gov.*

NYC DCP. (2005). *Annual report on social indicators.* New York: NYC DCP.

NYE DOE (New York City Department of Education). (2007). *Progress report, 2006–2007, for Gregorio Luperón High School.* Retrieved from *schools.nyc.gov.*

NYC DOE. (2008a). *The class of 2007 four-year longitudinal report and 2006–2007 event dropout rates.* Retrieved from *schools.nyc.gov.*

NYE DOE. (2008b). *Progress report, 2007–2008, for Gregorio Luperón High School.* Retrieved from *schools.nyc.gov.*

NYC DOE. (2010a). *Students with disabilities and English language learners.* Retrieved from *schools.nyc.gov.*

NYC DOE. (2010b). *Summary of NYSED Regulation 100.5 and Chancellor's Regulation A-501.* Retrieved from *schools.nyc.gov.*

NYS ED (New York State Education Department). (2010). *Education statistics from New York State.* Albany: Office of Information and Reporting Services. Retrieved from *www.emsc.nysed.gov.*

Oakes, J. (2002). *Education inadequacy, inequality, and failed state policy: A synthesis of expert reports prepared for Williams v. State of California.* Los Angeles: UCLA Institute for Democracy, Education, and Access. Retrieved from *escholarship.org.*

OECD (Organisation for Economic Co-operation and Development). (2008). *Review of national policies for education: Dominican Republic.* Paris: OECD. Retrieved from *www.oecd.org.*

Oettinger, G. S. (1999). Does high school employment affect high school academic performance? *Industrial and Labor Relations Review, 53*(1), 136–51.

Ogbu, J. U., and Simons, H. D. (1998). Voluntary and involuntary minorities: A cultural-ecological theory of school performance with some implications for education. *Anthropology and Education Quarterly, 29*(2), 155–88.

Orfield, G., and Eaton, S. (1996). *Dismantling segregation: The quiet reversal of* Brown v. Board of Education. New York: New Press.

Orfield, G., and Lee, C. (2005). *Why segregation matters: Poverty and educational inequality.* Cambridge, MA: The Civil Rights Project, Harvard University.

Orfield, G., and Yun, J. (1999). *Resegregation in American Schools.* Cambridge, MA: The Civil Rights Project, Harvard University.

Osterman, K. F. (2000). Students' need for belonging in the school community. *Review of Educational Research, 70*(3), 323–67.

Padilla, R. V. (2005). Latino/a education in the twenty-first century. In P. Pedraza and M. Rivera (Eds.), *Latino education: An agenda for community action research* (403–24). Mahwah, NJ: Lawrence Erlbaum.

Pallas, A., and Jennings, J. (2009). "Progress" reports. In Ravitch et al. 2009 (99–105).

Pennycook, A. (1994). *The cultural politics of English as an international language.* London: Longman.

Perreira, K. M., Chapman, M. V., and Stein, L. G. (2006). Becoming an American parent: Overcoming challenges and finding strength in a new immigrant Latino community. *Journal of Family Issues, 27*(10), 1383–1414.

Pessar, P. (1995). *A visa for a dream: Dominicans in the United States.* Boston: Allyn and Bacon.

Pessar, P., and Graham, P. (2001). Dominicans: Transnational identities and local politics. In N. Foner (Ed.), *New Immigrants in New York.* New York: Columbia University Press.

Petree, J., and Vargas, T. (2005). *Dominicans in Switzerland: Patterns, practices and impacts of transnational migration and remittances linking the Dominican Republic and Switzerland.* Lausanne, Switzerland: INTER Institut du développement territorial, LaSUR Laboratoire de sociologie urbaine.

Phillipson, R. (1992). *Linguistic imperialism.* Oxford: Oxford University Press.

Phillipson, R. (2003). *English-only Europe? Challenging language policy.* London: Routledge.

Pianta, R. C. (1999). *Enhancing relationships between children and teachers.* Washington, DC: American Psychological Association.

Pita, M. D., and Utakis, S. (2002). Educational policy for the transnational Dominican community. *Journal of Language, Identity, and Education, 1,* 317–28.

Podair, J. E. (2002). *The strike that changed New York: Blacks, whites, and the Ocean Hill–Brownsville crisis.* New Haven, CT: Yale University Press.

Pomeroy, C., and Jacob, S. (2004). From mangoes to manufacturing: Uneven development and its impact on social well-being in the Dominican Republic. *Social Indicators Research, 65*(1), 73–107.

Portes, A., and Grosfoguel, R. (1994). Caribbean diasporas: Migration and ethnic communities. *Annals of the American Academy of Political and Social Science, 533,* 60–69.

Portes, A., and Rumbaut, R. (1990). *Immigrant America: A portrait.* Berkeley: University California Press.

Portes, A., and Rumbaut, R. (2001). Not everyone is chosen: Segmented assimilation and its determinants. In *Legacies: The story of the immigrant second generation* (44–69). Berkeley: University of California Press.

Portes, A., and Zhou, M. (1993). The new second generation: Segmented assimilation and its variants. *Annals of the American Academy of Political and Social Science, 530*(1), 74–96.

PREAL. (2006). *Informe de progreso educativo República Dominicana; Programa de la Promoción de Reforma Educativa de América Latina y el Caribe.* Retrieved from *www.preal.org/Biblioteca.asp.*

Provasnik, S., and Planty, M. (2008). *Community colleges: Special supplement to the condition of education 2008.* Washington, DC: U.S. Department of Education.

Putnam, R. D. (1995). Bowling alone: America's declining social capital. *Journal of Democracy, 6*(1), 64–78.

Qin-Hilliard, D. B. (2003). Gendered expectations and gendered experiences: Immigrant students' adaptation in schools. *New Directions for Youth Development, 2003*(100), 91–109.

Quiroz, P. (2001). The silencing of Latino student "voice": Puerto Rican and Mexican narratives in eighth grade and high school. *Anthropology and Education Quarterly, 32*(3), 326–49.

Raley, J. D. (2004). "Like family, you know?": School and the achievement of peer relations. In Gibson, Gándara, and Koyama 2004 (150–73).

Ramírez, D. (1992). Executive summary. *Bilingual Research Journal, 16*, 1–62.

Ravitch, D. (2000). *Left back: A century of battles over school reform.* New York: Simon and Schuster.

Ravitch, D. (2009a). A history of public school governance in New York City. In J. Viteritti (Ed.), *When mayors take charge: School governance in the city* (171–86). Washington, DC: Brookings Institution.

Ravitch, D. (2009b). Introduction. In Ravitch et al. 2009 (1–6).

Ravitch, D. (2010). *The death and life of the great American school system: How testing and choice are undermining education.* New York: Basic Books.

Ravitch, D., Meier, D., Avitia, D., Bloomfield, D. C., Brennan, J. F., Dukes, H. N., et al. (2009). *New York City schools under Bloomberg and Klein: What parents, teachers, and policymakers should know.* New York: Class Size Matters. Retrieved from *www.lulu.com.*

Reitz, J. (Ed.). (2003). *Host societies and the reception of immigrants.* San Diego: Center for Comparative Immigration Studies, University of California at San Diego.

Reyes, A. (2006). Reculturing principals as leaders for cultural and linguistic diversity. In K. Téllez and H. C. Waxman (Eds.), *Preparing quality educators for English language learners* (145–56). Mahwah, NJ: Lawrence Erlbaum.

Reyes, L. (2006). The Aspira Consent Decree: A thirtieth-anniversary retrospective of bilingual education in New York City. *Harvard Educational Review, 76*(3), 369–400.

Rhodes, J. E. (2002). *Stand by me: The risks and rewards of youth mentoring relationships.* Cambridge, MA: Harvard University Press.

Rich, L. M. (1996). The long-run impact of teenage work experience: A reexamination. *Review of Black Political Economy, 25*(2), 11–36.

Richardson, L. (2000). Writing: A method of inquiry. In N. Denzin and Y. Lincoln (Eds.), *Handbook of qualitative research* (2nd ed., 923–49). Thousand Oaks, CA: Sage.

Riches, C., and Genesee, F. (2006). Cross-linguistic and cross-modal aspects of literacy development. In F. Genesee, K. Lindholm-Leary, W. Saunders, and D. Christian (Eds.), *Educating English language learners: A synthesis of research evidence* (64–108). New York: Cambridge University Press.

Ricourt, M. (2002). *Dominicans in New York: Power from the margins.* New York: Routledge.

Rivera-Batiz, F. (2000). Underground on American soil: Undocumented workers and U.S. immigration policy. *Journal of International Affairs, 53*(2), 485–502.

Rivera-Batiz, F. (2002). *The socioeconomic status of Hispanic New Yorkers: Current trends and future prospects.* Washington, DC: Pew Hispanic Center.

Rivera-Batiz, F. (2008). International migration and the brain drain. In A. K. Rutt and J. Ros (Eds.), *International Handbook of Development Economics.* Northampton, MA: Edward Elgar.

Roffman, J., Suárez-Orozco, C., and Rhodes, J. (2003). Facilitating positive development in immigrant youth: The role of mentors and community organizations. In D. Perkins, L. M. Borden, J. G. Keith, and F. A. Villarreal (Eds.), *Positive youth development: Creating a positive tomorrow.* Brockton, MA: Kluwer Press.

Rogers, D. (2008). *Mayoral control of New York City schools.* New York: Springer.

Rolstad, K., Mahoney, K., and Glass, G. (2005). The big picture: A meta-analysis of program effectiveness research on English language learners. *Educational Policy Review, 19*(4), 572–94.

Romaine, S. (1994). *Language in society: An introduction to sociolinguistics.* Oxford: Oxford University Press.

Rong, X. L., and Brown, F. (2002). Socialization, culture, and identities of black immigrant children: What educators need to know and do. *Education and Urban Society 34*, 247–73.

Rosenbaum, E., and Cortina, R. (2004). *The schooling of immigrants in New York: Graduating high school cohort of 1999* (RSF Project # 88-03-01). New York: Russell Sage.

Rosenbaum, E., and Rochford, J. A. (2008). Generational patterns of academic performance: The variable effects of attitudes and social capital. *Social Science Research, 37*(1), 350–72.

Rubinstein-Ávila, E. (2007). From the Dominican Republic to Drew High: What counts as literacy for Yanira Lara? *Reading Research Quarterly, 42*(4), 568–89.

Rueda, R., Monzó, L. D., and Higareda, I. (2004). Appropriating the sociocultural resources of Latino paraeducators for effective instruction with Latino students: Promises and problems. *Urban Education, 39*(1), 52–90.

Ruiz, R. (1984). Orientations in language planning. *Journal for the National Association for Bilingual Education 8*(2), 15–34.

Ruiz-de-Velasco, J., and Fix, M. (2000). *Overlooked and underserved: Immigrant students in U.S. secondary schools.* With B. Chu Clewell. Washington, DC: Urban Institute.

Rumbaut, R. (2006). Severed or sustained attachments? Language, identity and imagined communities in the post-immigrant generation. In P. Levitt and M. C. Waters (Eds.), *The changing face of home: The transnational lives of the second generation* (43–95). New York: Russell Sage.

Ryan, R., Stiller, S. P., and Lynch, J. H. (1994). Representations of relationships to teachers, parents, and friends as predictors of academic motivation. *Journal of Early Adolescence, 14*(2), 226–49.

Sabia, J. J. (2009). School-year employment and academic performance of young adolescents. *Economics of Education Review, 28*(2), 268–76.

Sagás, E., and Molina, S. E. (Eds.). (2003). *Dominican migration: Transnational perspectives*. Gainesville: University of Florida Press.

Sarroub, L. (2005). *All American Yemeni girls: Being Muslim in a public school*. Philadelphia: University of Pennsylvania Press.

Scheckner, S., Rollin, S. A., Kaiser-Ulrey, C., and Wagner, R. (2002). School violence in children and adolescents: A meta-analysis of the effectiveness of current interventions. *Journal of School Violence, 1*(2), 5–32.

Schultz, K. (1996). Between school and work: The literacies of urban adolescent females. *Anthropology and Education Quarterly, 27*(4), 517–44.

Schwartz, A. E. (2005). Immigrant children in New York City public schools: Equity, performance, and policy. Paper presented at the New York City Council Committee on Immigration, New York University. Retrieved from *wagner.nyu.edu*.

Schwartz, A. E., and Stiefel, L. (2006). Is there a nativity gap? The achievement of New York City elementary and middle school immigrant students. *Education Finance and Policy, 1*(1), 17–49.

SEE (Secretaría de Estado de Educación). (2008). *Plan decenal de educación 2008–2018*. Retrieved from *www.oei.es*.

Selinker, L. (1972). Interlanguage. *International Review of Applied Linguistics, 10*, 209–31.

Selinker, L., and Han, Z. H. (2000). Fossilization: Moving the concept of empirical longitudinal study. In E. Elder (Ed.), *Studies in language testing/experimenting with uncertainty: Essays in honor of Alan Davies*. Cambridge: UCLES.

Sengupta, Somini. (1997). It may take 7 years, but more students are finishing high school. *New York Times*, April 27. Retrieved from *www.nytimes.com*.

Serra, C. (2007). Assessing CLIL at primary school: A longitudinal study. *International Journal of Bilingual Education and Bilingualism, 10*(5), 582–602.

Shohamy, E. (2006). *Language policy: Hidden agendas and new approaches*. New York: Routledge.

Shore, C., and Wright, S. (Eds.). (1997). *Anthropology of policy: Critical perspectives on governance and power*. New York: Routledge.

Short, D., and Boyson, B. (2000a). *Newcomer database for secondary school programs in the United States: Revised 2000*. Washington, DC: Center for Applied Linguistics.

Short, D., and Boyson, B. (2000b). Newcomer programs for linguistically diverse students. *National Association of Secondary School Principals Bulletin, 48*(619), 34–42.

Shukla, S. (2003). *India abroad: Diasporic cultures of postwar America and England.* Princeton, NJ: Princeton University Press.

Siegel, S., and Skelly, E. (1992). An open letter: New York to Adelaide. In G. Boomer, N. Lester, C. Onore, and K. Cook (Eds.), *Negotiating the curriculum* (78–90). London: Falmer Press.

Singleton, D. (2001). Age and second language acquisition. *Annual Review of Applied Linguistics, 21,* 77–89.

Sizer, T. (2004). *Horace's compromise: The dilemma of the American high school.* New York: Houghton Mifflin.

Slavin, R., and Cheung, A. (2005). A synthesis of research on reading instruction for English language learners. *Review of Educational Research, 75*(7), 247–84.

Smith, M. P. (2007). The two faces of transnational citizenship. *Ethnic and Racial Studies, 30*(6), 1096–1116.

Smith, R. (1997). Transnational migration, assimilation, and political community. In M. E. Crahan and A. V. Bush (Eds.), *The city and the world: New York's global future* (110–32). New York: Council on Foreign Relations.

Smith, R. (2001). "Mexicanness" in New York: Migrants seek new place in old racial order. *NACLA Report on the Americas*, 35(2).

Smith, R. (2006). *Mexican New York: Transnational lives of new immigrants.* Berkeley: University of California Press.

Smith, R., Cordero-Guzmán, H., and Grosfoguel, R. (2001). Introduction. In H. Cordero-Guzmán, R. Smith, and R. Grosfoguel (Eds.), *Migration, transnationalization, and race in a changing New York.* Philadelphia: Temple University Press.

Sørensen, N. N. (1994). *Telling migrants apart: The experience of migrancy among Dominican locals and transnationals.* Copenhagen: Institute of Anthropology, University of Anthropology.

Spanakos, A. P., and Wiarda, H. (2003). The Dominican Republic: From nationalism to globalism. In F. Mora and J. Hey (Eds.), *Latin American and Caribbean foreign policy* (104–19). Lanham, MD: Rowman and Littlefield.

Stanton-Salazar, R. D. (1997). A social capital framework for understanding the socialization of racial minority children and youth. *Harvard Educational Review, 67*(1), 1–40.

Stanton-Salazar, R. D. (2001). *Manufacturing hope and despair: The school and kin support netowrks of U.S.-Mexican youth.* New York: Teachers College Press.

Stanton-Salazar, R. D. (2004). Social capital among working-class minority students. In Gibson, Gándara, and Koyama 2004.

Stanton-Salazar, R. D., and Dornbusch, S. M. (1995). Social capital and the reproduction of inequality: Information networks among Mexican-origin high school students. *Sociology of Education, 68*(2), 116–35.

Stanton-Salazar, R. D., and Spina, S. U. (2003). Informal mentors and role models in the lives of urban Mexican-origin adolescents. *Anthropology and Education Quarterly, 34*(3), 231–54.

Stiefel, L., Schwartz, A. E., and Conger, D. (2003). *Language proficiency and home languages of students in New York City elementary and middle schools.* New York: The Urban Education Project, New York University.

Street, B. (1984). *Literacy in theory and practice.* Cambridge: Cambridge University Press.

Street, B. (1996). Literacy, economy, and society. Literacy across the Curriculum, 12(3), 8–15.

Street, B. (2005). At last: Recent applications of new literacy studies in educational contexts. *Research in the Teaching of English, 39*(4), 417–23.

Stritikus, T., and Nguyen, D. (2007). Strategic transformation: Gender identity negotiation in first-generation Vietnamese youth. *American Educational Research Journal, 44*(4), 853–95.

Suárez-Orozco, C., Pimentel, A., and Martin, M. (2009). The significance of relationships: Academic engagement and achievement among immigrant newcomer youth. *Teachers College Record, 111*(3), 712–49.

Suárez-Orozco, C., and Suárez-Orozco, M. (1995). *Transformations: Migration, family life, and achievement motivation among Latino adolescents.* Palo Alto, CA: Stanford University Press.

Suárez-Orozco, C., and Suárez-Orozco, M. (2001). *Children of immigration.* Cambridge, MA: Harvard University Press.

Suárez-Orozco, C., Suárez-Orozco, M., and Todorova, I. (2008). *Learning a new land: Immigrant students in American society.* Cambridge, MA: Belknap Press of Harvard University Press.

Sunderman, G. L., and Orfield, G. (2006). Domesticating a revolution: No Child Left Behind and state administrative response. Harvard Educational Review, 76(5), 526–56.

Swail, W., Cabrera, A., and Lee, C. (2004). Latino youth and the pathway to college. Washington, DC: Pew Hispanic Center.

Swain, M. (1996). Discovering successful second language teaching strategies and practices. *Journal of Multilingual and Multicultural Development,* 17(2–4), 89–104.

Sylvan, C., and Romero, M. (2002). Reversing language loss in a multilingual settings: A native language enhancement program and its impact. In T. Osborn (Ed.), *The future of foreign language education in the United States* (139–66). Westport, CT: Greenwood Publishing Group.

Tatum, B. D. (1997). *"Why are all the black kids sitting together in the cafeteria?" and other conversations about race.* New York: Basic Books.

Theroux, K. (2007). Small schools in the big city: Promising results validate reform efforts in New York City schools. *Carnegie Reporter, 4*(3). Retrieved from *carnegie.org.*

Thomas, W. P., and Collier, V. P. (1997). *School effectiveness for language minority students.* Washington, DC: National Clearinghouse for Bilingual Education, George Washington University.

Thomas, W. P., and Collier, V. P. (2002). *A national study of school effectiveness for language minority students' long term academic achievement: Final report.* Retrieved from *crede.berkeley.edu.*

Thorne, S. L., and Black, R. (2007). Language and literacy development in computer mediated contexts and communities. *Annual Review of Applied Linguistics, 27*(1), 133–60.

Torres-Saillant, S., and Hernández, R. (1998). *The Dominican Americans*. Westport, CT: Greenwood Press.

UNDP (United Nations Development Programme). (2008). *Human development report: Dominican Republic 2008*. Santo Domingo: UNDP, Human Development Office. Retrieved from *www.pnud.org.do*.

UN-INSTRAW (United Nations International Research and Training Institute for the Advancement of Women) and UNDP. (2010). *Migration, remittances, and gender-responsive local development: The case of the Dominican Republic. Executive summary*. Santo Domingo: UN-INSTRAW. Retrieved from *www.un-instraw.org*.

U.S. Census Bureau. (2000). *Census 2000 demographic profile highlights: Summary file 2 and Summary file 4*. Retrieved from *factfinder.census.gov*.

U.S. Census Bureau. (2006–2008). *2006–2008 American Community Survey three-year estimates*. Retrieved from *factfinder.census.gov*.

U.S. Census Bureau. (2007). *2007 American Community Survey one-year estimates*. Retrieved from *factfinder.census.gov*.

U.S. Census Bureau. (2009). *2009 American Community Survey*. Retrieved from *factfinder.census.gov*.

U.S. Census Bureau. (2009). *2009 American Community Survey one-year estimates*. Retrieved from *factfinder.census.gov*.

U.S. DOE (United States Department of Education). (2007). *Guidance on regulations regarding assessment and accountability for recently arrived and former limited English proficient (LEP) students)*. Retrieved from *www2.ed.gov*.

Valdés, G. (1996). *Con respeto: Bridging the distances between culturally diverse families and schools—an ethnographic portrait*. New York: Teachers College Press.

Valdés, G. (2001). Heritage language students: Profiles and possibilities. In J. Peyton, J. Ranard, and S. McGinnis (Eds.), *Heritage languages in America: Preserving a national resource* (37–80). McHenry, IL: Center for Applied Linguistics and Delta Systems.

Valdés, G. (2004). Between support and marginalization: The development of academic language in linguistic minority children. *Bilingual Education and Bilingualism, 7*(2 and 3), 102–32.

Valdés, G. (2005). Bilingualism, heritage language learners and second language acquisition research: Opportunities lost or seized? *Modern Language Journal, 89*(3), 410–16.

Valenzuela, A. (1999a). "Checking up on my guy": High school Chicanas, social capital, and the culture of romance. *Frontiers: A Journal of Women Studies, 20*(1), 60–79.

Valenzuela, A. (1999b). *Subtractive schooling: U.S.-Mexican youth and the politics of caring*. Albany: State University of New York Press.

Valenzuela, A., Prieto, L., and Hamilton, M. P. (2007). Introduction to the Special Issue: No Child Left Behind (NCLB) and Minority Students; What the Qualitative Evidence Suggests. *Anthropology and Education Quarterly, 38*(1), 1–8.

Van Hook, J., and Fix, M. (2000). A profile of the immigrant student population. In J. Ruiz-de-Velasco, M. Fix, and B. Chu Clewell (Ed.), *Overlooked and underserved: Immigrant children in U.S. secondary schools* (9–33). Washington, DC: Urban Institute.

van Lier, L. (2000). From input to affordance: Social interactive learning from an ecological perspective. In J. Lantolf (Ed.), *Sociocultural theory and second language learning* (245–60). Oxford: Oxford University Press.

van Lier, L. (2005). *The ecology and semiotics of language learning.* Dordrecht, Netherlands: Kluwer Academic.

Vargas, K., and Kelly, M. (2007). *Informe estudio cualitativo: Maternidad y paternidad en la adolescencia* (report). Santo Domingo: CONAPOFA.

Vargas, T. (2006). ¿Qué ocurre en la cotidianidad de los barrios urbano-marginales después que se instala barrio seguro? *AREITO, Periódico HOY Digital.*

Vargas, T. (2010). *Migración, remesas y desarrollo local sensible al género: El caso de República Dominicana.* Santo Domingo: UN-INSTRAW, UNDP. Retrieved from *www.un-instraw.org.*

Vasconcelos, D. (2004). *Sending money home: Remittance to Latin America and the Caribbean.* Washington, DC: Inter-American Development Bank Miltilateral Investment Fund. Retrieved from *www.iadb.org/news/docs/remittances-en.pdf.*

Vavrus, F., and Bartlett, L. (Eds.). (2009). *Critical approaches to comparative education: Vertical case studies from Africa, Europe, the Middle East, and the Americas.* New York: Palgrave Macmillan.

Vélez, W. (2007). The educational experiences of Latinos in the United States. In H. Rodriguez, R. Saenz, and C. Menjivar (Eds.), *Latinas/os in the United States* (129–48). New York: Springer.

Vernez, G., and Abrahamse, A. (1996). *How immigrants fare in U.S. education.* Santa Monica, CA: Rand.

Villalpando, O. (2003). Self-segregation or self-preservation? A critical race theory and Latina/o critical theory analysis of a study of Chicana/o college students. *Qualitative Studies in Education, 16*(5), 619–46.

Villenas, S. (2007). Diaspora and the anthropology of Latino education: Challenges, affinities, and intersections. *Anthropology and Education Quarterly, 38*(4), 419–25.

Viteritti, Joseph. (2009). New York: Past, present, future. In J. Viteritti (Ed.), *When mayors take charge: School governance in the city* (206–34). Washington, DC: Brookings Institution.

Walqui, A. (2000a). *Access and engagement: Program design and instructional approaches for immigrant students in secondary schools.* Washington, DC: Center for Applied Linguistics.

Walqui, A. (2000b). *Strategies for success: Engaging immigrant students in secondary schools.* Washington, DC: Center for Applied Linguistics. Retrieved from *www.cal.org.*

Walqui, A. (2006). Scaffolding instruction for English learners: A conceptual framework. *International Journal of Bilingual Education and Bilingualism, 9*(2), 159–80.

Walqui, A., García, O., and Hamburger, L. (2004). Classroom observation scoring manual. Unpublished guide created for WestEd, San Francisco.

Walsh, C. E. (1991). *Pedagogy and the struggle for voice: Issues of language, power, and schooling for Puerto Ricans.* New York: Bergin and Garvey.

Waters, M. C. (1999). *Black identities: West Indian immigrant dreams and American realities.* Cambridge, MA: Harvard University Press.

Watkins-Goffman, L., and Cummings, V. (1997). Bridging the gap between native language and second language literacy instruction: A naturalistic study. *Bilingual Research Journal, 21*(4), 381.

Weller, N. F., Cooper, S. P., Basen-Enquist, K., Kelder, S. H., and Tortolero, S. R. (2003). School-year employment among high school students: Effects on academic, social, and physical functioning. *Adolescence, 38*(151), 441–58.

Wei, Li. (2009). Polite Chinese children revisited: Creativity and use of code-switching in the Chinese complementary school classroom. *International Journal of Bilingual Education and Bilingualism, 12*(2), 193–211.

Willis, P. (1981). *Learning to labor: How working class kids get working class jobs.* New York: Columbia University Press.

Wong Fillmore, L. (1991). When learning a second language means losing the first. *Early Childhood Research Quarterly, 6*, 323–46.

Wortham, S., Murillo, E. G. J., and Hamann, E. T. (Eds.). (2002). *Education in the new Latino diaspora: Policy and the politics of identity.* Westport, CT: Ablex.

Zehler, A., Fleischman, H., Hopstock, P., Stephenson, T., Pendizick, M., and Sapru, S. (2003). *Descriptive study of services to LEP students and LEP students with disabilities.* Arlington, VA: Development Associates. Retrieved from *onlineresources.wnylc.net.*

Zentella, A. C. (1997). *Growing up bilingual: Puerto Rican children in New York.* Malden, MA: Blackwell.

Zentella, A. C. (2005). Premises, promises, and pitfalls of language socialization research in Latino families and communities. In A. C. Zentella (Ed.), *Building on strength: Language and literacy in Latino families and communities* (13–30). New York: Teachers College Press.

Zhou, M., and Bankston, C. I. (1998). *Growing up American: How Vietnamese children adapt to life in the United States.* New York: Russell Sage.

Ziffer, A. (2005). *Los procesos participativos de planificación y gestión educativa: La experiencia del Plan Decenal de Educación en la República Dominicana.* Santo Domingo: Programa Regional de Becas CLACSO.

Zúñiga, V., Hamann, E., and Sánchez García, J. (2008). *Alumnos transnacionales: Las escuelas mexicanas frente a la globalización.* Mexico, DF: Secretaria de Educación Pública.

Index

curriculum affected by, 127, 134–35, 136, 138, 149, 243
decontextualized language of, 126, 134, 149
design of, 121, 134, 242
as graduation requirement, 122–23, 127, 134, 213
pass rate at Luperón, 87, 134, 240
preparation and strategies for, 98–99, 129, 147–49, 213, 224
students interviewed and, 219, 225, 229
urgency associated with, 109, 134–35, 136
enrollment data, 2, 6, 35–36, 76–77, 221, 228, 231
EOPs (Educational Opportunity Programs), 225, 227
ERIC (Education Resources Information Center), 46
Escamilla-Toquica, C., 157
ESEA (Elementary and Secondary Education Act), 54
ESL achievement test. *See* New York State ESL Achievement Test
ESL instruction
for adults, 111, 112
anti-bilingual climate and, 53
approaches to, 13, 146–49, 239, 242
content-area instruction and, 74, 238
policy mandates and, 59–60, 65
and separation from mainstream, 7, 55, 135
staffing of, 77
translanguaging in, 135, 136, 142–45, 200
Espaillat, Adriano, 71
Espinal, Evaristo, 72, 74
ethnic segmentation. *See* segregation, linguistic and scholastic

facility, of Luperón. *See* building site, of Luperón
family, school as, 81–83, 103–4, 190, 203–7, 236, 246
family complexity, 39, 115, 156, 160, 161, 163–64, 249n14

family members. *See* aunts; fathers; grandparents; mothers; parents; siblings and cousins
family obligations
dropouts and, 214, 216, 228–30
sense of, 158–59, 168, 192, 195, 237
fathers
authority of, 162–63, 178, 214
migration of, 154–56, 159, 229
and mobility, 162–63, 174, 175, 177, 178
multiple families of, 160, 163–64
and safety, 180, 181
separation from, 104
strained or nonexistent relationships with, 158, 214, 216, 218
See also parents
Feagin, J. R., 161
federal government, 3, 5, 7, 11, 51, 53–58, 116, 222. *See also* No Child Left Behind
Feinberg, R. C., 209, 244
Ferguson, G., 117, 240
Fernández, César, 23, 24, 25
Fernández, Joseph, 72, 74, 75
fighting, 105, 180, 197
Fine, M., 46, 60
Fischer, K., 17
Fishman, J. A., 16
Fix, M., 1, 7
fossilization, 13
Foster, K. M., 19, 151
founders of Luperón, 32, 72–85, 88–90, 136, 232
research process and, 24, 78
four-year school, Luperón as, 10, 85–86, 88–91, 95
and four-year graduation rate, 60, 86, 87–88
Fry, R., 5, 6, 213, 220, 223, 228–29, 231, 247nn2–3 (chap. 2)

Gándara, P., 176–77, 234, 239
gangs, 93–94, 106, 113, 163
García, Ofelia
on dynamic bilingualism, 14, 123, 149
at Luperón, 22–23, 24–25, 98, 148
on speech community model, 116
on translanguaging, 17, 117, 124, 134